Appearance and reality in politics

APPEARANCE AND REALITY
IN POLITICS

WILLIAM E. CONNOLLY

Professor of Political Science
University of Massachusetts, Amherst

Cambridge University Press

Cambridge
London   New York   New Rochelle
Melbourne   Sydney

Published by the Press Syndicate of the University of Cambridge
The Pitt Building, Trumpington Street, Cambridge CB2 IRP
32 East 57th Street, New York, NY 10022, USA
296 Beaconsfield Parade, Middle Park, Melbourne 3206, Australia

First published 1981

Printed in Great Britain by The Anchor Press Ltd
and bound by Wm Brendon & Son Ltd
both of Tiptree, Essex

British Library Cataloguing in Publication Data
Connolly, William E
Appearance and reality in politics.
1. Political science
I. Title
320.9′181′2   JA66   80-41241
ISBN 0-521-23026-8

Contents

Acknowledgements   *page* vii

Introduction   1

1 The politics of political explanation   7
   The actual and the possible in electoral politics 7. The political import
   of alternative philosophies 18. The positivist rejoinder 23. The
   rationalist derailment 28. A critique of pure interpretation 34

2 The underdetermination of subjects by structures   41
   The political context of structural theory 41. Theory without
   anthropology 43. The mode of production as structure 46. The
   reinsertion of anthropology 48. The primacy of politics 58

3 Appearance and reality in politics   63
   Penetrating appearances 63. Hidden injuries and structural constraints 67
   The reality of appearances 82

4 The public interest and the common good   90
   The two orientations 90. The circle of liberalism 94. The dialectic of
   dissolution 101. Politics and the common good 109

5 Some theories of state crisis   120
   The priority of the state 120. Reform of the welfare state 122. The fiscal
   crisis of the state 127. The cultural contradictions of capitalism 142

6 Personal identity, citizenship, and the state   151
   The quest for personal identity 151. Citizens and looters 157. Personal
   identity, electoral politics, and the state 161

Contents

7 Socialism and freedom   173
   Socialist ideals and political strategies 173. The classical debate
   reconsidered 180. The assumption of indefinite community 186. Some
   institutional revisions 188. Liberalism and socialism 191

Notes to the text   195

Bibliography   211

Index   215

Acknowledgements

Several of the chapters in this study were delivered as papers while I was a Visitor at Nuffield College in 1977. I want to express my gratitude to the students and faculty at Nuffield for inviting me. The formal and informal discussions we pursued helped me to clarify many ideas in this book. Thanks are due too to the Earhart Foundation which provided a grant to defray travel and research expenses during this period.

1977 was an exciting year to be a Visitor in political theory at Oxford University. Charles Taylor was beginning his first year as Chichele Professor of Politics and Philosophy at All Souls; Sheldon Wolin was a Visiting Professor at Balliol; John Gray was starting his first year at Jesus College; and Steven Lukes had just returned from a year in the States. They joined Alan Montefiore, William Weinstein, Ronald Beiner, Michael Sandel, and me in a series of lively discussions and seminars. Each of these theorists offered incisive commentaries on particular chapters in this text. The seminar discussions enlivened my sense of the vitality of the theoretical enterprise, and the critical commentaries helped me to refine some of the central themes in this book.

I have received help from this side of the Atlantic as well. Fred Dallmayr, David Kettler, and Brian Fay have commented on portions of earlier drafts. And numerous colleagues in and around Amherst have also contributed to my thinking. Michael Best collaborated with me on an earlier version of chapter 2, and his imprint can be found at several points in this study. George Kateb, Jean Elshtain, Glen Gordon, Michael Shapiro (visiting from the University of Hawaii), Morton Schoolman, Michael Gibbons, Dennis Wakefield, Vivien Goldman, and Bradley Klein also offered advice and ideas which proved to be valuable. Finally, Deborah Connolly helped to prepare the index.

Acknowledgements

Chapter 2 is a slightly revised version of 'Politics and Subjects: The Limits of Structural Marxism,' by M. H. Best and W. E. Connolly, in *Socialist Review*, vol. 9, no. 6 (November–December 1979), pp. 75–100, reprinted here by permission. Chapter 3 is a revised and extended version of 'Appearance and Reality in Politics,' in *Political Theory*, vol. 7, no. 4 (November 1979), pp. 445–68, published by Sage Publications, Inc. A condensed version of parts 1 and 2 of chapter 5 previously appeared in *The Public Interest*, pp. 43–61, a pamphlet published by the American Political Science Association, 1977, and reprinted here by permission. Chapter 7 is a revised and extended version of 'A Note on Freedom under Socialism,' reprinted from *Political Theory*, vol. 5, no. 2 (November 1977), pp. 461–72, by permission of the publishers, Sage Publications, Inc.

WILLIAM E. CONNOLLY

University of Massachusetts
Amherst
September 1980

Introduction

I propose in this study, first, to examine a series of intimate connections between the quest for personal identity, the construction of political interpretations, the performance of the welfare state, and the legitimacy of that state in the eyes of citizens to whom it is formally accountable through elections. Secondly, I hope to show that an interpretive approach to political inquiry, because of the nature of the institutional practices to be understood, provides the best basis for comprehending this complex web of connections. This text is situated where the philosophy of social science and political theory intersect; it is nourished by the belief that its particular point of concentration permits one to make a distinctive contribution to issues on both sides of this academic boundary.

The first two chapters focus explicitly on this intersection. They explore the philosophy of political explanation and the politics of philosophies of explanation, trying to see how each bears on the other without denying reason a place in either field. The first chapter examines the political background and implications of alternative philosophies of explanation, and presents a preliminary case for the interpretive approach to political inquiry. The second confronts the challenge to interpretive theory posed by one version of structural theory. I contend that the theory presupposes notions of the subject (the person) and of social relations which it purports to eliminate from social theory. The internal critique of the philosophical premises of structural theory and the external critique of its political implications allow me to introduce a structural dimension into the framework of interpretive theory.

Chapter 3 provides the hinge upon which the text turns. The ambiguous posture of one constituency in American politics is subjected to interpretation. The account reveals how an interpretive theory, modified to include a structural dimension and a theory of personal identity, can respect the political understandings of participants even while showing those understandings to contain misrepresentations of the order. Exploring the risks and defeats imposed on dissident movements, we are better able to understand why a variety of injured constituencies strives to save appearances, to ward off interpretations which would draw them into the orbit of dissident movements. The intent is to explain the gap between the appearance the order presents to participants and its real structure, while treating the appearances as partly constitutive of the practices misrepresented.

The explanation of the disjuncture between appearances and realities is incomplete until a theory of the state is developed which coheres with this general account. The next three chapters are devoted to this assignment. Chapter 4 examines how discrepancies between the imperatives of an order and the implicit aspirations of segments of the populace can foster a dialectic of social dissolution. The field upon which the processes of social dissolution can operate is broadened today because of a tightening and extension of the web of social interdependencies and because of the corollary expansion of the necessity to coordinate social institutions through conscious political means. The liberal politics of the public interest, striving to close the gap between priorities of the order and dispositions to action within the populace, introduces a series of political interventions in the market and accelerates the scope of direct bureaucratic controls. The liberal *theory* of the public interest lacks the conceptual resources to comprehend the dialectic of dissolution and the *politics* of the public interest contributes to the regimentation its proponents oppose. The absence of theorizing today about the common good, that is, about a set of purposes, priorities, and limits which deserve the allegiance of the citizenry, is a symptom at the level of theory of the split in practice between the imperatives of the order and the disaffection of the populace from them.

Chapters 5 and 6 consolidate this thesis and specify it more closely. It is argued, first, that there is something of value inside each of three disparate theories of the state. But none of these theories, representing respectively radical, liberal, and neo-conservative modes of thought, provides sufficient theoretical resources to comprehend the double relation the state bears to its citizens and its economy. Each theory needs to be infused with a deeper understanding of the dialectic of disaffection from the civilization of productivity; only then can we understand how that dialectic exacerbates inflationary pressures, impairs the performance of the corporate economy, helps to expand the size of the welfare state, and sets up the bloated state to be the most visible target of disaffection. Such an understanding presupposes a social epistemology at odds with the one governing the theories under examination.

In chapter 6 an attempt is made to explain more closely how and why the welfare state is set up to be the object of this pervasive disaffection and how the triadic relation of the state, the economy, and the electorate works to screen the underlying issues out of the official political dialogue. The quest by citizens to secure the appearance of dignity and integrity under unfavorable conditions combines with the dual accountability of the state to expand the role of the state, deflect political articulation of the underlying issues, and deplete the supply of civic resources the state can draw upon to play its enlarged role.

The critical interpretation which emerges supports the case for a sympathetic exploration of a socialist political economy. But socialist theory and practice contain dilemmas of their own, insufficiently acknowledged by their advocates. The hesitancy of the Left to confront these issues – even at the theoretical level – helps to convert implicit disaffection from the civilization of productivity into greater tolerance for authoritarian solutions endorsed by the Right. If citizens believe that the only alternative to the established order necessarily suppresses their freedom more completely, the belief will license tolerance for the selective expansion of the disciplinary apparatus of the state. Some of the priorities and premises in socialist theory are reassessed, though the reassessment is provisional and incomplete, trying to draw this theoretical orientation closer to the social undercurrents and structural limits of our civilization.

It is perhaps best to view this text as a collection of essays, each of which pulls together some of the threads left hanging in the others. Arguments which appear in one setting are extended or modified later, drawing upon considerations not yet available in the initial formulations. Thus an account of the sources of two-party politics launched in chapter 1 to illustrate the logic of interpretive theory is filled out in chapter 5 to help explain the simultaneous pressures for the growth and contraction of the welfare state. The gap between the formal expressions of allegiance to the larger order and the proliferation of symptoms which belie these expressions is elucidated in chapters 2, 3 and 6. But the account is not complete until the rationale inside the widespread repudiation of the socialist alternative is examined in the final chapter. The defense of presuppositions crucial to interpretive theory is a primary theme in chapters 1 and 2. But additional elements in interpretive theory are elucidated later. Presentations of the test procedures appropriate to interpretation, the obstacles to the reduction of defensible interpretations in each domain to one account, and the relation between the quest for personal identity and the construction of political interpretation emerge as subordinate themes in several later chapters. The full portrayal of the version of interpretive theory endorsed here is not provided until those dimensions have been incorporated into it. The essay format proves most appropriate for the development of these and other themes, because the relation of each part to the whole cannot easily be exhibited through a linear progression.

I have benefitted immensely from the opportunity to present early drafts of these essays to students and faculty at several universities. Many criticisms and comments expressed during these occasions have found their way into the final version of this text. One recurrent challenge, though, deserves special notice: 'Isn't a more optimistic portrayal of current trends and alternatives possible? Doesn't this interpretation inspire criticism of the established order and pessimism about the prospects for political action to correct its evils? Doesn't it place an intolerable burden on the Left?'

My first response is to confess that I remain unsettled about how thoroughly the trends identified here permeate the institutional interior of advanced capitalism. They are pervasive enough, I believe, to receive close theoretical attention. But perhaps they will reveal themselves eventually to be more ephemeral than they appear in this text.

But inside this uncertainty is a suspicion: today the impulse to optimism constitutes a turn to falsification. And theoretical falsification generates, in its turn, a profound despair, or its sibling, a consuming cynicism.

The intimate relation between thought and action is now widely appreciated among social theorists. Thus if theory implies an orientation to action, an unnecessarily pessimistic theory cuts into the

4

nerve of political efforts which might otherwise succeed. Hence the challenge. But this familiar charge – familiar particularly to those who have levelled it against others – implies a less familiar corollary.

The wish to reassure dissidents pursuing a precarious political course might authorize a theory which misrepresents the structure of the established order. Conduct informed by such illusions eventually generates the most shattering disillusionment of all. The New Left, for all its energy and achievements, surely was a victim of this dialectic. Its spirit was pure; its life was short. Its collapse produced a vacuum on the Left, a nervous muddle in the middle, and a legacy of bitter memories and tactical innovations to the Right.

Critical thought today must cultivate a temper which can be sustained without artificial injections of optimism because it comprehends pressures and energies filtered out of the explicit political dialogue. The Right speaks in its own way to contemporary symptoms of disaffection. But tendencies within liberalism and radicalism deny, evade, or contain these expressions. These are dangerous games to play.

A critical temper resistant to the cycle of illusion and dissillusionment periodically gripping the Left might also begin to engage constituencies now disengaged from the prevailing terms of political discourse. This is its hope. But there are no guaranteees that it will be realized even if its interpretations are sound. Since the aspiration for engagement cannot be achieved by the aspirants alone and since the false hope that it can often authorizes falsified interpretations, the readiness to remain disengaged when necessary is part of the process by which the cycle of illusion and disillusionment is broken.

The politics of political explanation

The actual and the possible in electoral politics

The inclusion of disabled persons within the orbit of affirmative action laws might be treated by many as a political decision, but fewer would interpret the rules which differentiate between the able and the disabled to be a set of political constructions. The first outcome contains at least two features which appear to distinguish it from the second: reform groups actively support the inclusion of the disabled within the affirmative action pool and the rationale in support of this selective dispensation is contestable. Those contesting it might ask, for instance, Why are the sons and daughters of the poor excluded from these ranks? They also face pervasive obstacles to personal achievement produced by forces beyond their control.

A more radical orientation would seek to politicize more completely the socially established meaning of 'disability.' What, its proponents will ask, are the standards of success and achievement against which a set of traits are defined as disabilities? Perhaps these standards would become objects of political struggle if their implications for the classification and treatment of people who do not measure up to them were articulated more openly. The relation between the enunciation of standards and the production of disabilities (or deviances or perversions) is certainly close. The absence of an acute sense of smell would constitute a disability in a setting where its perfection was essential to the discrimination between carcinogenic and noncarcinogenic food. Masturbation would be defined as a perversion where the authorized purpose of sexuality was limited to reproduction. And a variety of speech disabilities would disappear if the social expectation of speed and efficiency in verbal communication were relaxed.

This connection between standards and disabilities complicates the politics of reform; for reformers who visibly defend people with recognized disabilities invisibly and uncritically defend the social priorities and standards which constitute those disabilities. There is thus some basis to the radical charge that reformers help to perpetuate the class of people they intend to protect.[1]

I will not pursue these particular contentions here. My point is to call attention to a process by which social priorities and standards commonly treated as non-political at one moment (perhaps they are seen to be traditional or rational or part of human nature itself) can be politicized overtly at another moment, first, by showing them to be more specific to a particular order than previously believed, secondly, by exposing negative implications residing within them for specific classes of people, and thirdly, by showing how the benefits or status received by privileged constituencies rest upon the perpetuation of these conventions. And once such a practice has been politicized explicitly (feminist, gay, and minority politics constitute recent examples) those implicated will generally acknowledge that the previous relationship contained a covert political dimension all along. Viewed retrospectively, the politicizing agents can be said partly to have exposed a political dimension residing inside the practice and partly to have produced it.

A similar dynamic can be detected within the philosophy of political explanation. Many social scientists today admit that the specific explanatory theory one adopts contains a political dimension: it supports as rational or desirable a particular range of policies and strategies, and it undermines the legitimacy of others.[2] But fewer social scientists concede that every philosophy of political explanation also generates political implications. I will contend that the politics of political explanation operates at this level too. My intent is to probe certain relations between the philosophy of political explanation and the politics of philosophies of explanation without dissolving either phenomenon into the other. Attention to this relationship eventually enhances the role that reason can play in political explanation. For in those persisting circumstances where the resources of pure reason remain insufficient to resolve the pertinent issues, awareness of the political implications of alternative philosophies of explanation converts some of the tacit supports of a particular orientation into explicit premises susceptible to further deliberation and assessment.

8

Two idealized accounts of why two-party politics persists in the United States will be formulated. Each account will be situated within a particular philosophy of social science which is itself idealized. The philosophical premises in each theory permit the identification of possibilities within the electoral system not clearly identified within the other,[3] and even where the identification of possibilities converges the two frameworks generate divergent implications for practical judgment. After drawing out these political dimensions more complex versions of the two philosophies of explanation are introduced, and a preliminary defense of one of them is offered. The defense will be converted into an offensive operation later, when hidden aspects of contemporary politics are examined through the lens of interpretive theory.

Why does the two-party system remain such a permanent fixture of American politics? The purposes in posing this question can vary widely. One might wish to know how to maintain an electoral system which seems to promote stability while it renders state officials accountable to the electorate. One might wish to devise a strategy by which a dissident minority could employ electoral politics to place its priorities on the political agenda. One might wish to show a governing elite how to manipulate electoral laws to disenfranchise a dissident constituency. But whatever the specific intent, and whatever one's theoretical predispositions, certain factors surely present themselves as candidates for incorporation into the explanatory account. Thus the range of issues susceptible to legitimate state control, the contours of the class structure, the extent to which ideological and/or ethnic groups are clustered in particular geographic areas or dispersed across the country, and the laws which govern the electoral process are all pertinent factors to consider.

There is good reason to start inquiry with the last factor. Maurice Duverger, in a classic study of political parties in a variety of states, has concluded that an electoral system composed of single member districts with plurality election (he calls it 'simple majority' election) is closely correlated with a two-party electoral system.

The simple majority single ballot system favors the two party system. Of all the hypotheses that have been defined in this book, this approaches the most nearly perhaps to a true sociological law. An almost complete correlation is observable between the simple majority single ballot system and the party system: dualist countries use the simple majority vote and simple majority vote countries are dualist.[4]

9

More recent studies tend to confirm this finding. Douglas Rae concludes that, though a variety of delicate adjustments in electoral laws generate detectable changes, these adjustments do not notably unsettle the 'fairly consistent association between single member districts plurality formulae and two-party systems.'[5] In a summary of recent studies of party politics in the United States, Jean Kirkpatrick concludes that though issues have changed significantly over the last three decades, though techniques of political campaigning now allow individual candidates to rise above traditional party machinery, and though the intergenerational transmission of loyalties and identifications has weakened, 'the Democrats are still the majority party, competition for office is almost always carried out under two – and only two – labels, and a majority of candidates still identifies with or "leans" toward either the Republican or Democratic Parties.'[6]

A model of explanation embodies an ideal; it tells us how the phenomenon would be represented if a complete explanation of it were provided. To assimilate the 'same factors' to different models of explanation is thus to represent them differently; and different representations generate different practical conclusions. We shall test this contention by incorporating the relationship described above between electoral systems and party systems first into a lawlike model of explanation and then into an interpretive mode.

According to the law-like model, a phenomenon is fully explained when, given a specified set of initial conditions, phenomenon A is shown to be associated invariably with phenomenon B; and A and B together are implicated in a deductive system of such relationships, enabling the investigator to formulate a set of significant counterfactual propositions concerning what would happen if A were varied in determinate ways while the initial conditions remained constant. The association between A and B is said to be law-like, or stronger than an accidental association, if the relationship is formulated within a larger theoretical system which generates counterfactual expectations when the antecedent factor is varied in specific ways; and the explanatory power of the theory is tested by ascertaining whether the expected variations do occur when the antecedent factors are so varied. The ability to predict changes that will occur if the variables are manipulated in particular ways increases, at least in principle, the ability of policy makers to produce desired changes in the political system through manipulation of the antecedent variables.[7]

It is not very difficult to see how the generalization we began with can be assimilated to this model. We can in fact identify three such generalizations:

1. If single member district, plurality election, then two-party system (SMD, PE = 2PS).

2. If multi-member district, majority election, then multi-party system (MMD, ME = MPS).

3. If single member district, majority election then multi-party system (SMD, ME = MPS).

The generalizations can be brought together within one theory by elucidating a theoretical principle which, in conjunction with a specified set of initial conditions, explains why each generalization holds. Thus: 'Each citizen votes for the candidate closest to his ideological orientation who has a reasonable chance of winning.'

The principle, along with the laws, will generate the expected results whenever a particular set of initial conditions is established. The initial conditions include: legalization of party organizations, election by secret ballot, inclusion of party affiliation on ballots, diffusion of ethnic and class membership across electoral districts, concentration of significant political issues at the level of the nation-state, etc.

The open texture of the theoretical principle (represented by 'closest to' and 'reasonable chance'), combined with the incomplete specification of the initial conditions, means that the explanatory theory of party systems is itself underspecified and incomplete by comparison to the law-like ideal of explanation. It is an explanation sketch on the way to meeting the conditions of an ideal explanation. It is nonetheless useful for our purposes because it approximates that ideal more closely than any other theory of significance in contemporary political science. For once the theoretical principle, the initial conditions, and the law-like propositions are brought together, the complex does appear to have rather impressive explanatory and predictive power. Holding the conditions and the principle constant, we can explain why each law holds. Law 1 (SMDPE = 2PS) holds in countries like the United States and England. Dissident voters realize that a vote for the third party, though it best represents their ideological orientation, would increase the likelihood of victory for the candidate from the majority party most distant from their views. Voters, guided by the principle articulated earlier, will thus distribute their votes between the two candidates with the greatest chance of winning; and that means, when the initial conditions are operative, that the votes will coalesce around the two largest parties, freezing minority parties out of representation. We can predict, moreover, that if the electoral system of the United States were converted into one in which there were single member districts, majority election, then the likelihood for emergence of a multi-party system would increase significantly. For the dissident voter could now maximize the potential effect of each vote by casting the first vote for the candidate closest to him ideologically (Law 3). And, assuming that enough voters followed a similar strategy and no candidate received an absolute majority, the minority candidate could then bargain with the two run-off candidates, throwing support to the one who made the most favorable policy concessions. Conversion to multi-member districts (Law 2) would support a multi-party system even more distinctly. For voters supporting minority parties could expect the minority candidate to win the third or fourth seat in their district, and they could further hope that a bloc of such seats in the Congress would be strategically located in the legislative process.

Putative counter-examples to these laws can be handled by reference to the initial conditions. Thus Canada, which has single member districts, plurality election, but a multi-party system, also concentrates a disaffected ethnic minority within one geographical region. It thereby provides not a counter-instance but a closer specification of the law's conditions of application.

The generalizations we have gathered into one theory approach a law-like status because each is a counterfactual to the others; they only approach that status because the loose specification of the principle and the initial conditions, and the range covered by terms such as 'party' and 'system' in the generalizations, render the relevant counterfactuals comparatively indeterminate. Nonetheless, political officials, comprehending this theory, can manipulate the pertinent antecedent variables to produce the sort of electoral system desired. If a relevant antecedent, such as the regional concentration of ethnic groups in Canada, is not now amenable to manipulation, advocates of this model might expect a law-like account of the factors sustaining regional concentration to identify means by which they could, in principle at least, modify this condition.

But the relationship between single member, plurality election districts and two-party politics can be given an alternative reading, one which accentuates a different set of possibilities. The theoretical principle articulated earlier is not, on this reading, construed to be a high level law which explains laws at a lower level; it is defined as a rule of rationality. Voters, *seeking* to maximize the impact of their vote, cast it with a general *understanding* of the electoral consequences flowing from the election system within which they vote. Remove that objective, and there would be no rationale for the rule; remove that understanding, and the rule would not be applied correctly in each specific context; and remove the application of the rule, and the 'laws' would not follow. Because the principle (now seen as a rule) requires a set of concepts, understandings, and commitments on the part of the voters, and because these states are thought not to be susceptible to explanation through deeper law-like generalizations, the electoral generalizations themselves assume a character closer to conventions than laws. The explanation now assumes the appearance of an interpretation, that is, an elucidation of the intersubjectively shared concepts, beliefs, and purposes which help to constitute these electoral practices. And the interpretive reading accentuates ingredients which (from its point of view) were suppressed in the first account.

The voters, to sustain the relationship between election rules and particular constellations of party competition, must possess a particular range of concepts and accept a restricted set of beliefs. They must know what it is to cast a vote, understanding the difference between voting, and, say, playing a lottery; otherwise we would not be able to characterize the individual act as a 'vote' or the cumulative result as 'an election.' The voters must believe that, in their society, elected officials can effectively promote objectives prized by voters, that the opposing parties offer alternative policies sufficiently divergent to constitute an electoral choice, that politicians are not so corrupt that the winners inevitably sell out to the highest bidder, that each ballot is indeed secret, and that those who vote for a losing candidate will not be punished severely. If several of these beliefs were to disappear, the ability to characterize the activity as an election would be jeopardized; some of the implicit beliefs which individuate the act of voting (e.g., casting it voluntarily, with the purpose of affecting government policy, in a context of choice between meaningful alternatives, without the threat of coercion) would disappear.

The electoral process and the rule of rationality governing it together presuppose a complex set of beliefs, concepts, and intentions on the part of participants. The law-like model can incorporate such mental states, but it interprets them as dispositions to conduct susceptible to a counterfactual analysis.[8] From the vantage point of interpretive theory, the conversion of beliefs into dispositions produces an explanation sketch which distorts how some beliefs are formed and misrepresents the capacities the human objects of inquiry have to reconsider established beliefs in the light of new reason and evidence.

To say that a quiet animal is dangerous is to say that it would attack if it were hungry or if other specified conditions were present. Such a counterfactual (or dispositional) analysis of a particular belief held by a person can take us some distance, particularly if the belief is attributed to another who is not aware of the attribution and whose character is generally known to us. Thus if a citizen of upright character believes that a particular candidate is corrupt, then, were he asked to contribute to the candidate's campaign he would refuse (except in exceptional circumstances), and were there an uncorrupt and otherwise acceptable candidate, he would vote against the corrupt one. A person who professed to hold a particular belief but who never acted in ways which seemed to express it could not be said really to hold it.

But the counterfactuals supported by beliefs are not merely more indefinite and context-dependent than those supported by the dispositional states we attribute to inanimate objects (e.g., this thing is flexible, hard, combustible); such an analysis is necessary, but insufficient to capture the phenomenon under scrutiny. I might describe another's implicit or unconscious beliefs by stating pertinent counterfactuals, but when another asks me about my beliefs, or I ask about my own, the double structure of believing is brought into prominence. I ask, 'Do I believe these local politicians are corrupt?' The question is answered to some degree by reviewing my own past conduct with respect to those officials. Do I avoid them? Do I refuse to support them in campaigns? Have I dropped out of local politics? All these questions, and many others, are appropriate ways to tease out of my past conduct a particular belief implicitly expressed in it. But once I have formulated the question to myself so bluntly I can now ask myself another one. Am I prepared to *endorse* the belief previously expressed in conduct? The second question leads me to consider evidence supporting or defeating it, to listen to arguments on both sides of the question, to ascertain whether it coheres with a stock of other beliefs I hold, to reach, in short, a conclusion guided by procedures appropriate to assess the rationality or irrationality of existing beliefs. And if I then decide that there are sufficient arguments and evidence against my earlier belief, I am committed to redescribe it now as a prejudice or an unsubstantiated thought which I will try to eliminate from the premises of my future conduct.

Because we see ourselves as creatures able to revise previous beliefs on the basis of new reason and evidence, and able to adjust future conduct to the results of those new considerations, a question posed to me (by myself or another) about my beliefs is a request both to characterize the belief implicit in my conduct and to see whether I will endorse it upon reflection. We acknowledge these two dimensions in our unwillingness to call a persisting thought known to be false a belief, in our desire to promote coherence between beliefs we endorse explicitly and those implicit in our actions, and in our efforts to avoid manipulation and self-deception (or at a minimum the appearance of self-deception).[9] It is because the paradigm case of holding a belief is to endorse as warranted or rational a thought expressed in one's conduct that we are susceptible to self-deception and manipulation. If my conduct, for instance, expresses a belief advantageous to my reputation but inconsistent with available evidence, my evasion of the embarrassing evidence is itself a sign that beliefs are, for me, more than merely implicit dispositions to behave in certain ways under specified conditions.

The pertinence of the double structure of belief to the correlation between single member districts with plurality election and a two-party system can be brought out by exploring some hypothetical possibilities residing within that correlation. Suppose, first, that a significant faction, traditionally loyal to the Democratic Party, decides to vote for a third party because the platform of the minority party speaks more closely to its grievances and ideals. We can expect Democratic regulars to remind the dissidents how our electoral system works, how their support for a minority party will be counterproductive within the American system. The arguments appeal, not to law-like relationships, but to the irrationality of supporting a third party in this system; they point out that such action is irresponsible because it will promote a Republican victory. As the arguments are articulated more precisely the dissidents realize that the advice is sound because of the legal rules governing the electoral process, their beliefs about the importance of elections, and their wish to keep Republicans out of office.

Once the dissidents understand why their strategy is irrational in the context of these rules, beliefs, and objectives, they may decide to come back into the fold. But this new level of understanding also introduces alternative possibilities for future action. The dissidents may now insist that, to retain their allegiance, the Democratic Party must strive to revise the election laws once in office so that it will no longer be irrational for an ignored minority to challenge the dominant party in this way. Or, the dissidents may decide that since Party leaders keep them in line by threats of political disaster should they stray, they will break away in one election to show that they are a force to be reckoned with. 'We will contribute to the Party's defeat this time so that next time it will take our demands more seriously.' The charge of irrationality is not now quite so credible, or at least new arguments are needed to sustain it. The dissidents have adopted a new strategy based on new knowledge of the conventions supporting two-party politics in the current system and on the new belief that the Party uses these conventions to maintain their loyalty without responding to their demands. The charges of irrationality and irresponsibility (which are related but do not amount to the same thing) can now be levelled with some force against the Party. It knowingly threatens to lose a needed constituency and to guarantee a Republican victory by its (arguably) unnecessary refusal to admit a legitimate set of demands into its policy agenda. 'Respond to our demands or you guarantee your own defeat.' This is the tack adopted by the newly enlightened dissidents.

Once one faction pursues this strategy with some success, others may be moved to adopt a similar strategy. While Party leaders can concede something to several groups to keep the coalition together, they cannot make important concessions to all of them. For some of the concessions contradict others. As the Party makes contradictory promises to opposing factions, its credibility begins to fade; and as its credibility fades its formal concessions begin to mean less and less.

Suppose now that the dialectic we have sketched were actually pushed to an extreme point. The Democratic Party progressively undermines its credibility by making promises it cannot keep, while the Republican Party retains credibility but supports policies incapable of attracting a firm and stable majority of the electorate. A significant minority, reviewing these developments, might conclude that the electoral process itself is a farce. Adopting at first the stance of non-voters they might eventually conclude that more affirmative action is needed to dramatize their point and to delegitimize in the public mind a process which is already, they think, illegitimate. Since elections, they conclude (truly or falsely) do not make an important difference, they decide to place bets publicly on the outcome, giving prizes to those who come closest to guessing the result for a large number of contests. Those participating will enter the voting booth blind-folded, pulling levers randomly. Each participant will announce to the poll watchers, while entering the booth, 'this is a blindfold vote,' so that the public and 'elected' officials will know that the election has become a lottery.

If a sufficiently large minority were to follow this strategy, the two-party system, in one highly extended sense, would remain intact : two sets of 'candidates' would still be organized around two 'party' labels, and in each district one of them would be declared the winner. But appearances mislead here. For many of the beliefs and intentions which help to constitute an election have been drained from the process. To continue to use *our* concepts of voting, election, and two-party system to characterize this new practice is to misrepresent it. Public officials can no longer claim credibly to represent those who participated in the lottery which placed them in office.

We are not, of course, either predicting or advocating this development. But to see that it is *possible*, because of the constitutive role of the concepts and beliefs which form the background of our two-party system, is to discern potentialities within the actual arrangements not clearly recognized within the law-like model of explanation. And that recognition carries implications for attempts to understand the existing dynamics of party competition. First, it suggests a way to account for less dramatic shifts in our electoral politics over the last two decades. For there has been a movement away from party identification and toward non-voting. Secondly, it locates a set of possibilities within the present system whose non-occurrence deserves explanation. To explain why these possibilities have not occurred is to extend our understanding of how the two-party system works; it is to comprehend more closely what it takes to sustain allegiance to two-party politics in the contemporary American system.

I will provide tentative answers to each of these questions in later chapters, answers which are generally congruent with the interpretive mode of political understanding.

The political import of alternative philosophies

The difference between these models, as characterized so far, is that the first seeks law-like explanations of individual behavior and institutional relations while the second contends that because context-specific concepts and beliefs are constituent ingredients of social life and because the participants sharing those ideas have the capacity to criticize them through reasoned judgment, an interpretive dimension must be incorporated into any viable account of political life.

If, as I shall contend, the latter dimension is ineliminable from social life and inconsistent with premises inside the law-like model of explanation, why do many social scientists continue to deploy the law-like model as a standard against which the output of the social sciences is appraised? Put another way, why have so few moved explicitly to the interpretive mode of social and political inquiry?

Let me state two premises without now providing supporting arguments.[10] First, the United States (and other advanced industrialized states) today requires massive coordination of its populace to sustain economic productivity and social stability while the civic virtue which might provide spontaneous support for such coordination is severely depleted. Secondly, state subsidy of research for higher education in general, and the social sciences in particular, is tied to the expectation that they will identify levers of social coordination and management deployable in these circumstances.

If the deficit in the supply of civic virtue is connected to a widely held belief that the state does not, and perhaps cannot, speak effectively to the grievances of diverse constituencies, then a social science establishment might seek to (*a*) provide rational grounds for altering those beliefs, (*b*) justify those beliefs while pointing toward new relationships between the state and the economy which would enable the state to respond more effectively to legitimate

18

grievances and rekindle civic virtue, or (*c*) bypass attention to the rationality or irrationality of established beliefs by identifying levers which, when pulled, will produce the desired behavior and/or the needed beliefs within the established order. It is not inevitable that the third option will overrun the first two, but in conjunction with the prestige afforded to the law-like model by its apparent success in the natural sciences, it does present an attractive alternative. The needs of the state, its rationale for financing the enterprise of social science, the desire of social scientists to justify that investment, and the wish of social scientists to avoid complicity in the manipulation or coercion of 'client' populations clustering around the welfare state converge to make it attractive. The belief in the law-like model helps to maintain apparent coherence among those objectives and wishes. Moreover, social scientists in the current setting who wish to establish a close connection between thought and action can do so most securely by adopting a model of thought congruent with state imperatives for technical planning and control.

From the vantage point of assumptions about human agency, freedom and rationality within interpretive theory, the contemporary social scientist faces a dilemma: to serve the expected function effectively the social scientist is pressed to identify means by which the policies necessary to effective state performance can be mystified to a populace which might otherwise repudiate some of them. For conduct is always mediated by beliefs, and to the extent that state priorities go against the settled convictions of important constituencies the social scientist's desire to be a policy scientist offering practical advice will collide with the desire to avoid complicity in the manipulation and coercion of client populations.

The law-like model appears to circumvent this predicament. It apparently allows one to achieve practicality and to avoid complicity. Since it construes beliefs embedded in behavior (or in some versions the behavior identifiable as separate from beliefs) to be produced by specifiable factors in the way that a brain hemmorhage produces the incapacity to speak, the identification of levers of control which bypass the rational faculties of participants or which determine the results of deliberation is not usually seen to be manipulative or coercive. The model cannot, of course, be deployed so bluntly, since it is part of my thesis that social scientists who adopt it in their scientific work also unavoidably adopt distinctions and modes of reasoning incompatible with it in their everyday lives. Social scientists from a variety of epistemological camps would concur in describing a relationship as coercive if someone did something only to avoid a threatened sanction, but they might divide in their assessments if the person's wants and beliefs were subsequently brought into line with the initial demand.[11] The law-like advocate would of course ask what new beliefs and desires could be inferred from the new behavior; but the interpretive theorist would ask further whether the altered beliefs and desires expressed in the new mode of behavior were generated by rational, non-rational, or irrational means.

The law-like model encourages the social scientist to become an expert who knows things about the tendencies and motives of people which they do not know about themselves; this knowledge can then be used to predict behavior under specified conditions and to identify the conditions under which the behavior could be produced. But to play the role of expert, the predictions must be fairly reliable, and to render the predictions reliable the expert is encouraged to keep established correlations outside the sphere of public discourse. For given the reflexive capacities of the human objects of inquiry, widespread awareness of the antecedents of their own behavior might provoke them to revise future patterns of conduct. The awareness could diminish both the ability to test the law-like claim (since one of its preconditions has changed) and the ability to use the knowledge effectively in social policy.

Commitments to the law-like model, to the role of the expert in possession of such knowledge, and to the production of reliable correlations, converge to surround the knowledge obtained with an aura of mystery, a mystery enhanced by the technical language in which the knowledge is couched. The aura of mystery supports social control by cutting off reflexive reactions to new knowledge on the part of those who are the objects of inquiry. It also enlarges, at least as seen from the vantage point of interpretive theory, the sphere of manipulative politics.

Consider one extreme example. According to a recent study, advertising experts are trying to increase sales in selective markets through new forms of subliminal advertising. Clothing sales through mail-order catalogues seem to increase if the word 'SEX' is etched lightly ('embedded') at strategic points in the advertisements and if latent homosexual desires among consumers are reinforced subliminally through the visual design of the ads. Similarly, liquor sales apparently increase among that small proportion of buyers who consume over 70 per cent of the product when the word 'DEATH' is embedded in liquor advertisements and when death masks are etched into the visual designs.[12] The effect on the consumer must be produced at a pre-conscious level, since explicit awareness of this technique would produce a counterproductive reaction.

The researcher's purpose is to generate a particular belief, such as the belief that a brand of liquor is smooth or dry, by embedding in the overt message the covert idea that the death wish will be fulfilled by dry liquor. Because the science in which the inquiry is couched treats a belief as simply the disposition to act in specified ways, the test of success in producing the desired belief is the willingness of the consumer to buy the product after exposure to the advertisement. In everyday discourse, a set of concepts such as persuasion, manipulation, coercion, force and conditioning differentiate the ways of generating beliefs by reference to the alternative ways these relationships bear on the freedom and reason of the recipient; and this internally integrated set of notions contains a set of moral presuppositions about the comparative legitimacy of each mode of influence.[13] But these concepts and presumptions have been displaced by the surface grammar governing the science of advertising; its distinctions are organized around considerations of comparative effectiveness, intensity, durability, and cost efficiency. The vocabulary in this second field of discourse stifles the voice of moral restraint by stripping it of the conceptual field in which it is articulated.

Many social scientists, representing diverse social epistemologies, would in fact oppose this particular instance of consumer manipulation. But the law-like model lacks the theoretical rationale to justify this conclusion. The policy scientist who is dazzled by the law-like model of inquiry and who also criticizes blatant cases of manipulation does so because the presuppositions built into daily discourse assume priority temporarily over those operating at the surface of the scientific discourse. Failure to recognize this ambiguity allows the social scientist to have it both ways : to condemn periodically from one vantage point that which is legitimized from another.

In less stark cases, the perspective of the social scientist is more likely to prevail. Thus to subsume the correlation $SMDPE = 2PS$ under the law-like model is to treat the collateral beliefs necessary to its operations as dispositions to action. When the correlation is presented to a wider public it is treated as embodying beliefs not in need of further examination. The recipients are likely to construe the relation as a fixed fact of political life rather than a convention partially sustained by their own revisable premises of action. The law-like rendering of the correlation in this way discourages participant exploration into the rationality of the beliefs which underpin it. This ambiguity between the presuppositions one adopts in one's role as a social scientist and those one adopts while immersed in other social roles disappears in interpretive theory; its presuppositions cohere with those we make in daily life about our capacities as reflective creatures able to reconsider established beliefs and projects through reasoned deliberation, and able to incorporate the results of those reassessments into future orientations to conduct. Moreover, the concepts in its inquiry articulate with those in social life. The advertising technique is interpreted as a form of manipulation within the discourse of interpretive theory. And the theory supports a moral presumption against the advertising strategy.

It is not my thesis that the law-like theorist must *intentionally* support a politics of manipulation in the current political setting. For particular practitioners may intend merely to produce knowledge within the framework available to them; they may have no interest in the uses to which it is put, or they may believe mistakenly that it is not inherently more susceptible to some uses than to others. Nor is it my thesis that the advocate of the law-like model must describe a particular range of knowledge uses through the vocabulary of manipulation and mystification, for the manipulative implications are most sharply defined within a social epistemology rejected by that theorist. Nor is it my thesis that every social scientist who characterizes research findings in the terminology of the law-like model is a thorough or consistent devotee of that model. In the actual practice of social science many, perhaps most, social scientists adopt an unconsciously ambiguous posture. Their language often suggests commitment to the law-like model when the point is to emphasize the objectivity, precision, predictive power, and policy relevance of the enterprise, and it often suggests wariness of the implications of the model when the point is to warn consumers, advise citizens, or to protect freedom of scientific inquiry. It *is* my thesis that in the current political setting this ambiguity itself helps to sustain a relationship between the enterprise of social science and the manipulative, coercive use of the fruits of that enterprise. For the model supports beliefs consistent with the role social scientists are expected to play in contemporary politics and the social scientist's desire to meet role expectations supports belief in the law-like model of explanation.

By characterizing the opposition between these two divergent social epistemologies as the politics of political explanation I mean to emphasize, first, that each orientation does bear general political implications; secondly, that pressures accurately described as political shape the background within which the debate proceeds; thirdly, that here, as elsewhere in politics, reasoned argumentation can make a difference to the conclusions finally endorsed by practitioners; and, fourthly, that even though interpretive theory has strong arguments in its support, the inability of either side to resolve definitively some perplexing issues converts this domain into a field upon which theoretical controversies flourish. The discussion to follow will be organized around the last two points.

The positivist rejoinder

By 'positivist' I mean a doctrine which either denies that there is an internal relation between belief and action, or treats the beliefs of the human objects of social inquiry as dispositions to behave in specified ways. Such a positivist might be expected to offer three replies to the argument presented here.

First, it might be claimed that the criticisms of the law-like model can be handled by treating the background concepts and beliefs necessary to correlations between electoral rules and party systems as the initial conditions for the occurrence of the laws. Secondly, it might be claimed that social scientists do not seek universal laws but probabilistic laws, and that the latter are not susceptible to criticisms offered against the former. Thirdly, and most seriously, it might be claimed that even though a coherent explanation must incorporate this background of shared concepts and beliefs, that background itself is in principle susceptible to a deeper explanation consistent with the basic presuppositions of the law-like model. I will reply briefly to each of these rejoinders.

The requisite concepts and beliefs can be treated as initial conditions necessary to operation of the generalizations. But if that background is as large as we have suggested, then the form of the law-like model would be saved at the expense of losing its distinctive character. Before we have explained why these laws hold we must explain how the beliefs necessary to them are maintained: the most fundamental questions are thus shifted from the center of the theory to the periphery. If the beliefs are unexplained, the explanatory account is trivial; if the explanation includes reference to the reasons the participants do or might give in support of them, and to an assessment of the rationality of those supporting reasons, an interpretive dimension is inserted into the explanatory scheme.

Secondly, the search for probabilistic generalizations, or even tendency statements, *is* more realistic in the social sciences than the quest for invariant laws, partly because of the open texture and ambiguous implications of the constitutive ingredients of social practice, and partly because of the impressive capacity for reflexivity on the part of those who serve as the objects of social inquiry. The central question remains: How are these probabilities or tendencies to be interpreted? Are they incomplete law-like explanations perfectible in principle through closer specification of their conditions of application? Or, are they interpretive accounts of institutional relations which remain porous and revisable because of the distinctive character of the human objects of inquiry? 'Tendency statements' are sometimes articulated through the vocabulary of the law-like model, but more often the authors are unclear about what sort of model of explanation provides the standard against which the explanatory power of those claims is to be appraised. The model of explanation to which these tendency statements are appropriately to be assimilated depends on the outcome of the debates we have already launched.[14]

The third rejoinder raises the most fundamental issues. To reply we must make some revisions in the interpretive model as so far elaborated. It seems clear that certain moods and desires are produced by bypassing the deliberative processes of reason (even unconscious reason) and that the reflexive comprehension of these causes is either beyond the current capability of the agents or, if attained, is incapable by itself of generating a deliberative reaction to the initial causes. Thus, hypoglycemia can cause depression. Although awareness of the cause might allow one to modify some of the thoughts which are part of the depressive state, apparently a new set of depressive thoughts will predictably replace them. In this case, awareness of the cause can increase the patient's willing-

24

ness to accept medical treatment, and the treatment may allow the agent to be guided in the future by considerations of reason and evidence in shaping a larger portion of beliefs. But awareness of the cause cannot suffice to eliminate its effects. The variety of such influences, the variable extent to which each is susceptible to reflexive self-understanding, and the extent to which the agents are then capable in principle of adjusting their actions to the new understandings is indefinitely large. The possibilities with respect to hypnosis are different from those for repression; those for secondary repression are different from those for primary repression; and those with respect to neurosis emerging from conflicting parental relationships may be different from overtly similar patterns of behavior produced by the inherited protein Pc 1 Duarte.[15]

These qualifications, and others to come, mean that an inter-pretive theory restricted to the self-understandings of participants cannot provide a complete account of actions and practices. But they do not touch the claim that an interpretive dimension must form a part of any sufficient explanatory account. This latter claim could be refuted by demonstrating that the concepts, beliefs and reasons through which we conventionally comprehend our own conduct can be explained through a more basic set of concepts, disconnected from the presuppositions of interpretive theory.

Donald Davidson and Wilfred Sellars are two prominent American philosophers who have explored this possibility sym-pathetically. Sellars, for instance, has contended that while the 'manifest image' of human agency and action is not *reducible* to a more basic image, the 'scientific image' of the human being as 'a complex physical system' can in principle account for behavior and relations at the manifest level.[16] The manifest image is not elimi-nated, but *in principle* is explicable by a basic theory incorporating presuppositions quite divergent from those contained within it.

The rich set of arguments developed to support and refute this position cannot be summarized here; but a central conclusion shared by most parties to this debate does restrict its application to the practice of contemporary social science. While the disputants generally agree that no *a priori* argument can disprove the future possibility of realizing the science projected by Sellars, they also agree that no such account is even remotely close to realization today. *We* do not *now* possess the theoretical and conceptual resources to explain the manifest image in terms of the second model. Because a successful explanation would require a conceptualization of this 'complex physical system' beyond our current powers, current attempts to achieve this displacement with available concepts necessarily oversimplify the phenomena to be explained.

Stuart Hampshire, acknowledging that we cannot now guarantee the future impossibility of such a displacement, reminds us that the concepts of mechanism and physical system it requires 'must be understood more generously, as potentially standing . . . for physical structures, and for types of physical processes, which are not yet recognized, or even envisaged, in contemporary physics.'[17]

Given the current state of our knowledge of human beings and social relations we must, at least for the foreseeable future, differentiate the mode by which we explain the physical *preconditions* for forming beliefs, appraising their rationality, adjusting conduct to beliefs, and reflexively adjusting old habits of conduct from *the mode employed to comprehend these performances themselves when they are functioning well.* We cannot now formulate one mode of explanation to cover both explanatory tasks.

In each of the following cases an antecedent factor is closely associated with a subsequent state.[18] But in each case the relationship varies in two respects from that found in others. (1) An incurable disease impairs an agent's ability to make complex calculations. (2) A previous tradition of use depletes the soil and limits the supply of food available to the participants. (3) An unconscious memory limits an agent's ability to relate to authority figures in a rational way. (4) A conscious and unjustified belief about the manipulative intent of another limits an agent's willingness to trust the other. (5) A conscious and justified belief about the manipulative intent of another limits an agent's willingness to trust the other.

Each relationship varies from most of the others in the degree to which the agent must be aware of the antecedent factor before it can contribute to the subsequent state, and in the alterations which could (or sometimes must) follow if the agent were to recognize the antecedent more fully. In case 1 the relationship does not require the agent's awareness as one of its conditions, and the agent might even be incapable of recognizing it. Recognition, were it to occur, would make a minimal difference to the relationship, though the agent might now refrain from trying to think thoughts known to be beyond his capacity. In case 2 certain beliefs and objectives are inherent in practice of cultivating, but the agent's awareness of the relation between the practice and the result is unnecessary for the antecedent to produce it. Were the agents to recognize the relation, they would revise beliefs implicit in their previous practice and they might be able to take preventative measures previously unavailable to them. In case 3 the agent must possess a range of concepts such as 'parent' and 'authority' before the relationship can be operative; he must also hold certain unconscious beliefs about the intentions of authority figures and how they bear on his own identity aspirations. In this case a more explicit recognition of the antecedent would itself help to unravel the relationship; for to recognize the unconscious memory is to call into question the propriety of reacting to all authority figures in only one way. The term 'recognize' does not do justice to the treacherous process by which one comes to see such previous conduct in a new light, nor can we safely assume that the recognition itself, if complete, would be sufficient to dissolve the old pattern of conduct. But the recognition would surely alter the relationship in some way; the agent might, for instance, decide to *try*, by whatever means available, to revise future conduct more completely. In case 4 not only is the attitude of distrust caused by the antecedent belief, but the belief helps to constitute the attitude itself; without this belief, or others like it, we could not characterize the attitude as one of distrust. The realization that the belief is unjustified – emerging perhaps from the belated understanding that the other forms intentions through a set of concepts unfamiliar to oneself, and that the other is trustworthy but unfamiliar with one's own settled expectations – will dissolve the attitude and alter the relationship. The project now might be to comprehend the point of view of the other more closely and to teach the other more about one's own point of view. In case 5 the relationship requires the belief which enters into it; and once the justification for the belief is provided no further explanation of the relationship is needed. Moreover, only marginal advances in one's self-consciousness about the relationship are possible in this case, such as defining more closely considerations which were previously implicit and diffuse. Such an alteration in self-consciousness would sharpen and crystallize the previous relationship, and it might establish preconditions to its eventual alteration. But the more articulated recognition would not by itself reconstitute the previous relationship in a significant way.

In social and political life, each sort of relation occurs between antecedent and subsequent state. The law-like model, in its pure form, fits most closely the first; but further up the list, it becomes more important to interpret the intersubjective context and the particular intentions and beliefs of the specific agents involved within that context. As these considerations become more pertinent, the possibility of a more self-conscious awareness on the part of the participants takes on added significance. In these sorts of cases, awareness of the antecedent conditions on the part of participants frees them to form new intentions and projects, though it does not guarantee their achievement. Reflexivity, to varying degrees in alternative contexts, increases the freedom of the reflexive agents. Interpretive theory, because it brings out the intersubjective dimension of social reality, contributes to reflexivity on the part of the participants. Its philosophical assumptions respect the capacities of the participants for freedom and reason, and actual interpretations advanced within its frame can enhance the realization of these capacities. This political dimension of a philosophy of political explanation, once it is explicitly stated, provides a consideration in its favor. It does so, at least, for those who construe reason and freedom to be laudable human achievements.

The rationalist derailment

In defending interpretation against the law-like ideal of explanation, it may appear that the interpretive orientation is susceptible to assimilation by a rationalist or 'rational choice' mode of explanation. The rationalist ideal of explanation is similar to the interpretive model in stressing the importance of rational determination of conduct and in seeking, therefore, to explain conduct through the reasons agents adopt for pursuing it. The orientation differs in its insistence that universal criteria of rationality joined to stable features of human preference schedules suffice to account for established patterns of conduct. Rational choice theories, seen from the vantage point of interpretive theory, unjustifiably universalize standards which are particular to specific historical settings; they treat departures from these standards as irrational; and they then justify action to 'rationalize' those spheres of life not in conformity with the particular standards illicitly universalized.

I. C. Jarvie's criticism of the version of interpretive theory advanced by Peter Winch provides a convenient forum for considering these issues. I intend first to defend Winch against Jarvie's criticisms and then to defend Winchcraft against its own quest for purity.

In a much discussed essay, 'Understanding a Primitive Society,'[19] Winch argues that though witchcraft is irrational in our society, and though it is also very difficult for us to comprehend what the practice amounts to in a primitive tribe like the Azande, our correct understanding of the rationale adopted by the participants themselves will show it to be a rational set of practices. It is rational for them but not for us.

Consider, first, Jarvie's interpretation of the Winch argument. As Jarvie sees it, Winch admits that the assumptions in Zande witchcraft do not correspond to reality as we conceive it, but Winch then contends that the assumptions do cohere with the conception of reality adopted by the Azande themselves. Adopting a version of cultural relativism, namely the principle of honoring different strokes for different folks, Winch concludes that we are unjustified in criticizing the conventions which form an intrinsic part of the Zande way of life, and, thereby, unjustified in criticizing the practice of witchcraft situated within these conventions. Here is Jarvie's summary of Winch's argument:

magical beliefs . . . may well be tied into a whole system of other beliefs, a veritable world view in which disputed beliefs play an essential and theoretical role. This system constitutes an ongoing way of life and it shows grave lack of understanding to single out elements of it and attempt to adjudge them not in accord with objective reality. *They may not accord with reality as seen from the standpoint of our language and culture, but they can hardly be said not to accord with the same reality they themselves conceive (and) they themselves embody.*[20]

Jarvie has little trouble demolishing the argument so interpreted. For the beliefs apparently embedded in the practice of witchcraft are full of inconsistencies. And when these inconsistencies are pointed out to them the Zande 'use *ad hoc* devices to evade them.'[21] In Zande society the intellectual norms of conjecture and criticism are underdeveloped, but Winch cannot see this, according to Jarvie, because he sees no rational way to adjudicate between the different standards of rationality embedded in each society. Jarvie then shows that there are universal criteria of rationality appropriate to every society, even though some people within every society, and some entire societies, recognize them less fully than others. These criteria consist of formal rules such as the rules of non-contradiction and identity, and they involve further the critical capacity to 'learn from experience, and especially from mistakes.'[22] Appealing to these standards we can detect inconsistencies in Zande conceptions of witchcraft. The rules for detecting witch substance, for instance, carry the implication that everyone must be a witch, while it is crucial to the practice of witchcraft that only some members be defined as witches. We can see this, though the Azande cannot, for

whereas, on the one hand, our explanation comes from an open and critical intellectual system in which ideas about the world are constantly scrutinized, criticized and revised to meet these criticisms, on the other hand, Zande magic is part of a closed and unrevisable system of beliefs.[23]

Jarvie has misread Winch's argument. First, Winch does not repudiate universal criteria of rationality. He thinks it quite appropriate to ask whether Zande beliefs are self-contradictory. He notes, for instance, that 'there are some situations . . . *where what appears to us* as obvious contradictions are left where they are, *apparently* unresolved.'[24] And he agrees that rationality is 'limited by certain formal requirements centering around the demand for consistency.'[25] But he also insists that these formal requirements do not *suffice* to guide judgment and conduct in specific historical contexts.

But these formal requirements tell us nothing about what in particular is to *count* as consistency, just as the rules of propositional calculus limit, but do not themselves determine what are to be the proper values of p, q, etc. We can only determine this by investigating the wider context of the life in which the activities are carried on.[26]

This move in Winch's argument also forms the centerpiece of interpretive theory.

Secondly, Jarvie implicitly attributes to the Azande (and to Winch's interpretation of them) a point of view which has achieved great primacy in our society. He is so captivated by the instrumental orientation to nature that he automatically construes Zande witchcraft to be a misguided attempt to bring nature under their more complete and reliable control. Examined from that point of view, witchcraft could not fail to appear irrational or, at least, to express a very low level of rationality. The participants seem never to learn from experience how ineffective their rituals are. But, according to Winch, the Azande are not trying to control nature; they are expressing recognition of the limits to human control over the most profoundly important issues of life and death. The ritual expresses feelings of revenge and expiation; it reconciles the participants to misfortunes over which they can have little or no influence. Interpreting Zande witchcraft as merely a technique to control nature is like interpreting the exchange of wedding bands in our society as merely an attempt by each partner to exert magical influence over the other to remain faithful.

While there may be irrationalities in this practice and while (though Winch does not formulate this possibility clearly) the ritual may be poised ambiguously between expressing a spiritual meaning and promoting magical influence, we are not in a position to appraise its rationality until we understand internally the point of view from which it is formed. It is difficult for us to do so because we do not have practices which cohere nicely with the Zande practice of witchcraft. In the essay Jarvie criticizes, Winch has suggested in advance why it is so difficult to examine alternative ways of life from a point of view unfamiliar to us. 'Our blindness to the point of view of primitive modes of life,' he says, 'is a corollary to the pointlessness of much of our own life.'[27] To paraphrase Jarvie's own indictment of the Azande, his unreflective attribution to them of a priority operative in our society impairs his ability to learn from previous experience and from mistakes embedded in contemporary institutions.

Jarvie creates theoretical closure in the name of critical rationalism by universalizing a point of view prevalent in our society. He thereby depletes the critical arsenal available to critical rationalism, losing an opportunity to reappraise from another point of view practices and objectives uncritically accepted in advanced civilizations. The objective he has universalized without argument further allows him to define as irrational social relations and institutions in his own society which do not conform to it. This illicit universalization of a particular is part of the process by which the 'rationalization' of traditional practices of work, education, and childrearing is legitimized in contemporary society.

A few examples might illuminate the pertinence of Winch's orientation to the interpretation of contemporary practices and the dangers inherent in an orientation which implicitly treats basic priorities of the researcher as the priorities appropriate to all rational agents. Consider three contentions advanced by an alien who strives to comprehend selected features of our way of life before deciding how to treat us. (1) 'They claim to eat pigs and cows because the meat is nutritious; but they refuse to eat the equally nutritious meat of cats and dogs.' (2) 'Professors distribute copies of essays written by others to students, but students are forbidden to hand in such essays to professors.' (3) 'Those housewives oppose abortion in the name of the sanctity of human life but they also favor capital punishment for people convicted of murder.'

The first two practices lose the appearance of irrationality once the specific context within which they occur is articulated. In the first case, the alien must be brought to understand our idea of a pet, the role that pets play in our lives, and how, given those relationships, animals must not serve both as pets and food. In the second, the alien-critic must be brought to understand our notion of plagiarism, how it is located within a practice of intellectual life, how contributions to knowledge earn the esteem of other practitioners, and how, thereby, the pretense to have made such a contribution is inconsistent with the ideals of intellectual life. To place the concepts 'pet' and 'plagiarism' in context is to dissolve the initial appearance of contradiction. Though new challenges could be introduced (e.g., to the presumed differentiation between persons and animals or to the very idea of an author), the original desire to explain an irrational practice has given way to an understanding of a coherent practice in terms of its rationale. The alien's new understanding of this rationale permits him to treat us as more than savages incapable of reflective engagement with him.

The third example deserves a slightly more involved elucidation. Assume the aliens to be members of our own society and the anti-abortionists to be housewives in working-class families. The appearance of contradiction does dissolve when we fill out the elements on each side of the equation. The working-class mothers construe abortion to be the willful killing of an innocent person and capital punishment to be the willful killing of one who is guilty of a serious crime. Moreover, their critics, who favor abortion and oppose capital punishment, are interpreted by them as repudiating the standards of responsibility which 'made our country great.' For the critics, interpreted from this standpoint, would punish the innocent more severely than the guilty.

This closer specification of the position of anti-abortionists allows the critics to understand it in terms of its rationale. But this corrected account, even if true, does not exhaust the possibilities for interpretation and criticism. Why are the anti-abortionists *so* oriented to questions of guilt and innocence? Perhaps they secretly view themselves to be innocent and unrecognized victims of forces beyond their control. And perhaps they believe (consciously or unconsciously) that to voice this view would constitute an accusation against those closest to them – against husbands, parents, children and bosses. If they further believe these intimate associates to face enough troubles and self-doubts of their own, they may seek legitimate targets upon which to project these accusations. Such an interpretation would help to explain both why the issues of innocence and guilt are so prominent in the evaluations of abortion and capital punishment, and why the anti-abortionists express their convictions with such fervour and intensity.

An interpretation along these lines would not suffice to justify the orientation which initially appeared to be irrational. Doubt might still be cast on the rationale for treating the fetus as a person to whom the predicates 'innocence' and 'guilt' are applicable. But the interpretation does bring the perceived position of the anti-abortionist to a level of rationality comparable to that of the pro-abortionist; it enhances the prospects for each party to reconsider more critically implicit premises and priorities in its initial stance. It thereby undercuts the judgment that these opponents can only be treated as one would treat an irrational adversary.

Rationalism, in at least two of its forms, unwittingly supports the perspective of the alien who must explain and react to strange practices without comprehending the rationale within them. In the name of reason, it construes the unfamiliar to be unreason; in the name of criticism, it closes off avenues to self-criticism; in the name of the universal it celebrates the provincial. To avoid recognition of deficiencies in this perspective the rationalist must either treat a particular set of ends and priorities as if they were universally acknowledged by all peoples, or treat particular character traits and purposes prevalent in one society as if they reflected orientations that all people everywhere would endorse if only they knew themselves more thoroughly. There *may* be such ends and traits, but the rationalist mode of inquiry, because it inhibits the internal understanding of alternative ways of life, inhibits our ability to ascertain to what extent there are. It tries to establish on *a priori* grounds that which must be established through historically specific inquiry. In doing so, it fosters a reified view of one set of social processes, identifying them as the universal norm against which others are to be appraised; it construes practices deviating from these universalized standards as irrational or representing lower levels of rationality; and, particularly when the alien life impinges on the interests of the parties sponsoring the inquiry, it legitimizes the control, discipline or confinement of those sunk in such irrational practices.

A critique of pure interpretation

Jarvie is worried that the mode of interpretation commended by Winch makes criticism of any way of life impossible; and many others share this concern.[28] I contend that Winch seeks to open contemporary practices to critical reflection through exposure to the rationale inside alien practices and that this position implies the possibility of identifying irrationality both in our way of life and others. The crucial defect in Winch's position is that he fails to ask how explanation is to proceed once an irrational belief or practice has been identified. Exploration of this issue will soften further the fixed lines of dispute between 'interpretive' and positivist' modes of inquiry.

There are significant affinities between Winch and Hegel. Though Winch anticipates internal coherence within alien ways of life, and Hegel expects established ways of life to break down because of internal incoherencies, each believes that social practices are intersubjectively constituted, that any theoretical account of such practices must incorporate the self-interpretation of the participants, that universal (or 'abstract') criteria of rationality are insufficient to guide theoretical and practical judgment, and that the interpretive account which emerges will be teleological in character.[29]

Hegel sought to avoid the dilemma of epistemology which, he believed, plagued rationalist and empiricist philosophies; and he also aimed to transcend the philosophical skepticism which commonly haunts former advocates of these positions. The dilemma can be stated briefly: The attempt to judge ordinary consciousness by an external standard must bump into one of two unwanted implications. Either the defense of the external criterion of knowledge against which ordinary consciousness is criticized invokes the criterion again (a vicious circle), or it refers to another criterion itself in need of grounding (an infinite regress). Thus Descartes, in testing ordinary beliefs against the standard of clear and distinct ideas, presupposes the validity of that standard. And every attempt to resolve doubts about the standard without recourse to received opinion will bump into one of these two limits. Hegel strives to avoid this dilemma by adopting the mode of consciousness to be examined as the starting point of inquiry, and this starting point includes the theory of knowledge accepted within that life. Examination of a particular form of consciousness then shows how it breaks down internally; how, for instance, the explicit standard of knowledge accepted contradicts minimal criteria implicitly presupposed by the participants, or how a set of vague social objectives, once realized concretely, are recognized to contain implications incompatible with the original pursuit. In showing how ideas and practices break down internally, how they lose their life and legitimacy, the theorist invokes only criteria and standards of achievement accepted by participants.

I do not wish to defend Hegel's entire project nor to deny that he invokes some criteria implicitly shared in every way of life.[30] But the approach, similar to Winch's in so many respects, does sometimes generate internal critiques of existing practices. And Winch must accept this implication if his own procedure in criticizing faulty social epistemologies is to be redeemed.

Hegel's criticism of skepticism (or his elucidation of the self-criticism it eventually comes to) draws this implication out nicely. Skepticism, emerging within a way of life where the attempt to translate one's thoughts into practice is continuously obstructed, where, therefore, one's freedom of action is severely impaired, celebrates freedom of thought by severing it from constraints imposed by the external world. If such a world cannot be known, then it cannot constrain one's thought. Skepticism 'procures for its own self the certainty of its freedom' and 'generates the experience of that freedom.'[31] But in doing so it becomes enmeshed in contradictions between the formal assertions it makes and those implicitly affirmed in conduct. 'It affirms the nullity of seeing, hearing, etc., yet it is itself seeing, hearing, etc. It affirms the nullity of ethical principles, and lets its conduct be governed by those very principles. Its deeds and its words always belie one another.'[32] Since deeds express thoughts, the thoughts expressed at one level continually contradict those invoked at the other; and since to live is to carry out deeds, one cannot consistently live in accordance with the skepticism formally adopted.

Winch accepts a similar critique of skepticism; moreover, his critique of positivist social epistemologies is remarkably similar in form. For he contends that the positivist necessarily presupposes in everyday life ideas about self and others which are incompatible with those supported by the positivist idea of a social science. Since the first set of presuppositions, Winch believes, cannot be consistently eliminated by people engaged in social relationships, and since it has not been demonstrated that the second set must be true, the rational solution is to give up the formal doctrine.[33]

But social inquiry, as a practice, shares pertinent characteristics with other social practices. Both, for instance, embody conduct intimately connected with the interpretations of those engaged in it. It follows that a way of life, as well as a way of social science, may embody a disjuncture between the explicit interpretation the participants give of an activity and the interpretation implied by their actual conduct, or between the critical tests available to participants and their refusal to apply them to selective areas of life. Winch is subject to criticism for his failure to *emphasize* that the form of critique he applies to the practice of social science may also be applicable to other social practices. And this modest defect contributes to a more serious one. For once such a disjuncture is identified the next task is to *explain* why it persists.[34] And the appropriate explanation will necessarily transcend the boundaries of pure interpretation.

Winch's understandable hesitancy to criticize tribal societies and his unwillingness to explain why contemporary social scientists remain immune to the criticisms he advances allow him to ignore the limits to pure interpretation implied by his own work. If we shift our focus again to the study of contemporary society, these limits to pure interpretation will emerge.

One cannot explain the phenomenon of McCarthyism in the 1950s by remaining faithful both to the interpretations advanced by McCarthyites and to those advanced by their critics or victims. Each interpretation contains beliefs profoundly at odds with those contained in the other. It cannot be the case that the dissidents both threatened and did not threaten the institutions of freedom, or that they were and were not dupes of an international communist conspiracy. The notions, 'dupe,' 'freedom,' 'communist,' 'dissident,' and 'conspiracy' take on partially discrepant meanings within each interpretation, to be sure. But if one side, say the McCarthyites, stretches these terms far beyond their normal range to give greater plausibility to its charges, the extended definitions, when recognized, will strengthen the plausibility of the thesis but weaken the legitimacy of the reaction. And if the terms are kept within the normal range by both parties, each interpretation will stand in sharp opposition to the other. To explain McCarthyism we must conclude that at least one of these opposing self-interpretations is unjustified, in that it ignores available counter-evidence or advances inconsistent claims; and we must then explain why the participants adopted such unjustified beliefs as premises of action in these circumstances.

The explanation will go beyond an account of the rationale given by participants to an account of why they adopt this unjustified rationale. Similarly: if the available evidence is uncertain between these opposing interpretations, we must explain why the beliefs of the participants were nonetheless so strong and unqualified. An interpretation of McCarthyism, because it must incorporate the consciousness and conduct of opposing parties, necessarily goes beyond at least one of the established interpretations. While tied to the life world of the participants, while exploring the rationale inside each set of actions and reactions, it cannot avoid appraising the rationality of those reactions. One limitation to pure interpretation is thus set by the oppositional mode of contemporary politics.

The mode of explanation shifts when we judge a practice to be irrational or unjustified. If we conclude, for instance, that the McCarthyites held distorted beliefs in the face of strong and contrary evidence, we might try to show how the leaders identified with a spectrum of the populace whose traditional roles and prestige were threatened by the growth of bureaucracy, the displacement of the small firm by the corporation, the expansion of organized labor, and the expanded role of the United States in international affairs. To warrant political efforts to restore the previous way of life it was necessary to believe that these new forms were unnecessary and reversible. The belief that a communist conspiracy had taken over the unions and the bureaucracy provided the sort of belief needed. For if this conspiracy produced the changes opposed, then a purge of the conspirators might permit a return to the desired condition. And since it was a secret conspiracy it would be necessary and reasonable to draw inferences about the conspiratorial motives and intentions of the conspirators from fragmentary evidence.

Such an explanation reverses the relation between belief and its rationale found in pure interpretation. Rather than understanding the belief in terms of its rationale we show how the rationale is constructed to vindicate a needed belief; and we then show how the belief is protected to vindicate the pursuit undertaken. We are moved to this reversal because we find the rationale provided to be inconsistent with other defensible beliefs adopted by participants, or unjustified by procedures for testing beliefs available to the participants.[35]

The limits to pure interpretation are reached each time we judge an action or practice to be irrational or unjustified.[36] But that judgment essentially involves a prior process of interpretation. And the explanation of why the irrationality persists displays a certain coherence among the beliefs, priorities, and actions of the participants. This secondary interpretation of coherence amidst irrationality is possible because the professed commitment by participants to socially established norms of rationality delimits the ways in which they can sustain the irrational practice or action. Moreover, every time we transcend pure interpretation in an account that also becomes available to the participants, we enlarge its possible future scope. Those who find their current beliefs and conduct explained by reference to unrecognized antecedents are now in a better position to recognize them. They can criticize defects in the account, or revise their beliefs and projects in light of these new considerations. The objects of inquiry re-emerge as engaged participants. Our impressive capacity for clarification, correction, evasion, resistance, and ambivalence in such instances presupposes our endorsement of a set of standards to which beliefs and conduct properly conform. It is always possible, and sometimes likely, that participants will adjust previous beliefs and conduct to accord with those standards once defects in their previous habits are depicted convincingly.

Among the impediments to the revision of beliefs in the light of new evidence, one seems to be particularly important. If the ability to convert the new beliefs into premises of action is impaired severely, the very identity we seek to confirm as persons who maintain congruence between professed beliefs and the beliefs implied by conduct will place the new candidates under extreme pressure.

The wish to appear as responsible agents who say what they mean and do what they say, can, in these circumstances, encourage the agents to adjust what they believe to that which they are allowed to do.

I might revise my beliefs about the techniques advertisers use and then participate in consumer boycotts of advertisers using such manipulative techniques. Here the change in belief is matched by corollary possibilities for alterations in conduct. But suppose we became convinced that our view of nature as merely a deposit of resources to be exploited for human use supports an impoverished set of social relations in work and exchange. Suppose, too, that a deeper understanding of the principles of natural science convinces us that the very texture and complexity of the laws of nature justify an aesthetic orientation to it. We now wish to draw nourishment from nature in ways which express respect for its natural beauty. This new orientation might be difficult to express while participating in the established institutions of work, exchange, and consumption. Moreover, the close interdependence of this institutional structure might foil efforts to bring its practices closer to our new convictions. In this setting either our professed convictions would be nullified by those expressed in conduct or we would acknowledge that our behavior is alienated: it constantly appears to embody convictions we do not really endorse. The inability to adjust actions and practices to new convictions might eventually encourage participants to repudiate the convictions. The new set of beliefs lose credibility because they cannot find expression in institutionally sanctioned conduct.

Structural theorists contend that such constraints are so powerful and complete in any social formation that they determine the 'intersubjectivity' of the role bearers. Here the reflexive moment disappears; interpretation congeals into the articulation of structural determinants. I shall argue that these theorists exaggerate the role of a limiting condition which can be assimilated into interpretive theory.

The limits to pure interpretation, once posed, generate a series of adjustments in the logic of interpretive theory. But the adjustments accentuate the interpretive dimension in two respects: The recognition of limits to interpretation in a particular setting involves the practice of interpretation; and the construction of an account which transcends pure interpretation enhances the future prospects for a closer fit between the explanation provided and the self-understanding of the participants.

These theoretical implications carry political import. By acknowledging in its mode of explanation the capacity for reason and freedom among the human objects of inquiry, an interpretive account is primed to bring out the rationale implicit in established practices and to encourage rejoinders and reconsiderations on the part of those whose conduct is subjected to interpretation. Because its mode of comprehension invites reflexive reaction it is engaged openly in the political life it interprets.

2

The underdetermination of subjects by structures

The political context of structural theory

Socialist movements in capitalist societies, as the history of the nineteenth and twentieth centuries shows, can be derailed in a variety of ways. An investment strike by private capital can fuel unemployment, discouraging dependent workers and encouraging political elites to reinstitute programs that support private profit-making. A stratified workforce can become bitterly divided, provoking some segments to support the official intimidation of others. The population at large, frightened by the uncertainty which accompanies such a transition, can press for a return to the status quo ante. Domestic military and police forces, taking advantage of new anxieties and instability, can step in to restore the old order. A foreign state, threatened by the emerging example of socialism, can finance internal disruption, limit the supply of essential trade items, or intervene militarily.

Even success can be destructive. Revolutionary regimes, struggling to eliminate obstacles to the realization of a new order, can terrorize dissidents at home and drain socialist movements elsewhere of energy and conviction. Finally, socialist intellectuals, striving to visualize an end to the alienation and exploitation around them, can undermine inadvertently their own cause by promising a future too pure to remain credible, upon reflection, to potential supporters.

If the course of capitalist development did not generate consequences which weaken allegiance to it, if it did not erode traditional social ties, threaten workers with job insecurity, propel people into careers that are debilitating and devoid of worthy social purpose, upset the equilibrium of the ecosystem, convert many young people into delinquents, and treat many old people as wards of the state, then this maze of road blocks and obstacles surely would have exhausted socialist sentiments by now. But one index of the power-ful pull of anti-capitalist sentiment[1] is the emergence, within a generation after each disillusionment, of a new wave of oppositional movements. Each new movement strives to renew the struggle while avoiding retrospectively recognizable defects in the theory and practice of its immediate predecessors.

The 'structural' version of Marxist theory, inspired by Louis Althusser,[2] must be comprehended within such a political context. Its political function has been to protect a new generation of socialists from despair. Althusser is reacting, first, against the voluntarist interpretation of Stalinism, whereby the particular character, strategy and motives of Stalin himself were treated by western radicals as the primary sources of Soviet repression; and, secondly, against the voluntarist and humanist orientation of an earlier wave of western radical movements symbolized in France by theorists such as Jean-Paul Sartre, Albert Camus, and André Gorz and represented during the 1960s by New Left politics in the United States and western Europe. Althusser insists that the apparent voluntarism in each case is controlled by deeper structural deter-minants. Theories which do not grasp these determinants are in-herently ideological; they are subjective reactions to the conditions of existence, rather than in-depth accounts of a determinate social formation.

Whatever its virtues and defects as a theoretical production, structural theory is an understandable response to such a prolonged series of political defeats for the Left. First, it discredits a series of radical theories (e.g., existential Marxism, New Left Democracy, critical social theory) which prevailed during a recent round of political defeats. Secondly, by replacing the dialectical relation between theory and practice with the idea of an autonomous theoretical practice generating internal criteria of knowledge, it insulates socialist hopes and aspirations from embarrassing develop-ments within actual capitalist systems. Thirdly, by treating capitalism as a structured whole resistant to wholesale transformation until its structural preconditions of existence are broken internally, the theory provides solace to radical voluntarists who have failed to break the order by political means. Fourthly, since persons (or subjects) are treated as effects of structure within structural theory, the theorist is able to project a possible future in which structural alterations will initially produce modes of behavior needed to displace capitalism and later produce modes congruent with the role imperatives of communism. And, fifthly, by treating Stalinism as a particular effect of the Soviet system, rather than in any way expressive of theoretical ambiguities within Marxism itself, the theory relieves doubts among socialist intellectuals about the viability of their own ideals.

The power of structural theory to mesmerize critical intellectuals is (or perhaps was) located in the ambiguous relation between the elimination of subjective categories from Marxist theory and the escape from subjective despair by critical intellectuals. But commitment to the theory which promises to purge itself of this 'philosophical twaddle about man' is precarious.[3] For the sources of enchantment to it cannot be acknowledged without casting doubt on the truth of the contentions which make it enchanting.

This ideological dimension of structural theory, which joins a series of bourgeois predecessors in purporting to have gone beyond ideology, must be attended to even while we examine the power of its intellectual claims. For in important instances theoretical contentions are stated with an intensity and a mood of certainty which the sustaining arguments do not justify. On such occasions, the gap between the mood of the assertion and the mode of the argument requires explanation.

We will first examine Althusser's claim to have constructed a Marxist theory without reference to a human subject. We will then explore the Althusserian concept of structure, contending that the conceptualization fails on its own terms. The critique will support a revised understanding of the structural dimension of social life whereby structure is defined as a porous set of institutional interdependencies in which participants retain some capacity for reflexivity. In the last section we will return to the political rationale for Althusser's theoretical anti-humanism, trying to purge critical theory of this apology for ruthlessness in politics.

Theory without anthropology

Many contemporary theorists, writing either as Marxists or as leftists engaged in a dialogue with Marxism, insist that an intersubjective dimension must be incorporated into any theory capable of grasping the structure of advanced capitalist systems. The work of theorists such as Jean-Paul Sartre and André Gorz serves as the explicit target of Althusser's attack. Jurgen Habermas and Charles Taylor are two others who seek to provide epistemic grounds for an interpretive theory with critical potential.[4] All of these theorists, though their works diverge in important respects, share a set of general orientations. They contend that a social order is constituted in part by an intersubjective background of concepts and beliefs; that a structural dimension of these practices helps to account for constraints, contradictions, and possibilities immanent within an order; and that it is sometimes possible to discern within an order implicit aspirations for a reconstituted society more worthy of the allegiance of the participants. They believe that a social theorist must initially strive to comprehend the self-interpretations of participants in order to individuate the actions and institutions to be explained, but they also insist that a complete explanatory account may transcend the interpretations accepted by participants. They intend their own theories to be politically engaged, seeking to alter the self-interpretations and orientations to action which now prevail, so that a larger constituency will resist authoritarian pressures within the existing order and become better attuned to the quest for a more democratic order.

Though Althusser does not discuss any of these theorists in detail, though he ignores the structural dimension within each theory, and though he often treats this mode of thought as if it *reduces* social relations to relations between free, disembodied subjects, it is just this complex of ideas which he seeks to debunk. Each of these theorists, on the Althusserian reading, is trapped within the 'ideology of the subject.' For each inserts anthropological categories referring to human needs, intentions, projects, understandings, and choices into the explanatory side of social theory, whereas the structural theorist realizes that the ideas, behavior, and purposes of role-bearers must be conceptualized strictly as objects to be explained. The 'naive' version of this humanist disease, according to Althusser, is expressed in bourgeois theories of action where such notions as preference, utility, rationality, freedom, consent, and interests are given explanatory status. A more subtle, Marxist humanism employs such defective notions as alienation, praxis, needs, and species-life to comprehend social relations; and it draws further upon such dyadic contrasts as false consciousness/self-consciousness, appearance/reality, sphere of necessity/sphere of freedom to contrast the present with standards to be realized in a possible future. Both types of theory are 'humanist.' They employ anthropological categories in explanation; they articulate a theory of human powers and potentialities to explain the present and to set a normative standard for appraising it. The following statements from Althusser and Balibar indicate both the substance of their opposition to 'humanism' and their tendency to construct a caricature of the theories they oppose.

. . . the *relations* of production (and political and ideological social relations) are irreducible to any anthropological inter-subjectivity – since they only combine agents and objects in a specific structure of the distribution of relations, places and functions, occupied and 'supported' by objects and agents of production.[5]

. . . the structure of the relations of production determines the *places* and *functions* occupied and adopted by the agents of production, who are never anything more than the occupants of these places, insofar as they are supports (*Traeger*) of these functions.[6]

Marx's thesis does not mean that in the modes of production other than capitalism the structure of the social relation is *transparent to the agents.*[7]

. . . the reverse side of . . . economism is humanism or bourgeois liberalism. This is because ideas find their foundations in the categories of Bourgeois *Law* and legal ideology materially indispensable to the functioning of Bourgeois Law : liberty of the Person, that is, in principle, his right freely to dispose of himself, his right to his person, his free will and his body.[8]

The economism/humanism pair, when it is introduced into Marxism does not really change . . . ; it takes on a Social-Democratic accent, one which raises not the question of the *class struggle* and its abolition . . . , but that of the defence of Human Rights, of liberty and justice, even of the liberation and free development of the 'personality' or the 'integral personality.'[9]

The Althusserian project, as embodied in *Reading Capital*, is to define the capitalist mode of production as a structure and to show how this structure can be theorized without resort to concepts and assumptions that express the 'ideology of the subject.'

The mode of production as structure

Althusser specifies three elements present in every mode of production: labor power, the object of labor, and the means of labor. He then specifies two 'connectives' which combine the elements in specific ways: the labor process, which involves the transformation of natural objects into use values, and the social relations of production, which involve specific types of relations among the agents of production.[10] For Althusser, the labor process as a 'material mechanism is dominated by the physical laws of nature and technology.' With respect to the relations of production, Althusser stresses that the 'relations between men and men are defined by the precise relations existing between men and the material elements of the production process.' He asserts that 'By combining or *interrelating* these different elements . . . we shall reach a definition of the different *modes of production* which have existed and can exist in human history.' According to Balibar's initial formulation, these elements and connectives form a 'table of invariants in the analysis of forms.'[11] The invariant elements assume different combinations in different modes of production, such as the feudal, the capitalist, and the communist. Later, however, Balibar cautions that each element requires further elaboration before its role in any specific mode can be characterized closely enough. The elements, then, are not literally 'invariant.'

A first approximation of how these elements combine to form an economic structure that produces commodities and reproduces itself, is provided in Balibar's quotation from *Capital*:

Whatever the social form of production, laborers and means of production always remain factors of it. But in a state of separation from each other either of these factors can be such only potentially. For production to go on at all, they must *combine*. The specific manner in which this combination is accomplished distinguishes the different epochs of the structure of society one from another.[12]

In what sense does a particular combination of these elements constitute a structure? And how are we to conceptualize the thesis of structural determination whereby the operation of the elements is determined by the structure of the whole? Some of Althusser's formulations seem to bypass the concept of structural causality in favor of a more traditional conception of linear causality. Thus he says that 'the "means of labor" determine the typical form of the labor process considered: by establishing the "mode of attack" on the external nature . . . they determine the *mode of production*, the basic category of Marxist analysis (in economics and history); at the same time they establish the level of *productivity* of productive labor.'[13] But most statements by Althusser and Balibar which establish the agenda for this theory suggest a view of structure and causality distinguishable from a linear view of causation. For example:

. . . economic phenomena [are] *determined by a (regional) structure* of the mode of production, itself determined by the *(global) structure* of the mode of production.

. . . the only way to the essence of the economic is to construct its concept, i.e., to reveal the *site* occupied in the structure of the whole by the region of the economic, therefore to reveal the articulation of this region with other regions (legal–political and ideological superstructure), and the degree of *presence* (or effectivity) of the other regions in the economic region itself.[14]

It would be impossible to follow the logic of these statements literally. That would require the specification of the economic, political, and ideological instances and the way in which each articulates with the others. But the political and ideological instances have not been defined yet 'by the structure of a combination.' Presumably, we can break into the structure at the economic level. That is, at least, the level which Althusser and Balibar have tried to define in structural terms: the goal is to locate each element in a particular position so that other elements can articulate with it only in one specific way; the whole can then become operative only if each element meshes with all others in the specific way open to it.

In capitalism the worker, as possessor of labor power, is separated from effective control over the means of production. Workers cannot gain access to these means without submitting to the directives of the owner-managers; and those who control the means require labor power before the means can be set into motion. When these separated elements are combined through commodity exchange (labor contracts) in the market, market competition and production for profit exert continual pressure for reduction of unit labor costs. Pressure to reduce costs is converted into imperatives to expand labor productivity, and the expansion of labor productivity is produced by intensification of the division of labor, mechanization, and the displacement of craft occupations by less skilled work tasks. These effects, in turn, make it increasingly difficult for workers to run the new productive arrangements independently. Even if they were to obtain physical access to the means of production, they would lack the skills and knowledge required to operate them. Once some elements of the structure are installed, labor and the means of production can only be connected through commodity exchange in the market; and only if they are so connected can production and reproduction of the system occur. Because each capital investment must either reduce labor costs or lose out in the market, the surviving capital and labor role-bearers are impelled to maintain a 'capitalist mode of production' which is 'constantly *in the process* of transition from manual labor to mechanized labor.'[15]

The historical process by which these elements were separated and combined, that is, the transition from feudalism to capitalism, requires an analysis of another sort; but once the elements are initially combined in this way the structural imperatives of the mode assert themselves. The comprehension of origins (diachronic or historical analysis) and the comprehension of system reproduction once the elements are articulated in a particular way (synchronic or structural analysis) form two separable modes of inquiry because the process by which a mode is created diverges from the process by which it thereafter produces and reproduces itself.

The reinsertion of anthropology

Though this is a minimal characterization of the mode of production as the 'effectivity of the structure on its elements,' it is sufficient for our purposes. The account is sufficient to show that the *boundaries of structural theory must be transcended in the very process of theorizing the parameters of a structural whole*. This contention will be established in two stages.

Marx draws an important distinction between labor and labor power which is not explored by Althusser or Balibar. In capitalist society the worker appears to own his labor power, and clearly cannot employ it productively until it is sold to the capitalist under prevailing conditions. But the appearance of ownership is deceptive: to be a living being and to possess only the capacity for labor is to be in a state of need. For 'if his capacity for labor remains unsold, the laborer derives no benefit from it, but rather he will feel it to be a cruel nature-imposed necessity that this capacity has cost for its production a definite amount of the means of subsistence and that it will continue to do so for its reproduction.'[16] The worker is an owner in the thin sense that he is a 'free owner of his own working capacity and his own person,' but the laborer is also 'deprived of everything necessary for the realization of his labor power.'[17]

This *need* impels the worker to accept the available conditions of work; it therefore helps to explain the articulation of the elements in the capitalist mode of production. Without this need the articulated elements could not slide into gear. But to refer to human needs on the explanatory side of theory is to introduce, however mildly, a whiff of anthropology into structural theory. This raises the question: What can be done now to prevent an anthropological stink? To raise the question is to create a demand for criteria to establish when it is and when it is not legitimate to introduce anthropological assumptions into a structural theory.

Consider now how the anthropological dimension expands. In *Reading Capital* and *For Marx*[18] Althusser constructed a sharp disjuncture between theory, which is scientific and autonomous, and ideology, which articulates to social and economic practices without being susceptible to tests of truth or falsity. Ideology expresses 'not the relation between the workers and their conditions of existence, but the way they live the relation between them and their conditions of existence.'[19] Those sunk in ideology can never use it as a dialectical vehicle to true theory; for in ideology the real relation is 'inevitably invested in the imaginary relation, a relation that *expresses* a *will*, a hope, or a nostalgia, rather than describing a reality.'[20] If this irrevocable disjuncture between theory and ideology were not affirmed by Althusser, anthropological categories would be reinserted immediately into structural theory; for there would be some possibility that the real conditions of existence, now opaque to the participants, could become more transparent to them. Their orientations to political practice would then shift in accordance with the new understanding, and the consequences of that revised practice would provide grounds for further revising understanding, and so on. The possibility for a dialectic of self-consciousness would thus be lodged within social practice. The postulated disjuncture between theory and ideology closes off this potential dialectic of self-consciousness. But the price of closure is high. Althusser has to hold, for instance, that even in a communist society the role-bearers could not become free subjects, 'Let us admit,' he says, 'historical materialism cannot conceive that even a communist society could ever do without ideology.'[21] With the introduction of that disjuncture he gives up even a modest version of Marx's aspiration to see an order in which 'the practical relations of everyday life offer to man none but perfectly intelligible and reasonable relations,' and in which production is 'consciously regulated' by 'freely associated men . . . in accordance with a settled plan.'[22]

But the disjuncture between theory and ideology cannot serve its intended purpose. My charge is this: without an anthropological dimension in theory, it is inexplicable why the role-bearers require ideology to bear the roles imposed by capitalism; with such an anthropology, the view that theory is not and cannot be made available to participants in ways that influence their future conduct must be revised profoundly. Structural theory does not eliminate, rather it suppresses, the anthropological dimension. And once the suppressed premise is exposed, structural theorists must re-engage the very issues they have sought to expunge from theory – issues such as the nature of human subjects; the relation between individual subjects and intersubjectivity; the structural limits to the emergence of self-consciousness; the connection between consciousness and political practice; and the moral inhibitions to both social control and revolutionary action. We shall now show how the split between theory and ideology is undermined by the considerations which purport to establish it.

Let us assume a capitalist system functioning according to Althusserian assumptions. Its human bearers are entering into a variety of relations such as laboring, investing, contracting, managing, consuming, and so forth. The bearers accept an ideology that makes their life experiences more bearable to them.

What capacities must the role-bearers have? What other possibilities are built into the possession of these capacities? Why cannot they 'bear' these roles without ideology? These are questions we will pursue.

Take the worker. Surely to enter into a wage contract he must be capable of understanding a whole set of complex, background ideas such as 'acting intentionally,' 'reaching an agreement with another,' 'acting in accordance with a standard,' 'being held responsible for living up to agreements,' 'property rights,' and 'working for pay.' But to understand these one must comprehend an indefinitely large set of ideas which helps to fix their meanings by contrast and comparison. A very young child, for example, does not have such capacities sufficiently developed. Unable to take the role of the other, the youngster does not know how to promise or to enter into a contract, nor does he really understand our distinction between work and play. Even if such a child were to acquire the body of an adult, it would be of marginal use as the bearer of multiple roles in a capitalist society. With extremely close (and costly) monitoring it might do some sorts of work. But the monitoring would be necessary not only on the job but at home, in consumption, paying taxes, on the streets, and so on. To accommodate such children in adult roles, the system would then require a huge number of monitors who did have the capacities necessary to comprehend the complex beliefs, concepts, rules, threats, and delayed consequences essential to effective role performance. It is a pity in a way. If young children could serve as role-bearers, the ideology required to keep them working and consuming in the right proportions would be simple indeed.

To possess the complex concepts (and complex beliefs yet to be considered) appropriate to these roles *is to have the capacity to form alternative concepts and beliefs*. If I understand how to promise I also understand how to refuse to do so, how to break a promise, how to express regret. That set of understandings is sharpened through possession of a related set, such as lying, acting out of charity, offering a bribe to another, or threatening another; and to understand each of these is to comprehend the standard of conduct lived up to or down to in performing it. Similarly, to understand what it is to enter into a wage contract is to have the capacity – even if it is selectively *developed* in particular contexts – to understand what it is to change the terms of a contract, to enter into collective contract arrangements, to convert the contract into a life-long reciprocal commitment, to alter the roles of the respective contractors, or to replace the contract form altogether. To comprehend enough to carry out the complex roles in capitalist society is to have the capacity to imagine quite different roles.

If the agents have these complex capacities and concepts, surely in principle they could be brought to comprehend the relations of production approximately as Althusser does. Their understanding might never reach the same level of precision or subtlety. But to understand the established ideas of wage, profit, markets, and

contracts, is to be able to understand potentially the ideas of exploitation, labor as a commodity form, and surplus value. Nothing about
the mental capacities of these role-bearers requires them to live at
the level of ideology. They have the capacity to understand
Althusser's theory.

We must expect the structural theorist to express impatience with
these initial contentions. 'Of course,' it might be replied, 'the
bearers possess some such set of skills and capacities, but the direction in which they can develop and the kinds of actions bearers
actually take (their attempts or only their achievements?) are structurally determined.' But to reject this minimal anthropology is to
omit the preconditions for successful performance of the roles
required by the theory, while to accept it is to place the theorist
under severe pressure to add further anthropological elements in
order to save the structural theory of ideology.

The workers are capable of understanding the actual operation
of the system, but, according to the theory, they live at the level of
ideology.[23] Certainly, if workers were willing to play the required
roles while recognizing things as they really are, ideology would be
redundant at best. Indeed, *if* ideology is not necessary to the identity of the role-bearers, it would surely be pernicious in its effects
on role performance. The system would operate more smoothly if
its bearers, though aware of its real structure and its contradictory
tendencies, were quite willing to accept its role requirements. Serfs
would not need to see their plight as God's will; laborers would
have no need to see exploitation as free exchange.

What characteristics of the bearers make ideology functional for
role performance? Equally important, what is it about the bearers
that encourages them to accept ideology in these circumstances?

Social relationships among people embody a set of reactive attitudes, or, as Marx put it, following Hegel, they embody 'reflexive
relations.' Attitudes such as resentment, love, hate, gratitude, indignation, regret, and guilt are formed in reaction to actions of others
interpreted by the respondent as intentional and voluntary. Resentment expresses such an attitude toward another because of the
other's action-attitude toward me; indignation is a reaction to
another's action-attitude toward another; and guilt is a reaction
toward one's own previous attitude-action. To resent another is
typically to assume that the other intentionally and unjustifiably,
say, damaged one's reputation in a manner that justifies a punitive

reaction on one's part. Expressions of resentment and of the other reactive attitudes invoke standards accepted by the expressers, and the standards embody judgments about interests, rights, justice, and propriety. A theorist could try to prove that such reactive attitudes, though endemic to social life as we live it, always rest upon fallacious metaphysical assumptions about agents and their capacities, but that is not the point now. For the participants in the social life of complex societies do make such assumptions about themselves and others. Agents who apply such standards in personal relationships have the capacity to apply them to collectivities, to reassess prevailing standards critically, to formulate new standards and judgments. The actual and potential self-interpretation of those expressing reactive attitudes creates a systematic need for ideology. For it is not difficult to expect that, in a context of unconstrained discourse, workers, whose reflexive relations in daily life invoke normative standards, might conclude that the system of exploitation is unjust or that a system generating internal contradictions is illegitimate.

The *function* of ideology is now clear enough. It constrains the political reflection of those who see themselves entering into reflexive relations and expressing reflexive attitudes in daily life. The structural theorist must tacitly acknowledge this; otherwise there is no need on the part of role-bearers for an ideology first to interpret the prevailing order in terms of standards acceptable to them and, secondly, to debunk alternative standards whose application would threaten the legitimacy of the system.

Ideology plays a function in the system, but why do the agents internalize it? If system x, given the characteristics of its role-bearers, requires ideology to operate smoothly, the requirement does not itself explain why it is met. The ideology appropriate to role performance and the actual ideology of the role-bearers could fly apart, undermining the willingness of workers to bear those roles.

Further assumptions about the agents will close this potential gap. First, the workers have certain stable and intense interests in attaining food, shelter, clothing, and security for themselves and their families; and once this mode of life is locked into place, these interests can be secured only by accepting the roles it generates. Secondly, those who 'play' the required roles seek to retain some rough congruence between the beliefs and aspirations appropriate to their life situation and the beliefs and aspirations they actually adopt. Thirdly, efforts to reform the system in a piecemeal way, so that discrepancies between role requirement and role performance can be resolved in favor of the latter, prove to be self-defeating. If all of these assumptions were true one would expect workers over the long term to internalize beliefs and aspirations congruent with established roles.

The first assumption seems inherently plausible. The third is central to the theory we are examining. So we shall explore the second more closely.

Consider a young dissident who takes a job where the established roles of dissident and worker collide. He lacks ready access to dissident groups or texts. As a dissident he has a simple concept of exploitation and believes that owners exploit workers. The dissident also believes that deference to managers is a form of bad faith and that a collective struggle is needed to reconstitute the system of production, authority, and distribution. But the dissident also works. The worker must be punctual, obey the commands of the boss, adjust work rhythms to the pace of the machinery, accept wages as the incentive to work, live up to the terms of the wage contract, and adjust overt attitudes and behavior in a thousand ways to established rules, norms, and expectations.

Even though the two roles clash, one can try to 'live' one and 'play' the other. But this is far from easy : if one is isolated; if there is no chance of finding a role consistent with one's real beliefs; if family and friends emphasize the importance of continuing in the present role; if others, naturally expecting one to accept the appropriate beliefs and norms, feel deceived and unjustly treated when one repudiates them; and if one's own sense of moral integrity is threatened when overt conduct is persistently at odds with one's underlying commitments, the dissident beliefs themselves will come under tremendous pressure.

The pressures are not merely psychological : psychological, epistemic, and moral pressure are interwoven. If I hold belief x but fail to express it or to act on it for a long period of time, it becomes increasingly a private view. As a shadow of a belief, not readily amenable to closer specification and clarification in inter-subjective discourse, it gradually approaches the status of a private memory or a dream. A private memory is indefinite and uncertain because there is no public way to inspect again the events it reports. A belief is similarly diluted, uncertain, and jeopardized as long as it is disconnected from its holder's public statements and activity and as long as there is no wider group with whom to share and express it.

The worker's current conduct expresses a set of definite beliefs and norms he does not hold, while his real beliefs, abstracted from his concrete life-activity, are increasingly shadow-like in character. Facing *social* pressure to identify himself as others do, *epistemic* pressure to adopt clear beliefs subject to public tests, and internal *moral* pressure to achieve congruence between inner beliefs and outer conduct, he can respond affirmatively by adopting gradually the beliefs appropriate to his role. The others can simply be allowed to fade away.

By the time the worker reaches this point, he need no longer see himself (at least consciously) as either a coward or a victim. For he has come to believe that economic growth is in the interests of all; that such growth requires private profit; that productive labor is necessarily organized in authoritarian, routinized ways; that the only incentive to work is the promise of private material gain; that to contract one's labor power is to enter into free exchange; that one set of bosses is approximately as good as another; that equal opportunity in an unequal system fosters both social justice and economic growth; and that young dissidents who challenge these views have had little experience in the *real* world.

Since his overt conduct and conscious beliefs are now integrated, the worker sees himself as a free agent who accepts the established conditions of life as desirable in some respects and intrinsically unavoidable in others. But, according to structural theory, he now lives at the level of ideology.

Notice: if the system were not as tightly structured as structural theorists claim, or if the agents were to have a clear comprehension of the inner connections between roles and beliefs, the worker could respond to pressure to establish congruence between them in a variety of ways. Anyone who understands these connections, then, could seek out associates and roles more compatible with his or her initial orientation; one might tap latent militance in others; one might study radical theory to deepen and protect the initial orientation against these pressures; one might strive to live with these ambiguities and thus go crazy, or strive to live with them and thereby identify openings and strategies for change not previously discerned by others. Human beings are not *simply* natural objects.

They have the potential to comprehend epistemic and existential predicaments facing them and can, individually and collectively, strive to avoid, deflect, delay, transcend, or eliminate these predicaments.

Structural theory cannot characterize an operative structure, in particular cannot account for its need for ideology and the receptivity of the role-bearers to it, without drawing upon an anthropological theory.[24] It is because the anthropology implicit within structural theory makes contact with tacit assumptions the participants make about themselves in daily life that it can be suppressed by structural theorists. We fill in what they leave out. But the anthropology must be suppressed, and we must do the filling in, if the central pretensions of structural theory are to be preserved. For once an anthropology has been inserted into the theory, the theory must include space for reflexivity on the part of the role-bearers who form the objects of inquiry. Their ability to comprehend the inner connections among role performance, their own beliefs, and their pursuit of identity affect the possible directions in which the structure might develop historically.

Similarly, an intersubjective theory must contain a structural dimension. Particular institutions of work, family, markets, and state, each of which is partly constituted by the self-interpretations of participants, also combine together into an interdependent totality. None of the parts can be reconstituted significantly unless the others to which it is linked are also reconstituted; and some of the parts, developing along a relatively autonomous trajectory, may come to stand in a contradictory relation to the others. Thus, to give an example of structural interdependence, a market economy is not consistent with the institution of the extended family because the labor mobility (free labor) required by the first institution nullifies the preconditions for continuation of the second.

Another example can be found in the structural connections among instrumental work, restrictive forms of community life, and consumption configurations. The capitalist workplace is the site of perpetual tension between the pursuit of profit by employers (entailing strategies of scientific management, detailed specialization, bureaucratic regulation, and wage incentive ladders) and the demand for dignity by employees (involving job security, a role in decision-making, challenging job assignments, and the production of socially useful goods). The resolution of this tension in favor of the profit imperative helps to channel patterns of consumption. If work does not confirm a sense of the worker's dignity, and if the expansion of the market undermines the preconditions of local community life, the possession of commodities becomes a crucial means available to the worker to secure a semblance of dignity; and mass spectator sports and shopping malls provide a deformed expression of collective identity.[25] One can see this operating on a more general level. Labor mobility, individualized career patterns, and the breakdown of stable communities encourage the production of a particular kind of commodity. Commodities which can be consumed by individuals are favored over those which require the common involvement of a larger collectivity. The automobile, the private home, individualized therapy, and personal recreational facilities acquire primacy over functional equivalents presupposing the existence of collective units of consumption. These constraints upon feasible modes of consumption in turn can contribute to inflationary tendencies; for individuals will demand the means to achieve the particular gratifications available to them in the established order of things as a condition of bearing the burdens imposed on them.

Structural relationships like these can be converted into contradictory tendencies. Public policies to control inflation simply by curtailing consumption ignore the structural links between work, social life, and consumption, and will intensify problems of worker motivation and labor productivity as a consequence. But, at the same time, the attempt to replenish depleted motives to work by reconstituting work processes might improve the strategic position from which workers could oppose the system of production for private profit. The effort to maintain one aspect of capitalism may weaken another. Relations of this form can be stated only as contradictory *tendencies* because the options examined do not exhaust the set of possible options in the system. But they are *contradictory* tendencies because in each case the available response strengthens one imperative of the system while it undermines another.[26]

Connections and contradictory tendencies within a totality cannot be stated without reference to the self-interpretation of the participants, and without including the possibility that the explanatory account will inform the future self-interpretations of at least some of those participants. The participants can understand, for instance, the connections briefly delineated above between work, consumption units, commodity forms, inflationary tendencies, and state policies to reduce inflation. It is precisely because the intersubjective complex is *structured* that a shift in the ideas of participants does not in itself suffice to create the space for significant social change; but it is also because these relations are *intersubjectively* structured that the possibility for a more reflective politics resides within them.

The primacy of politics

Structural theory, it has been argued, presupposes an anthropology and an intersubjective dimension; and acknowledgement of these elements resituates the relation between theory and ideology. But Althusser himself has recently recanted the 'theoreticism' of his earlier work. He now denies that there can be a pure theoretical practice or that the structure of a mode of production can be grasped through formal theory. He now insists, in contrast to his earlier position, that theoretical and philosophical questions are to be settled 'in the last instance' by political considerations. Today, these political considerations are wheeled out to eliminate humanist categories and anthropological assumptions from structural theory. The dominant motif persists amidst a profound shift in its explicit rationale.

'Marx's theoretical anti-humanism,' says the new Althusser in *Essays in Self Criticism*, 'means a refusal to root the explanation of social formations and their history in a concept of man with theoretical pretensions, that is, a concept of a man as an *originating subject*, one in whom originate his needs (*homo economicus*) his own thoughts (*homo rationalis*) and his acts and struggles (*homo moralis, juridicus* and *politicus*).'[27]

The critical humanism also repudiated by Althusser, however, advances no such idea of an abstract, ahistorical subject; it claims instead that *inter*subjective relations *help* to constitute social life and that these relations are structured in ways not fully embodied in the self-consciousness of participants. The subject (or rational person) is thus a partial, precarious, historical achievement rather than a fully autonomous author of ideas and acts. The discrepancy between the position Althusser opposes and the stance actually adopted by his opponents generates our first question: Why does Althusser construct a caricature of critical humanism?

A second question must be posed as well. For the new statements expressing Althusser's anti-humanism are shrouded in ambiguity. Even while repudiating the ideology of the subject he now aims at 'a communist society where, one day, all men will be free and brothers.'[28] He rescinds, then, his earlier claim that every social formation, including communism, requires its role-bearers to live in the mist of ideology. But discourse about freedom is usually attached to an idea of agents who, actually or potentially, are free. Perhaps Althusser is articulating a new concept of freedom, one which does not require subjects capable of reflecting, making choices, forming projects, or reconsidering previous premises of action. But he neither formulates any such idea of freedom nor indicates how the negation of the subject is consistent with the affirmation of an ideal of freedom. Or perhaps he believes that the masses (as he calls them) are today pure role-bearers and that they can become pure subjects in a communist society. I doubt that it is possible to sustain such a disjunctive view. It is easier to try to eliminate the subject completely from social theory (as the early Althusser did) than to displace it *completely* from one society while claiming these negated capacities will flourish in another. Surely some shadow-like expression of these capacities must be manifested in the contemporary system, creating the possibility for an enhancement of self-consciousness. Our second question then is: Why is Althusser's new anti-humanism shrouded in ambiguity? Why does he appear to affirm for the future what he eliminates from the present, while remaining silent on the rationale for this disjuncture?

Consider the explicit answer Althusser now gives to the question, 'Why must humanism be eliminated from structural theory?' 'Because practically, i.e., in the facts, this expression is exploited by bourgeois ideology which uses it to fight, i.e., to kill, another, true word, and one vital to the proletariat: the class struggle.'[29] Philosophy fights 'against lying words; it fights against "shades of opinion."' [30] The meaning of these statements becomes more clear when we concentrate on a series of Althusserian dicta about the political rationale for philosophical positions. Thus: 'the philosophical fight over words is a part of the political fight';[31] and 'philosophy is, in the last instance, the *theoretical* concentrate of politics';[32] and the 'ultimate stake of philosophical struggle is the struggle for *hegemony* between the two great tendencies in world outlook (materialist and idealist)';[33] and, finally, 'between those who recognize' a break between the early, humanist Marx and the later, structuralist Marx and those who do not, 'there exists an opposition which, it must be acknowledged, is ultimately political.'[34]

We are now in a position to answer our first question. If the struggle for political hegemony has priority over the construction of a theory which can help to make the political judgment of participants more rational, then it is not important to ascertain whether intersubjective theory contains a moment of truth capable of qualifying structural theory. Hegemony can be attained without recourse to dialogue; it might be more effectively promoted if 'shades of opinion' are ignored.

Can we also detect a political rationale for the ambiguity residing in the new version of anti-humanism? I suggest the following reading. Both the affirmation and the denial of the subject are needed to justify the kind of politics Althusser supports. And the incompatibility between these two positions must be suppressed (consciously or unconsciously) to sustain that politics. The strategy is to eliminate anthropological categories from structural theory, to affirm the possibility of a future order which presupposes them, and to deflect attention from the discrepancy between two formulations.

Consider, first, the pressure to affirm the potential for reflective politics in contemporary society. Althusser's early theory denigrated workers by treating them as the mere bearers of roles living unavoidably within the mist of ideology. But once the role-bearers became alert to Althusser's account of their conduct, they could not be expected to align themselves with intellectuals who had characterized them in this way. It is difficult to see oneself as a role-bearer at the level of theory and a comrade at the level of practice, especially if the theory anticipates that workers will remain role-bearers in a communist society. Once workers have been exposed to the terms of structural theory, they must suspect that those who construe them as the mere supports of a structure will also be prepared to manipulate them whenever it seems strategically appropriate to do so. The new Althusser, impressed now by the primacy of politics, seeks to engage those who are to provide the human basis of a socialist movement. He now speaks of paying close attention to the ideas of 'the masses' and projects a future society in which they will be free.

But the humanist echoes in this new posture potentially inhibit the revolutionary agenda governing Althusserian politics. To acknowledge the idea of the subject is to pose moral questions about the use and abuse of allies and adversaries in political struggle. One may be obliged to convince allies of the justice and wisdom of one's strategies, and to renounce the use of terrorism against adversaries. Recognition of the other as a subject creates limits to action that are to be transgressed only in the most extreme circumstances. Althusser is quite aware of earlier debates among critical humanists in France, such as Camus and Sartre, which occurred during the period when he was solidifying his own theoretical perspective. He surely knows the argument by Camus, for instance, that rebellion, *because* it 'suggests a nature common to all men, brings to light the measure and the limit which are the very principles of this nature.'[35] Recalling the Althusserian dictum that the 'philosophical fight over words is part of the political fight,' we can see Althusser's failure to acknowledge the humanist presuppositions in his own theory as a refusal to accept the moral inhibitions to political struggle embodied in those presuppositions. A line – a political line – is drawn to separate the humanist fragments in one area of the theory from the anti-humanist sentiments in the other. The ambiguous orientation to the subject is not resolved; it is dissolved into a political solution.

Once the theoretical props to anti-humanism have been pulled away, once, that is, the theory of structural determination and the disjuncture between theory and ideology have been scrapped, the political props become more fully exposed to view. The political stance, because it ignores 'shades of opinion' separating it from other theories and from internal ambiguities within its own theory, inevitably degenerates into a manipulative political practice. 'We' must draw sharp lines for 'them' so 'they' will adopt the right political line, even if 'we' cannot ourselves establish such lines theoretically. The doctrine of the primacy of politics over theory degenerates into the opportunistic use of theory for political purposes; and the space for this opportunism expands indefinitely when the doctrine fails to recognize its allies and adversaries as subjects.

In giving a critical interpretation of Althusser's texts I have followed the course he pursued in his own reading of Marx's writings, first detecting 'absences' or 'silences' in the text and then filling them in with an account which makes sense of central formulations in it. Any such reading is contestable. I would welcome a more favorable reading as long as it reveals the theoretical ground for the continued repudiation of humanism in the *recent* Althusser texts and provides a more coherent interpretation of its political rationale. Attention to the political rationale is crucial because it provides the ground upon which Althusser's most distinctive claims now rest. It is time for Althusserians to break their silence on these issues, to state explicitly the political rationale for theoretical anti-humanism. It is also time for socialists with democratic commitments to break cleanly with Althusserian theory.[36] The other side of anti-humanism in theory is dehumanization in practice. The political implications of Althusserian theory, in conjunction with defects in the arguments designed to sustain the theory, support repudiation of its most distinctive contentions.

3

Appearance and reality in politics

Penetrating appearances

Certain social and political theorists, most notably Plato, Hegel, Marx, and Freud, distinguish a society's real structure from the appearance it presents to its participants. Bound up with this distinction are those between theory and ideology, thought and action, the actual and the possible, and consciousness and self-consciousness. The goal of theory, when these distinctions are prominent, is to pierce through appearances to the real structure, to allow (at least some) participants to see things as they really are, and either to reconcile the newly self-conscious agents to necessity or to encourage them to bring the society into closer harmony with their real interests.

The discrepancy between appearance and reality can assume a variety of forms. That which is particular may present itself as a universal, as when the calculating ethic appears universal to its bearers while it is really dramatically accentuated in their particular order. Or a causal relation can be inverted in consciousness, as when God appears to be the author of man while man is really the author of God. Or a partial truth can be mistakenly construed as the whole story, as when the appearance of free exchange in the market between labor and capital is really circumscribed by the need for labor to sell itself to those who control the means of production. Or the future vision which helps to unify society may actually be unrealizable, as when a populace identifies with the project of creating a society of affluence for the benefit of future generations while the future beneficiaries will not be able to sustain allegiance to the result once accomplished. And each of these forms can be reversed, as when a universal presents itself as a particular, and so on.

Not only the discrepancy, but also the connection, between

appearances and realities can vary. Thus the belief that God will continue to nourish the soil will not by itself provide the soil with nourishment if God refuses. But the belief that the future pursued in common now will prove satisfying to future generations helps to nourish present practices geared to that purpose, even if the future beneficiaries eventually will repudiate the actual achievement. A political theory must pay attention to both the discrepancies and the connections between appearances and realities.

Consider a simplified example of the sort of relationship to be examined here. A person thinks he is persuaded to participate in a strike by arguments another gives in good faith. But the agent giving the arguments consciously withholds some considerations which, were they known to our striker, would tip the balance in the other direction. The first person manipulates the second. This face-to-face relation of manipulation is in some respects a microcosm of the relations we will examine, but it deviates from them in other respects. It is similar, first, in that the appearance of persuasion to the first party is essential to the actual relationship of manipulation. The appearance is not a mere epiphenomenon which, if peeled away, will expose the underlying reality unchanged; it helps to constitute the reality it misrepresents. Secondly, a change in the appearance of the relationship will in some degree reconstitute the reality. If the recipient recognizes what has been going on, he may sever the friendship; or continue in it but seek to forestall manipulation in the future; or demand such changes unsuccessfully and find himself subjected now to coercion; or pretend he is still deceived to avoid open coercion. But a change in the appearance will in some way alter the real relation; moreover the stage will be set for efforts to revise it more fully. Thirdly, there may be some reluctance on the part of the recipient to recognize the real relation because he stands in a dependent status to the manipulator. The belief that he is persuaded supports the image he wishes to project to self and others as one who acts freely, while recognition of the reality would require him either to struggle against heavy odds to secure autonomy or to acknowledge his dependent status. The real relationship was not just invisible to him; he was an active participant in making it so.

But the simple model also omits dimensions of the macroscopic relationships to be examined. First, it is not necessary that some agents be in the know while others are not. Secondly, in the larger setting the appearances take the form of a complex web of concepts and beliefs in which each element receives some support from many others. It is more difficult to reach secure ground from which these tangled webs can be unravelled. This condition, in conjunction with the tendency of the identity of the participants to be bound up with the appearances they help to construct and defend, greatly complicates the task of tracing the relations between appearance and reality. Thirdly, because the institutional order is loosely structured so that a successful reform in one institution would have to be associated with a corollary series of reforms in others, a shift in the appearance the order presents may alter its performance without necessarily allowing the reconstruction or solidification now desired. This condition, in conjunction with the quest for identity on the part of participants, fosters ambivalence and ambiguity in the political self-interpretations of some constituencies.

Certain theoretical traditions are impaired in their ability to comprehend the relations between appearance and reality in politics. Their epistemic prejudices support the misinterpretation of such an order (should such an order exist). Thus the pure theory of interpretation, which identifies social reality with the interpretation of participants and presumes that the standards of rationality acknowledged within an order are fully appropriate to it, cannot comprehend a deep disjuncture between appearance and reality. Theorists working within this framework can expose modest discrepancies between implicit dimensions within a self-interpretation and its explicit articulation, but such discrepancies, important in their own right, do not suffice to comprehend the sort of relationships we are examining.[1]

Structural theorists, while sometimes oriented to the discrepancy between appearance and reality, nonetheless underplay possible complexities in the relationship. If the subjectivity and intersubjectivity of participants are treated merely as effects to be explained, and if the participants are treated as unable in principle to attain reflexive awareness of the theory which explains those effects, the theory which emerges may gloss over ambiguities and possibilities immanent within the order.

While doubtless preparing particular pitfalls for myself I will try to avoid the two identified by adopting the following strategy. We begin with an initial presentation of the political self-interpretation of a particular constituency. A series of hypothetical revisions is then introduced into the initial interpretation, each of which purports to comprehend dimensions of the order missed in the first account. The preliminary interpretation can be identified as the ideology of sacrifice and the hypothetical revisions as, respectively, the liberal, utopian, and structural moments. The ideology of sacrifice provides its bearers with a sense of dignity, though that dignity is preserved by misrepresenting important features of social life and is vulnerable potentially to invalidation by the action of other groups. Each of the hypothetical moments to follow captures a dimension missed in the initial interpretation, but none can sustain modes of conduct consistent with the wish of the participants to see themselves as free and dignified. The identity the participants seek to maintain is tied to a set of beliefs they struggle to secure: the belief that one voluntarily accepts the roles one plays; that these roles serve worthy private and public purposes; that one lives in a political order which is relatively transparent to its citizens and capable of promoting the collective ends they accept; and that the sacrifices persistently required in the order are necessary to the most worthy purposes of private and public life. The struggle to sustain these beliefs in turn generates implications for the political priorities, alliances, and conflicts established by the believers.

Lodged within the connection, first, between the effort to maintain a sense of dignity and the beliefs about the larger order needed to support that sense, and secondly, between beliefs about the order and their implications for political practice, is space for a potential disjuncture between the real structure of the order and the appearance it presents to a range of participants. This is the space we shall explore.

The intent of the total interpretation is to identify the pressures which generate the self-construction of the ideology of sacrifice, those aspects of social and political life screened out by that interpretation, and the consequences which would emerge were the invisible elements to become more visible to participants. The account is explanatory, not in revealing law-like relations among discrete elements, but in showing how structural limits *encourage* or *provoke* participants to adopt specific orientations to political conduct. The terms 'encourage' and 'provoke' identify precisely the loose and open quality of these relationships – terms like 'cause' and 'produce' are too imprecise. The porous texture and equivocal character of unreflective self-interpretations, the reflexive capacities of those who act on such interpretations, and the play or flexibility within the structural dimension of social life, together imply that a more formal account would gloss over uncertainties and ambiguities located within the object of inquiry.

The dialectic to be constructed is best viewed as a thought experiment. The preliminary portrait of the ideology of sacrifice is exaggerated; subordinate elements within it are suppressed. Each of the subordinate strains is then exaggerated in its turn so that, by identifying the political orientation implicit within each strain, we can ascertain why it remains underdeveloped in fact within the established order. This progressive introduction of counterfactuals eventually brings out more clearly how a dense and ambiguous background of undeveloped perspectives is condensed into an operative set of political practices. It provides a way to penetrate appearances without reducing them to epiphenomena or treating them as exhaustively constitutive of political reality.

After the entire interpretation has been offered we will return to the meta-theoretical level, probing the difficulties in ascertaining the extent to which such an account is valid or invalid.

Hidden injuries and structural constraints

Consider a group of white, married, male blue-collar workers in the United States today. Each is a principal breadwinner in a family with young children and each has a reasonable degree of job security. The breadwinner does not see himself as working simply to maximize his family's short range consumption opportunities. He voluntarily sacrifices now so that his children can escape the circumstances in which he finds himself.[2] He chooses to accept the work routines, authoritarian controls and overtime he dislikes in order to improve the mobility of his children. His claim to the respect of his wife and children grows out of this willingness to sacrifice, and the respect they give him lends dignity to his life activity.

This orientation to work and family helps to condition the worker's interpretive reaction to welfare recipients, intellectuals, student dissidents, feminists, deviants, and criminals. For the conduct and rhetoric of each of these types threatens to invalidate the ideology of sacrifice.

If the welfare recipient claims that unemployment is created by structural causes rather than by the personal defects of the recipient, the worker's very possession of a job may appear to be more a matter of luck than of self-discipline and desert. If the recipient calls for higher levels of support the worker's own sacrifice may begin to look foolish. If radicals claim that common crimes are implicitly acts of rebellion against an order that breeds criminals, they inadvertently condemn the worker for bowing passively to that order. Or: they mock his exercise of self-restraint by relieving the criminal of responsibility for stealing under existing social conditions. If feminists claim that women are imprisoned in the home, the worker's sacrifice is reinterpreted as a restraint on her freedom and dignity. If radicals treat equality of opportunity as a fraud they unwittingly undermine the worker's hopes for his children's future and render his sacrifice fruitless. If university students debunk the privileged way of life they are about to enter they ridicule the purpose which informs the worker's life activity. And even if the worker succeeds in projecting his children into higher circles they may then become, he fears, the kind of people who look down on people like him.

The worker is caught in a bind. To repudiate the ideology of sacrifice is to lose the claim to respect available under present circumstances, but to affirm it is to set the worker against the very constituencies with whom he must be allied if significant changes in this undignified life-situation are to be generated. The ideology of sacrifice generates political orientations that help to perpetuate the worker's plight while the plight generates pressures to perpetuate the ideology. Yet this bind itself cannot be acknowledged without undermining the identity available to the worker. The worker is thus under a double pressure, first, to accept the ideology and, secondly, to resist the suggestion that its role in securing his identity outstrips its truth value. If this ideology is to be secured he must claim that those who challenge it in various ways are either irresponsible or indulge themselves in utopian dreams.

It is important to see that the beliefs in the foreground of the ideology of sacrifice support a set of background beliefs concerning the necessity and desirability of the institutional structure within which it is forged. We have seen how the principle of equal opportunity, and thus the institution of labor mobility, is supported by this interpretation. It sustains a similar understanding of instrumental work. For if it were held that work could be organized in other ways the sacrifice would take on a new appearance. Its proponents would see themselves less as responsible agents making the most of the necessities of modern life and more as white Uncle Toms performing unnecessary and undignified tasks in a servile way. Distressing questions about the risks and responsibilities in organizing a political challenge to these forms would emerge. Moreover, instrumental work and the associated institutions of bureaucratic rationality, production for private profit, and sharply graded incentive systems, are justified in the name of economic growth. The ideology of sacrifice is most at home with itself if it does not question the viability of the end justifying these means. It supports thereby the priorities of the established order and the legitimacy of its dominant institutions.

Our portrayal has already moved beyond the self-interpretation of the participants toward an account of why they might strive to retain it in the face of contrary evidence. To fix that preliminary account we can say that while the reaction to criminals, feminists, environmentalists, and radicals does pick out discrepancies between the conduct of the target groups and that of the workers, it also magnifies these differences, distorts the motives of the target groups, and suppresses inner doubts on the part of the workers about the point of their sacrifice and the truth of the ideology sustaining it. The test of the claim that the self-interpretation involves a powerful element of self-deception is launched, first, by ascertaining if the workers' interpretation of the motives and situation of the target groups is inflated, secondly, if evidence available to correct this inflation is ignored, and thirdly, if the attribution of this defensive ideology of sacrifice to the workers helps to render intelligible conduct and conflicts which would otherwise remain vaguely mysterious.

Suppose that a range of workers acknowledges that this external account is approximately correct. They acknowledge that their previous beliefs about the accused and themselves formed a spiral of partial self-deceptions needed to secure a sense of dignity under adverse conditions.

We must expect this new interpretation eventually to support revisions in the personal identities and political commitments of those accepting it. They will externalize a range of doubts that had been internalized. They may begin to probe previously suppressed questions about the legitimacy of a system which, as they now see it, requires them to seek dignity in such undignified ways. Perhaps they will begin to locate themselves within the same class as many of those formerly accused of freeloading, to see the accused and themselves as members of a subordinate class which reaps the fewest rewards, receives insufficient space to carve out a dignified life, and is called upon to bear the largest sacrifices when the larger economy is under pressure.

The reinterpretation will reconstitute political alliances and cleavages; it will politicize grievances previously relegated to a non- or semi-political status such as the right to a job, class inequality, and the social preconditions of self-respect. The diminished sense of individual agency accompanying the demise of the ideology of sacrifice will be offset, at least initially and to some degree, by the enhanced sense of the working class as a potential agent of collective change. It ushers in the liberal moment.

This sense of collective agency and dignity is itself quite vulnerable to invalidation. For the changes sought cannot be superimposed on top of the established institutions. The institutions must be reconstituted as well. The right to a job cannot be guaranteed for everyone without setting an inflationary spiral into motion, reducing income levels and job security from another direction. Controlling inflation while retaining full employment, in turn, would require significant changes in the social infrastructure of consumption, accentuating collective goods (e.g., public transport, parks and recreational facilities, community housing, public health care) and reducing dependence on individual consumption (e.g., cars and single unit houses). The desired reduction in inequality could not be pushed very far without undercutting the flow of private investment into the system of production for private profit, and if that obstacle were surmounted its realization would require even more significant shifts from individualized to collective forms of consumption. Each of these changes in turn would require significant shifts in the role of the state, the status of private profit, the structure of work organization and incentives, and the mobilization of the economy around the expectation of constant economic growth.[3]

It is one thing to call for reforms within an established order and another to conclude that those reforms must be situated within a massive set of institutional changes. If the participants continue to believe that the established institutions, because they are essential to industrial society as such, are invulnerable to significant change, the initial sense of collective agency will dissipate. They may lapse into the old ideology. More likely, they will resign themselves to an inescapable fate while resenting even more deeply those dissident constituencies who unwittingly condemn them for their resignation.

The new, embryonic self-interpretation is inherently unstable. Its retention requires a deeper probing of doubts suppressed within the old view. The initial step is to reinterpret the established institutions, to see them not as a given set of 'natural' forms required to promote the necessary goals of economic growth and affluence, but as a set of potentially alterable human constructions requiring conduct and promoting ends which no longer automatically attract the allegiance of people implicated within them. The focus now is on the nature of these institutions and on the relation between the roles they impose and the changing aspirations of the role-takers.[4]

If a populace believes that the good life, the good life it can build in common, is one of affluence; if it believes that affluence will both satisfy in itself and create the freedom its recipients need to experience fulfilling relations and activities, the beliefs will legitimize those institutions promoting such desirable results. If the ends appear to be the natural ends of human life, the institutions essential to them will assume a nature-like appearance too. Complaints about the strains created by instrumental work, production for private profit, labor mobility, income stratification, accentuation of private over collective consumption, state subsidies for economic growth, the rapid obsolescence of old skills and old workers, environmental destruction, the dangerous dependence on crucial resources located in foreign countries, and the limits to intellectual development posed by technical education – these complaints will be muted and self-mocking in tone. For it would be irrational to favor the end and to oppose the means. Better to be ironic about the occasional inconsistency between one's appreciation of the good life pursued and lack of appreciation for the pursuit itself.

But it is because these practices are experienced and justified primarily as instruments to ends outside themselves that they are susceptible eventually to inner erosion. Such institutions can be drained of normative significance if

1. the ends pursued, once attained by a large minority, seem empty to the privileged beneficiaries;

2. many members of the subordinate population increasingly suspect that they and their progeny will sacrifice only so that others can enjoy this good life;

3. the very attainment of the previously postulated ends now

seems to destroy prized aspects of social life which the pursuers tacitly had assumed would remain intact.

Large numbers of people today, it can be argued, have moved toward one or more of these orientations. These are some of the very constituencies whose rhetoric and conduct placed the initial ideology of sacrifice under so much pressure.

For the institutions justified earlier by the future affluence and leisure they would generate are now largely intact. The future is now. The enthusiasm to build a life of affluence and free time for future generations can no longer be so readily mobilized once the gap between the original projection of vague aspirations and the concrete experience of the actual achievement is revealed historically.[5] The old purposes sustaining allegiance to the old role requirements cannot so easily sustain the innocent allegiance of a new generation of role-bearers. They must continue to work, politic, consume, rear children, invest, and bargain within these forms. But their allegiance to them weakens, their motivation to excel within them declines, and their performance deteriorates.

The expression of disillusionment varies across categories of age, class, occupational sector, region, race, and gender; its tonalities shift with variations in the level of international tensions and with the crests and troughs of the business cycle. But it does find expression. Its first clear manifestation was the youth movement of the 1960s, a movement in which those destined to fill privileged roles expressed disaffection from the role requirements, the larger purposes they served, and the sacrifices imposed by the whole complex on the subordinant population. Most other manifestations are, for reasons to be explained, indirect.

These manifestations include the problem of worker motivation in several sectors of the work force, the rise of the environmental movement, repudiation by many women of traditional household roles, the retreat by many into fundamentalist religion, the rise of hedonist movements, and – once the economic crunch set in – the competitive scramble amongst highly educated youth over the remaining slots in the few professions with intrinsically fulfilling work.[6]

This new interpretation of prevailing institutions and objectives crystallizes disaffection from the civilization of productivity while affirming the possibility of reconstituting the old institutions to serve new purposes. If it can also cast new light on old orientations, if it can retrospectively account for the ambivalence and exaggeration lodged inside the ideology of sacrifice, it can hope to become the new self-interpretation of those once gripped by that ideology. We shall test its power to account for the deep hostility toward the welfare state in a later chapter. Our concentration now will be on its ability to detect and explain the ambivalence within the old orientation, as it finds expression in charges hurled at a range of critics and victims of the system.

The accusations formerly advanced against radicals, welfare recipients, feminists, and minority activists did contain a moment of truth, for the conditions of existence of these constituencies do vary in some ways from those of the worker, and they often press their claims without attending closely to the worker's circumstances. But the intensity with which the accusations were levelled and the exaggerations they contained can now be comprehended overtly by those adopting the revised interpretation of the civilization of productivity. For these dimensions reveal a vulnerability within the accusers themselves. The tendency of the accusers, first, to exaggerate the differences between their own behavior and that of the accused, and, secondly, to deny the real grievances felt by these constituencies, protected a disorienting discrepancy within themselves between the beliefs and aspirations appropriate to their life situation and their declining allegiance to those orientations. The self whose indulgence was resented was in part the self of the other who appeared to escape the disciplines accepted by responsible people. But it was also that part of oneself which remained subjected to those disciplines and yet vaguely opposed to them. This ambivalence toward the roles with which one is intimately involved is difficult to acknowledge. To do so is to acknowledge a certain disaffection from the self one has become. And when one seems surrounded by those who believe that the imperatives of the civilization support the ends proper to humanity itself the overt expression of discontent with them must appear to be irresponsible or self-indulgent. One opens oneself to harsh charges to which there is no ready reply. Moreover, to express these discontents openly while continuing to carry out the same role assignments is to admit that one does not exercise self-discipline in pursuit of freely chosen ends. It is to call one's freedom into question.

To retain, thereby, the appearance of one whose outer conduct reflects inner convictions one is encouraged to adopt a hostile stance

73

to those whose conduct seems to express repudiation of those convictions. The denial of the grievances of Blacks and welfare recipients is part of the process by which those in marginally more secure circumstances subvert questions about their own dignity, integrity, and freedom. The state treats those others too permissively, one insists; and the insistence controls that part of oneself which one must not treat too permissively.

The situation portrayed here is fraught with irrationality. But the irrationality is not characterized adequately by saying that the participants resist necessary means to desirable ends or that policies recognizably in the interests of the collectivity are not in the interests of any individual. Contemporary social scientists have imposed more weight upon these formulae than they can bear. The tendency to force recognized irrationalities in the order into the frame of these timeless formulae is understandable. For they provide the most powerful categories through which those who lack a theory of intersubjectivity can come to grips with the symptoms of declining allegiance to the civilization of productivity. But the hegemony of these categories must be resisted. They legitimize ruthless policies designed to coerce those who appear to lack sufficient self-discipline to adjust private interests to collective imperatives or to accept necessary means to desired ends.

The central contentions advanced so far can be summarized by reference to three dimensions of irrationality within the civilization of productivity which are reducible to neither of these standard formulae.

First, a set of established social ends is progressively experienced by participants as empty or defeated by the institutional means now seen to be necessary to their attainment, while the institutional means to them are increasingly felt to be inescapable. The contradictory tendency here embodies a temporal or historical dimension whereby abstractly specified ends targeted for achievement in a distant future later decline in their ability to secure allegiance as their actual content is experienced concretely. And, as part of the same historical trajectory, the institutions which sustain those purposes are progressively solidified. The concrete experience necessary to crystallize disaffection, and the appearance of institutional intractibility, move in tandem.[7]

Secondly, the experienced inescapability of the institutional means to these ends conflicts with the wish of the workers to identify them-

selves as agents freely shaping their own lives. This potential contradiction can be alleviated, at least in appearance, by suppressing the inner disaffection from the ends themselves, by denying the progressive force of the evidence against them. In appearing now to affirm these ends one appears to adopt voluntarily the roles necessary to their attainment. This resolution stands at the level of appearance – which is not to say it is a mere idea disconnected from practice – to the extent that the overt affirmation is belied by other aspects of conduct in work, school, family, and politics. These inchoate expressions of disaffection stand as symptoms to the extent they are not incorporated into a coherent self-interpretation.

Thirdly, to identify with the institutions which impose these disciplines and appear so intractible it is helpful to view them either as nature-like in form or as rational means to universal ends. For it is never a constraint on our freedom as a politically organized populace to fail to change the unchangeable or to refrain from reconstituting that which is already rational. But this nature-like interpretation of, say, instrumental work and production for private profit preserves the sense of collective agency by misreading the constitution of the institutions. It denies the extent to which they are historical human constructions shaped in part by previous power constellations and priorities gripping many participants. This misreading bears long term political consequences. For, as we shall see in a later chapter, it sets up the welfare state to be the screen upon which the deeper disaffection from the civilization of productivity is projected; it increases the load imposed upon the welfare state in maintaining the civilization of productivity; and it depletes the supply of civic virtue available to the state in carrying out its expanded tasks of social coordination.

The irrationality at each of these levels supports those at others. The set together does not reside so much in the character of the participants or in the structure of the institutional complex abstracted from its participants. It resides, rather, in the disjunction between the quest for identity and an institutional complex, partially constituted by the concepts, beliefs and aspirations of its role-bearers, impaired in its ability to secure reflective allegiance to the purposes it must serve.

Pretend now that the newly revised interpretation becomes the self-interpretation of the youngest contingent of workers. They accept it partly because it makes better sense of blind spots and discrepancies in the old orientation and partly because it seems to orient them politically where the previous interpretation did not. Previously they were forced to conclude that, though the ideology of sacrifice was self-defeating, no other acceptable identity was available to them in the established order. Now they agree that the established institutional priorities cannot retain their reflective allegiance and that the institutions themselves are susceptible to change. The new forms envisaged are not merely to be instruments to ends outside themselves, but the instrumentalities must be infused to some extent with activities and relationships that are intrinsically fulfilling. It is not, they now say eagerly, that the sphere of necessity – organizing production, working, learning, rearing children, and politics – can be eliminated; but once the ends of productivity, private affluence and leisure are displaced from their overriding position, these practices themselves can be reshaped to create more room for fulfilling social relationships, collective consumption, and public deliberation over common areas of concern.

If the problem at this stage is seen to be one of public consciousness, then the point of politics is to change that consciousness. Encounter groups, experiments in community life designed to demonstrate the viability of new social forms, public demonstrations, and a politics of theater are likely to bloom. The point is to expose ideas and norms implicit in the old roles, to shock the audience into recognition of its own complicity in the way of life that breeds its discontent, and to articulate new ideas and norms to be insinuated inside new institutional arrangements. This is the utopian moment. It is, if you will, Charles Reich brought inside the factory gates.

The utopian moment contains a political insight. For to articulate implicit disaffection and to expose unrecognized complicity in a corrupt order is to increase the responsibility of those so implicated to change those institutions. My responsibility to contribute to the elimination of some undesirable outcome increases (other things being equal) as my *knowledge* increases of the implicit and reversible tendency of my previous conduct to support it. And this is the knowledge the new politics is designed to disseminate.

But the utopian moment is susceptible to shattering disillusionment. Technocratic elites, tied to the established order, will greet the new strategies with incomprehension and hostility. If the technocrats believe that the opposite of instrumental rationality in the pursuit of established ends is irrationality, if they therefore conclude that theatrical gestures impede the serious business of production and politics, then they must on principle refuse to 'reason' or 'bargain' with those who repudiate reason itself. Those who break the rules of the game must be broken. And this response, if widespread, sours the utopian initiative. Treated as irrational, it tends increasingly to live up to the charge. And it loses its ability to expose deeper irrationalities in the established order.

Underlying the inability to establish enclaves in the established order, and implicit in the repressive response, is a deeper reality. The institutions attacked, now that they are firmly established, have acquired a life of their own: the possibilities for change are now structurally constrained. Though the reinterpretation did improve selectively upon the view it displaced, though social institutions are constituted in part by the concepts, beliefs, and aspirations of the participants, changes in those beliefs and commitments cannot suffice to reconstitute an institutional complex. The interdependence and intermeshing of each institution with others creates an institutional structure strongly resistant to serious reconstitution. The growing discrepancy between the role requirements and the new aspirations can impede profoundly the performance of the old order, but this (by now) conscious disaffection does not automatically produce a political strategy sufficient to adapt that order to newly emerging objectives. The previous understanding of these institutions as an unchangeable part of nature, or as required by the criteria of reason as such, expressed in mystified form a truth overlooked in the reinterpretation.

Social relations are not *simply* communicative relations amongst (disembodied) agents. Two types of constraint operate on such relationships. First, social relations among human beings – who themselves embody natural needs for food and shelter and remain susceptible to the sorts of pains and injuries afflicting non-rational animals – require complex transactions between persons and nature if social life is to continue. No society can persist long if interruptions in such transactions do not soon propel new transactions into existence or allow the (perhaps modified) reinstatement of the old. An established heritage of skills, machinery, and organization mobilized in support of these transactions cannot easily be scrapped. Secondly, the institutions implicated in those transactions can become so intertwined that a significant change in one eventually

77

requires corollary changes in others if necessary transactions with nature are to continue. How tightly such contemporary forms are interlocked now is a matter legitimately open to controversy. But powerful constraints do flow out of this complex of institutional dependencies and interconnections.

Suppose that a new political coalition, mobilized to reorient the economy of growth, successfully elects candidates to the major governmental posts. Its representatives, facing a minority opposition in Congress, nonetheless have an initial majority strong enough to enact policies designed to propel the welfare state, situated in a privately incorporated economy of growth, into a socialist polity oriented to new aspirations. The elected officials must face in two directions at once. They must strive to enact programs congruent with their mandate while maintaining a level of economic performance sufficient to meet the needs of the populace.

To carry out its agenda the welfare state must generate sufficient tax revenues. The flow of tax revenues depends on the investment and production decisions of private owners. And those decisions in turn are influenced by the extent to which the welfare state supports the conditions of growth. The *dependency* of the welfare state on the economy it would reconstitute, combined with its increasingly *dominant role* in maintaining economic performance, presses it toward policies perpetuating the political economy of growth.

Suppose state officials, in alliance with organized workers, legally sanction a series of reforms in productive arrangements; they broaden work routines, extend participation in corporate decisions, and try to enhance the social utility of corporate products. If the reforms are instituted in an economy where private profit creation continues to be the basic motor of the system, a dilemma may emerge. Either the worker–consumer participants will have to adapt their policy agendas to the imperatives of private profit creation or the firms involved will falter nationally and internationally. If the participants adjust to these imperatives the reforms will be more apparent than real; if they do not the firms will soon face crises.

The answer would seem to be to nationalize the pertinent units first and then to institute the reforms. But the very national and international intertwining of these institutions gives corporate owners powerful leverage to defeat such attempts. They might transfer essential funds to foreign investments in anticipation of such moves, weakening the performance of the economy and arousing the fears of dependent employees. They might deploy the advantages available to any privileged minority in the policy-making process to delay or veto proposed changes. They might finance, say, disruptive strikes by truckers who feel threatened by these changes, interrupting thereby the nation's flow of goods and services. The possibilities here are quite large because of the complex interdependencies among the established modes of work, investment, distribution, consumption, state revenue creation, state efficacy in implementing policies, the military, the legitimacy of state policies, state accountability, the absence of accountability amongst economic units, and the international scope of capitalist enterprise.

As the performance of the system was impeded by these reactions, the state's response to it would itself be structurally constrained. It might be compelled to impose new disciplines and sacrifices on those least essential to corporate growth and least able to resist the impositions – on marginal workers in the market sector, the unemployed, welfare recipients, low level public employees, school children, the elderly, the sick, prisoners, the mentally retarded. It might have to sanction the extension of Taylorist modes of work and control into higher occupational levels in order to maintain productive efficiency and to discipline a work force losing the self-discipline it once exercised – even though the authoritarian, routinized mode of work is itself the source of much of the disaffection from the civilization of productivity.[8] It might have to tolerate high levels of inflation to cope with the imperatives facing it, even though inflationary spirals, with their corrosive effects on established income differentials, generate a large constellation of discontented constituencies each claiming to suffer unjustly by comparison to at least one other group previously behind it in the income hierarchy.

If the constraints were extremely tight – that issue remains open – the institutional result could eventually approach the shape of an historical dilemma. The future, once built, loses its normative grip on those implicated in it; but since its structure is largely established, powerful constraints to its reconstitution persist. Moreover, because the state is under pressure to promote growth, productive efficiency, and private consumption within the established order it is extremely difficult for a viable political movement to articulate the underlying disaffection in ways which could orient state action. The disaffection itself seems unreal to those gripped by it because it is not articulated as a set of concrete grievances within the established order. And it is not articulated partly because leaders competing for state office cannot identify existing state resources capable of responding to these issues.

It might not appear too difficult to get those who have already acknowledged disaffection from the civilization of work to move toward this newly revised interpretation. For they must expect any credible interpretation to explain why an advanced capitalist system perpetuates itself even amidst periods of instability and the periodic revolt of youthful constituencies. Moreover, looking to their own previous denial of disaffection, they might see inside it an implicit awareness that the established order is quite intractable. The ideology of sacrifice treated the established institutional matrix as nature-like, as the unchangeable background of politics: it thus recognized, if darkly, its structural resistance to significant change.

But if political interpretation involves both a quest for truth and a search for a secure identity, the newly revised interpretation faces a treacherous path. As it stands now, its strategic implications are underdetermined because its structural dimension is underspecified. Perhaps there are openings in this order not yet detected in the interpretation; or perhaps the constraints eventually will emerge as contradictions which must be resolved; or perhaps the preconditions for the evolution of a new order more congruent with newly emerging aspirations are undermined by the very efforts of the state to maintain economic performances. We can say, minimally, that the utopian moment is over for those who accept an interpretation in which structural interdependencies and constraints play an important role. We can also anticipate a reactive movement to stem the dialectic of disaffection, one which will struggle aggressively to suppress clear manifestations of discontent while repressing their more diffused expression in the wider populace. Those who would oppose such a regressive movement must strive to redefine public issues so that middle class liberals and radicals do not continue to press constituencies oriented to the ideology of sacrifice into a defensively aggressive posture.

This critical interpretation, when all its parts are assembled, treats prevailing appearances as forms in need of transcendence. But another reading might converge with this one at many points while insisting that participants must nonetheless become reconciled to the limits of the prevailing order. If those limits are treated as unbreakable necessities, that which is irrational within one account becomes rational in the next. Attention to this rejoinder, implicit today within new, defensive versions of liberalism, will help to bring out further dimensions in the interpretation advanced here.

The rejoinder goes something like this. There is a vacancy in the interpretation. The account is parasitic upon an idealized view of the previous history of capitalist development which is both unacknowledged and incorrect. This order – and others as well – has always been marked by struggle, selective oppression, resistance, cycles, and calamity. But the critical interpretation implicitly treats the past as a smooth surface which is only now subject to rupture. When we reconstruct appropriately our understanding of the past we will not be so critical of limits apparent in the present. For such limits, though not exactly the same ones, face every society.

There is a certain irony in this rejoinder, at least as it is offered in the context of American intellectual life. For it has taken two decades of radical reinterpretation to break the consensus reading of American history which previously prevailed within liberalism. Inside the irony is a misconception of the sort of account advanced here. The thesis is not that the growth of American capitalism has proceeded smoothly until certain flaws in its priorities became more visible to a range of participants. Rather, expressions of hope and solace previously available to defeated and forgotten constituencies are less available today. And the control of these constituencies is both more necessary to the maintenance of the order and more difficult than it once was.[9] These shifts insinuate themselves into our political life during periods of quiescence and unrest, infecting the performance of the dominant institutions and depleting the supply of civic resources we can draw upon in trying to shore them up.

But the major thesis of the new liberals refers not to the past but to the untouchable limits in the present. Earlier, optimistic versions, holding that the welfare state could maintain affluence and liberty while significantly reducing inequality and insecurity, are now giving way to this tougher doctrine; and this ideological shift serves to acknowledge some of the themes advanced here. The themes are then given a different reading. We must work within the admittedly narrow confines of this order because it is utopian to try to stretch the limits themselves. We must get tougher with those who impair or disrupt the system of productivity, doing so to preserve important virtues only it can preserve. Such an orientation recasts the relations between appearances and realities sketched here by relocating the lines which separate the rational from the irrational.

I do not believe that a definitive response can be made to this sort of rejoinder. But considerations can be advanced which support opening theoretical explorations and political movements it would close off. Theodore Adorno's reply to a similar thesis advanced under different circumstances provides the right launching pad:

Criticism of tendencies in modern society is automatically countered, before it is fully uttered, by the argument that things have always been like this. The accuser is further informed that . . . the grounds for his indignation are common knowledge, trivial, so that no one can be expected to waste his interest in them . . . Connivance makes use of the trick of attributing to its opponent a reactionary and untenable theory of decline – for is not horror indeed perennial? – in order by the alleged error in his thinking to discredit his concrete insight into the negative, and to blacken him who remonstrates against darkness as an obfuscator.[10]

Perfect, as far as it goes. It goes far enough to expose the potential for obfuscation accompanying efforts to treat evils within a particular order as universals, not far enough to establish the presumption in favor of treating them as particulars potentially susceptible to significant reconstitution. The case for retaining an open and exploratory orientation to future possibilities will be considered later in this study. For now it suffices to note that the interpretation advanced here incorporates a contestable position on that issue.

The reality of appearances

All of this might seem too laden with counterfactuals and counter-counterfactuals to be illuminating or realistic. Perhaps the consciousness of participants does enter into political relations, but *could* the participants become self-conscious in the ways suggested? I believe the question should be reversed. Given the capacity people in modern society have to think critically about the roles they play, the purposes they serve, and the assumptions underlying those activities, what sorts of impediments limit critical reflection into them? And how are the participants constrained from acting upon such reconsidered judgments once articulated? When the question is reformulated the multiplication of counterfactuals emerges as the most promising way, first, to explain why the ideology of sacrifice retains a powerful hold over large sections of the working class even though the identity it provides is so thin and vulnerable, and, secondly, to comprehend the complex obstacles facing any dissident orientation to thought and practice aiming to displace that ideology.

The ideology of sacrifice persists, despite the ambivalence within it, because a decade of tentative explorations by adventurous youth bumped into the various reactions and constraints we have identified. No secure enclaves could be found which allowed the participants to establish new bearings while launching families, working, preparing children for the future available in this society, and maintaining ties to an older generation whose own sense of achievement had been threatened by the exploratory forays. Some of these ties and responsibilities can be broken in pursuit of a better way of life, but it is extremely difficult to deny all of them over a long period of time if the political progress sought is consistently obstructed.

To specify the constraints facing such exploratory movements is thus to explain why disaffection from the civilization of productivity in fact finds only a limited and indirect political expression. Once the defining institutions of that civilization are wheeled into place even dissident political movements are pressed to define objectives congruent with the established order. But such a structural bias means that no organized movement *articulates* inchoate disaffection, crystallizing it into a coherent set of grievances and aspirations. The disaffection itself thereby remains vague and undefined. It tends to be denied by those experiencing it because it seems so unreal, so disconnected from the demands and possibilities of everyday life; and it seems so unreal because it lacks an institutional framework within which it can be translated into concrete proposals. When defenders of the established order then define the behavorial expression of these vague anxieties as the misbehavior of a new generation of hedonists and irrationalists, those who would otherwise explore such orientations in themselves tend instead to deny, to submerge, the doubts.[11] They may indeed attack dissidents who continue to project such irrational fantasies onto the public realm, and the attack may help to control such unspeakable tendencies in their own conduct and attitudes.

Epistemic pressures (the lack of articulation and specificity) and social pressures (the inability to secure identity over a lifetime outside of the established institutional forms) coalesce to block the explicit expression of disaffection while the very historical development of the institutions works to undercut allegiance to the ends they serve.

An interpretive account begins with the self-understanding of the participants, but it must eventually explore implicit beliefs, unexpressed doubts, vaguely articulated hopes, and repressed anxieties which help to account for their conduct. Moreover, these discrepancies must be explained, and one promising route (though it does not exhaust the possibilities) is to explore institutional interdependencies which encourage some understandings and aspirations, while rendering others inconsistent with the wish of the participants to see themselves as responsible agents freely choosing to play the roles available to them.

An interpretation wishing both to respect appearances and to reveal what they conceal can be disciplined, but it should not pretend to be politically neutral. For that which is implicit or repressed is not exactly like the explicit or the expressed minus the single difference that it is hidden or unstated. Implicit beliefs, hopes, and fears are vague and undisciplined. They are not public enough to be subjected to scrutiny, criticism and refinement from a variety of angles over a sustained period of time by a number of different people. Thus to clarify them is to give them a distinct shape and accent previously absent; to convince those to whom they are attributed to accept the new formulation is partly to draw out what was there already and partly to change it and its role in their lives. In the sphere of political reflection discovery and creation are not neatly separable. And since ideas, beliefs, and aspirations enter into political relations, that means that political reflection, once it is heard and heeded, or heard and repudiated, never leaves things as they were.[12]

The interpretive conversion of the implicit into the explicit, the identification of internal discrepancies, and the characterization of inchoate disaffection and aspirations, though anchored in the lives of the participants, will bear necessarily the imprint of one's own anthropology. The interpretation offered here, for instance, projects a multi-layered or faceted view of persons and social relations. It requires distinctions between explicit and implicit beliefs and between conscious and unconscious purposes; it affirms the possibility of deception, distortion, ambivalence, and projection in relations with others and oneself; it insists that some degree of self-consciousness, autonomous action, and moral integrity are possible human achievements; it recognizes an attenuated, historicized conception of natural human ends whereby some institutionalized ends cannot sustain the allegiance of a populace unless they are mystified or specified in futuristic terms. And if any of these ingredients had to be rejected on logical or experiential grounds, the interpretation within which they are housed would require revision.

One never confronts social reality in an unmediated way, then, for the appearance it assumes in the theory reflects to some extent the anthropology accepted by the theorist; and the anthropologically mediated interpretation, to the extent that it enters into the future thought and action of those whose conduct is subjected to interpretation, introduces new projects, alliances, and cleavages into political life. How can such a standpoint be disciplined by reason and evidence?

One can, first, compare the anthropology advanced to the one (or ones) accepted by the populace one is studying. This provides preliminary bearings. But the explicit convictions of the populace seldom exhaust their actual orientations; and, as we have seen, to bring out subordinate dimensions and presuppositions of such interpretations is to introduce additional elements in need of critical scrutiny. Moreover, even if the fit were tight, that would not guarantee the truth of both accounts. We have argued previously, for instance, that a populace can be moved at one time by vaguely specified aspirations without realizing that their later specification and realization will tend to undermine commitment to them. Such a test, then, is not only necessary, but necessarily contaminated by some of the very factors in need of critical scrutiny.

Secondly, one can show how a particular anthropology renders intelligible a range of ideologies and political conflicts which appear mysterious or merely unexplained from other standpoints. Such an account might draw upon an anthropology with some ingredients not presently acknowledged or recognized by the participants. Thirdly, and closely connected, one can show how certain assumptions help us to *identify* modes of behavior previously ignored and thus unexplained within other anthropologies. The persistent claim of Freudian theory to serious attention, for instance, flows from its impressive performance in these two areas, and the performance lends credibility to 'wild' assumptions within it that would otherwise be shrugged off.

Fourthly, one can compare, as anthropologists themselves do, the possibilities and limits identified as universals in a particular anthropology to actual forms of life *appearing* to be at odds with these expectations in some respects. Here too, though, appearances may still deceive; and the deception, once uncovered, may allow retention of elements initially jeopardized.

Fifthly, one can, as Peter Strawson and Jurgen Habermas have both done recently, explore presuppositions rooted in one's own reactive attitudes and speech acts to ascertain whether they square with assumptions explicitly incorporated into one's anthropology.[13] As part of this enterprise one can ask whether the assumptions made about others in explaining their conduct are consistent with those made in appraising it morally, and whether assumptions I make about myself as the author of an argument square with those I make about myself as a member of society whose conduct is susceptible to explanation.

Sixthly, one can explore the logic or illogic of notions central to an anthropology (notions such as rationality, self-deception, unconscious purposes, and autonomous action) to see whether each is internally coherent and whether all can be housed within the same framework.

None of these test-levels provides an ultimate court of appeal in the sense that conclusions reached there automatically override contradictory conclusions reached at other levels. With respect to our sixth level, for instance, a large number of philosophers previously argued that ideas such as self-deception and unconscious purposes were impermissible in scientific inquiry because they did not cohere with neutral requirements of scientific theory. But the apparent explanatory power of theories employing these notions justified resistance to this conclusion. And more recently revisionists have argued that the *rules of analysis* accepted in shuffling such notions outside the rubric of science (e.g., the analytic–synthetic dichotomy, a strict falsification principle) and the *restrictive analogies* within which these criticism were developed (e.g., self-deception as analogous to one person deceiving another, construing personal identity in terms of a 'simple' rather than a 'complex' model) distorted the findings emerging from the analysis of such notions.[14] Such rules and analogies themselves can be placed under pressure (seventh) when a theory not fitting these norms reveals strength in other respects.

But perhaps it can be argued that *for us today* some of these tests are more fundamental than others. For given our current powers of conceptualization and self-understanding, a set of implicit assumptions about ourselves built into the identity we seek to sustain could only be denied by lapsing into a series of pragmatic contradictions. If that were so, any explanatory theory of politics which explicitly or implicitly denies the validity of these assumptions must today be repudiated.

The reactive relations we enter into – as in my resentment when I conclude that another has slighted me intentionally and unjustifiably, or my indignation when I rebuke another who fails to abide by shared standards in his relations with a third person – presuppose my own belief in our common capacity to live up to shared norms, to pursue goals arrived at deliberatively, and to be held responsible for failure to live up to such standards. And the existential questions we periodically pose ('What shall I do? How shall I live my life?') presuppose a capacity for self-conscious criticism and for the reactive reconstitution of previous habits of conduct. Aware of ourselves as agents not exhausted by the multiple roles we play, we are aware of ourselves as agents able to subject those norms to reflective criticism and revision. We define ourselves today, to some degree, by contrast to earlier peoples less conscious of the historical variety amongst ways of life and thus more thoroughly inclined to view their individual and collective life as expressions of a fate given by God or Nature. The contrast helps to crystallize our sense of ourselves as responsible agents, capable of acting freely, and worthy, under the appropriate conditions, of being held responsible for what we do and what we become.

It is immensely difficult, perhaps now impossible, to give up the presuppositions built into the reactive relations and habits of self-conscious criticism we display in daily conduct. The attempt to do so would be blocked repeatedly by our tendency to affirm in conduct what we deny in abstract theory. The identity which supports the political self-interpretation we have explored critically is not itself to be repudiated. These are appearances which we must treat as realities.

Such a contention rests upon a reconstituted form of the transcendental argument, deviating from its classical predecessor in two respects: it does not insist that only one reading of the human capacities for reason, responsibility, and self-consciousness must be accepted by all contemporary theorists, but it does set limits within which alternative readings of these capacities and norms can be articulated now. And it does not claim that no future advance in our theories about nature and society could force a revision in these limits, but it does claim that our own reading today cannot remain internally coherent unless it falls within them.

Stuart Hampshire summarizes a qualified form of such a modified transcendental argument:

Within language as we know it, a limit is set to the possibility of varying the ways in which we think about our actions, by our nature as perceiving and thinking beings who are intentional agents moving among other things. One must start from the truisms that set these limits . . . We cannot claim an absolute and conditional finality for these truisms since the deduction of them is always a deduction within language as we know it. But the deduction only shows that we are not in a position to describe any alternative forms of communication between intentional agents which do not exemplify these truisms.[15]

Two implications flow from these contentions.

First, the self-identity attributed in this essay to the authors of the ideology of sacrifice is indeed a defensible, laudable vision of self supportable by reasoned argument. It is not this identification of oneself as a person worthy of being held responsible for one's actions and character that should be displaced (though its *social* preconditions and dimensions should be incorporated more fully into the self-consciousness of its bearers), but the established role imperatives which require many to construct the ideology of sacrifice to preserve a fragile, blunted form of that identity within the established order. The tendency of technocratic theorists to repudiate this underlying identity whenever its expression conflicts with prevailing role requirements is susceptible to criticism from this perspective. The technocratic theorist might argue that state officials, trying to manage a complex economy, should be released from the obligation to legitimize their policies to a wider populace or, more directly, that the conception of role-bearers appropriate to scientific explanation and social control is incompatible with the self-conceptions of the role-bearers themselves. Such an account, once its import is elaborated, must appear to us today to be quite implausible and to be thoroughly contemptuous of those whose conduct is to be explained. For the theorist, in constructing and defending the explanation, must claim to exercise the very capacities he strips from the human objects of inquiry. The self-identity of the one is affirmed while that of the other is repudiated; and no ground is provided for differentiating the one from the other.

Secondly, the best way to discipline those anthropological specu-lations which must somehow be incorporated into any social theory is to run coherence tests across the multiple test levels we have identified. Such a process will identify discrepancies to be resolved if the theory is to retain its acceptability, and it will render some anthropologies more plausible than others. But, because each iden-tified discrepancy can be resolved in a number of ways, because some ingredients in every anthropology refer to hypothetical limits and possibilities that have not yet been established historically, and because the introduction of a revised anthropology into the self-interpretation of participants might generate recognition of new limits or possibilities not clearly anticipated in current speculation, we must not expect any single, tightly formulated, anthropology to be so thoroughly grounded in experience and logic that every other candidate is eliminated from the running. Some orientations will appear more plausible than others and reasons can be specified in support of such a judgment.[16] But it is not to be anticipated that the number of legitimate candidates will reduce to one.

Political interpretation is not merely politically engaged, then, it is engaged in a special way. One's moral ideals and fears enter into theory through the very specification of its anthropological dimen-sion. The theory conveys a recommendation, underdetermined by available evidence, to crystallize our self-understanding in a par-ticular way in the hope, vain as it usually is, that this articulation will help to solidify the reality portrayed or to obstruct the outcome feared or to promote the achievement pursued. That is certainly a feature of the interpretation advanced here, as it is of those ranged against it. The warning conveyed by this particular interpretation found its most condensed expression in an earlier era: 'In our times we can neither endure our faults nor the means of correcting them.'[17]

4

The public interest and the common good

The two orientations

Not long ago the idea of the public interest was considered by most social scientists in the liberal tradition to be an unsuitable category for political inquiry. Since there was no specific interest which all members of the polity shared, the appeal to support a policy because it is in the public interest looked suspiciously like an attempt by one constituency to manipulate others. This prejudice against any idea of a public interest has dissolved at the same rate as the awareness of environmental issues has crystallized. Today most parties are convinced that some notion of a public interest is needed to cover those interests we share as citizens of a polity. There is now a vast literature purporting to tell us how to use the market or the bureaucracy to manipulate private incentives to produce 'public goods,' and to bring the private interest of persons and firms closer to the public interest.

The phrase 'the common good,' though, remains outside of these discussions; its exclusion reflects the legacy of previous theoretical prejudices. Political inquiry organized around an idea of the public interest generally defines the notion of interests narrowly, concentrating on desires and preferences already articulated by political constituencies. It tends to construe the public interest as an aggregate of a special subset of individual interests, those interests which a citizen might have simply by virtue of being a member of the polity. And discourse about the public interest does not assume that a policy in the public interest has any special priority over other aggregations of interest. If it is in the public interest to reduce pollution levels to improve the health of every or any citizen, it may still be in the 'net interest' of most participants to allow pollution to remain at existing levels. The interests the majority of the populace have in their private capacities as workers, owners, and consumers may outweigh the slight interest they share as random members of the public. Finally, inquiry into how best to promote the public interest tends to concentrate on how to eliminate the problem of the 'free rider.' This contemporary cowboy derives a benefit from a general policy without paying his share of the social cost to produce it. If most citizens most of the time are self-interested, it will be in the interests of each to be a free rider whenever possible, but the cumulative result of individual attempts to achieve this status undermines the efficacy of the policies in support of the public interest. Policies designed to promote the public interest, then, tend to draw on a particular set of legal penalties and market incentives to modify the behavior of potential free riders. The goal is to bring the individual interest of each more closely in line with the public purpose.

Inquiry into the common good revolves around a different center of gravity. What an individual wants and what is good for the individual may coalesce, but in any particular setting it is possible that the two standards will pull in different directions. The *common* good may refer to the aggregation of a particular set of individual interests, but the notion is not limited to this range of application. To appeal to the common good is to appeal to a set of shared purposes and standards which are fundamental to the way of life prized together by the participants. The participants have an obligation to respond to these appeals, even when the net interests of everyone, when each consults only his own interest, move in another direction. In a politics of the common good citizenship and civic virtue assume enhanced significance. Citizens are exhorted to support a proposed law because it supports the common good, and, once the law is established, the citizen is expected to follow its spirit as well as its letter. The citizen with civic virtue is asked to give presumptive priority to those dimensions of his own good shared with others, even though such a priority could not be justified by reference to his net interests taken alone. Supporters of such an orientation may acknowledge a set of basic rights which are not, except in the most extreme circumstances, to be sacrificed to the common good, but the bent of the orientation is to assess particular claims in the light of their bearing on common purposes and standards.

If reflection into the public interest is now in vogue translation of those issues into the vocabulary of the common good sends chills up the liberal spine. One is reminded of aristocratic orders in which the many sacrifice to a common good benefitting the few. The mind turns, as well, to more recent appeals to fascist collectivity in which 'blood rises up against formal understanding, race against the rational pursuit of ends, honor against profit, bonds against the caprice that is called "freedom", organic totality against individualistic dissolution, values against bourgeois security, politics against the primacy of the economy, state against society, folk against the individual and the mass.'[1] A politics tied to the rhetoric of the common good, a liberal must fear, will not only submerge the interests of the individual, it will suppress individual autonomy and rights and drown the ethic of tolerance. Radicals must also suspect appeals to the common good in a stratified society. For while such appeals draw sustenance from the conviction that we all are in this together, the policies invoked in its name invariably impose the greatest sacrifices on those stuck at the lower levels of the social order.

I wish to respect the moment of truth embedded in each of these objections and yet to argue, first, that a politics of the common good properly understood is indispensable to the life of a healthy polity in the contemporary world, and, secondly, that any mode of political inquiry which ignores the triadic relations between citizens, civic virtue, and the common good possesses insufficient conceptual resources to diagnose potential sources of dissolution and oppression within our own society. Fascism, one might say, can emerge as a perverse reaction to the attempt within a liberal regime to eliminate the politics of the common good. The route to be traversed here is treacherous, since a slip in any direction could sanction inadvertently some of the evils one seeks to avoid. Let me indicate in advance just why I think it is important to follow it. The points I make will apply to a variety of political economies, but I will focus on the particular ways in which they apply to representative democracy in advanced capitalism.

Two distinctive features of advanced capitalist democracies are pertinent. There is, first, the expanded potentiality in this order for self-consciousness among its citizens. The extension of literacy, the continuous access to mass media of communication and entertainment, the growth of international travel, the close and visible interdependence among contemporary states, the expanded use by policy planners of explicitly formulated social theories – all these developments can encourage the realization by citizens that we participate within an order which rests upon human convention rather than the unalterable dictates of nature. In saying that we can understand our institutions to be conventional I do not mean that any particular institution could be radically reconstituted if we were to will to do so. I do mean that any particular institution, taken alone, is susceptible to some degree of deliberate reconstitution and that the complex of institutions constituting our social order represents one among a small set of possibilities which might have formed the basis of our social life. The enhanced sense of the conventional nature of social existence accentuates the aspirations to appraise the comparative legitimacy of our own way of life, to compare it critically with other possibilities recognizable or imaginable to participants. The simultaneous extension of self-consciousness and the pressures for legitimation could only be curtailed in the contemporary world by repressive controls which deny citizens access to perspectives otherwise available to them. This is the respect, then, in which the preconditions of democratic politics also form some of the preconditions of fascism: an authoritarian regime *must* assume a fascist character only when there is among its populace the preliminary experience of democracy and the widespread understanding that other modes of life are possible.

The second distinctive feature is lodged more directly in our political economy: it consists in the progressive enlargement of those aspects of social life which must be coordinated, managed, or regulated by public means. If most features of our economic life (such as income distribution, employment levels, the type of work available, pensions, the type of commodities available to consumers, the comparative rates of development in different parts of the country) were once thought to be regulated impersonally by the market, it is now widely known that market transactions have become highly politicized. And if other areas of everyday social life (such as the sexual division of labor, the rules of child-rearing, the size of the family unit, the treatment of old people, the composition of the school curriculum, the ethnic composition of a neighborhood, the relationship between divorcees, the criteria for admission to higher education, even the role of the state in the larger social life) were previously governed to a significant extent by traditions unreflectively internalized by the populace, those traditions are today increasingly the object of political debate and public policy. I do

93

not suggest that there was previously no place for politics within market transactions and traditional relationships; I merely insist that both spheres are more intensely politicized today *and* that the populace is more acutely conscious of this politicization.

The convergence of these trends toward self-consciousness and the politicization of social life enlarges the sphere in which social coordination must be achieved by public means, confines the means by which public coordination can be achieved, and extends the range of rules, policies, regulations, and norms that need to be legitimized explicitly to those implicated within them. The dominant response to these developments, often favored by liberals, is to introduce incentives into the market through the political process so that individuals and firms are given monetary incentives to support the public interest. Another response, often favored by conservatives, is to regulate individual conduct increasingly by formal laws backed by the coercive power of the state. A third, celebrated within fascist doctrines, is to get the populace to identify completely and un-reflectively with the priorities established by the state through the combined use of manipulation and terror. And a fourth, celebrated previously by theorists in the republican tradition and preserved today in utopian images of socialism, is to promote civic virtue among citizens who identify reflectively with a way of life in common and who voluntarily adjust their political demands and daily conduct to the norms embedded in that way of life.

No contemporary society can cohere without the first and second modes of social coordination. I contend that these two modes, in turn, cannot suffice as modes of social coordination. They must be connected either to a civility tied to a mix of traditional and reflective commitments to a common good or to the terroristic suppression of reflective politics. The most profound illusion gripping contemporary liberals and rationalists is the idea that firm opposition to a politics of the common good can be sustained without inviting the regimentation and repression to which they are militantly opposed.

The circle of liberalism

Liberalism comes in many shapes and sizes. One of its variants pays close attention to the preconditions for civic virtue and the common good. John Stuart Mill, for example, insists that 'the first element of good government' is 'the virtue and intelligence of the human beings composing the community'; and that the 'most important point of excellence which any form of government can possess is to promote the virtue and intelligence of the people themselves.'[2] The specific virtues acknowledged by Mill remind us that it was easier to be both a liberal and a devotee of civic virtue in an earlier phase of the development of the civilization of productivity:

What, for example, are the qualities in the citizen individually which conduce most to keep up the amount of good conduct, of good management, of success and prosperity which already exist in society? Everybody will agree that these qualities are industry, integrity, justice and prudence . . . Whatever qualities in the government are promotive of industry, integrity, justice and prudence conduce alike to permanence and progress; only there is need for more of these qualities to make the society decidedly progressive than merely to keep it permanent.[3]

The virtues recognized by Mill cohered well with democratic politics in the developing civilization of productivity, and it was quite possible to believe that public commitment to that order and to those virtues would grow together. But this coherence no longer appears so readily sustainable. Another version of liberalism has therefore acquired prominence today. It seeks to retain the commitment to incrementalism, rights, tolerance, and freedom central to the liberal tradition, while breaking with the politics of civic virtue. This is the version of liberalism we shall examine.

From the depression in the 1930s to the middle of the Vietnam War, liberals, Ronald Dworkin reminds us, tended to support a familiar set of programs and principles. They favored economic growth, a reduction in economic inequality, freedom of speech, desegregation, separation of church and state, strong procedural protection for people accused of crime, and the decriminalization of victimless offenses against the prevailing morality. The liberal believed that a market economy, tempered by a welfare state accountable to the electorate, provides the institutional complex most favorable to the pursuit of these principles.[4] But, Dworkin says, these are a derivative commitment within liberalism; they are valued because they seem to support a more basic, constitutive principle of liberalism. Any of these positions could be revised if it turned out to inhibit fulfillment of the constitutive principle.

The constitutive morality of liberalism obligates the government to 'treat all its citizens with equal concern and respect.'[5] And this

95

principle, properly interpreted, requires the government to 'be neutral on what might be called the question of the good life.'[6] Liberal theory

supposes that political decisions must be, so far as possible, independent of any particular conception of the good life, or what gives value to life. Since the citizens of a society differ in their conceptions, the government does not treat them as equals if it prefers one conception to another.[7]

The constitutive morality of liberalism, as presented so far, is quite abstract. We need to know what institutional arrangements are most congruent with this principle and what sorts of policies are to be preferred once these institutions are intact. Dworkin believes that a market economy combined with a representative democracy holds the greatest promise. The market responds to producer and consumer preferences in allocating goods and services, and representative democracy offers a just way to reach 'collective decisions about what conduct shall be prohibited or regulated so that other conduct might be made possible or convenient.'[8]

In our society today the market imperfectly expresses the actual distribution of citizen preferences because of inequalities in class, race, and gender lodged within it. The liberal will thus favor redistributive policies through the state to remedy these biases to the extent that these remedies are consistent with the continuation of the market itself. Representative democracy, similarly, will be qualified by a strong constitution which keeps the basic rights of individuals outside the reach of majoritarian politics.

The liberal, operating within this familiar institutional setting, may support state intervention to allow the fulfillment of preferences at present closed off by the market. But what if the bent of the institutional order itself discourages the articulation of some preferences and nullifies the realization of others? The liberal may intervene in these cases, not because he thinks it is intrinsically important to protect, say, a landscape which is aesthetically pleasing, but because he believes the political economy left to itself might destroy the opportunity for citizens to form and express that preference in everyday life. 'He fears that this way of life will become unknown so that the process is not neutral amongst competing ideas of the good life, but in fact destructive of the very possibility of some of them.'[9] The principle of governmental neutrality between visions of the good life is consistent with active efforts to keep a variety of visions open.

This reading of liberalism, as Dworkin himself emphasizes, stands in opposition to any politics oriented to civic virtue and the pursuit of a common good. For in such a politics citizens call upon each other to support some practices and policies because they are thought to be intrinsically valuable, and to forgo others because they would undermine or jeopardize the way of life the citizenry seeks to live in common. From the standpoint of this alternative tradition one might criticize Dworkin's position by demanding a more concrete reading of what it means to treat people with equal respect and dignity, trying to tease out of the abstract principle a substantive morality of the common good. One might, alternatively, show the extent to which any particular institutional order must be committed with respect to different conceptions of the good life, showing that to commit oneself to a particular set of institutions is to commit oneself also to a conception of the common good.

These two critical strategies eventually intersect if either succeeds. I shall here pursue the second, with the intent of establishing the following conclusions. First, the principle is too indeterminate in its initial form to select among a variety of alternative ways of life. Secondly, once the principle is applied within a particular way of life, it can no longer remain neutral between preferred lifestyles. Thirdly, when the determinate principle is then extended again to allow a hundred flowers to bloom the rationale involved to support this result once again renders the principle too indeterminate. Fourthly, the implicit necessity to regulate and coordinate life-styles in accordance with the limits and imperatives of the order celebrated by Dworkin combines with his theoretical prejudice against civic virtue to sanction modes of behavorial management unanticipated and undesired by him.

Consider possible life-styles to which someone might aspire. One might wish to live in a society where the extended family provides identity, security and subsistence for its members; but extensive labor mobility, which is indispensible to the operation of a market economy, is inconsistent with such a way of life. One may wish to participate in a public life governed by shared religious beliefs and principles; but the separation of church and state must of course nullify that possibility. One may wish to decrease the consumption of those goods oriented merely to oneself or one's family unit (e.g., cars and private homes) and increase those consumed in common with a larger collectivity (mass transit and housing collectives); goods of the first set may be more consonant with a competitive market economy than goods of the second sort, especially if the market tends to undermine the durability of collective units needed to make the latter purchases. One may seek to be involved with others in a heroic enterprise or to maintain close ties with members of older and younger generations.

Each of these 'life-style' preferences involves essential reference to a larger institutional setting. To the extent that the system of political economy favored by Dworkin is inconsistent with them it cannot claim to be neutral between alternative preferences for a good life. And to the extent that the principle he supports is drawn upon to support one form of political economy over another it implicitly affirms some conceptions of the good life over others. The principle is either applied within a way of life which is still in need of legitimation as a whole or it is vacuous; it must either acquire determinacy and lose its ability to evaluate alternative systems of political economy or retain applicability to entire ways of life and lose its neutrality with respect to alternative conceptions of the good life within the social order. Dworkin evades this implication by concentrating implicitly on those life-style options which fall within the range of tolerance of our way of life. But this first evasion then generates a second, more serious one. For if the structure of every way of life encourages some life-styles, discourages others, and renders yet others unsustainable, every social order must, if it survives, develop ways to adjust the conduct of its members to its own range of tolerance. Dworkin says nothing about child-rearing, education, social taboos, market discipline, and profit imperatives as modes of social regulation; he says little about the role of legal coercion and public authority in this respect. But because the principle of neutrality is untenable these issues must be confronted somehow, and because of the commitments Dworkin does express, we can detect the forms of social coordination implicitly sanctioned within the theory.

Dworkin clearly could not place heavy stress on the regulation of conduct through laws backed by the coercive power of the state; for he wishes to strengthen the procedural rights of those accused of crime and to reduce the number of activities covered by the criminal law. And he cannot draw on resources available to a polity in which civic virtue flourishes. For part of the point of the liberal principle is to distinguish it from the ideal of 'a virtuous society' in which the members 'believe their community, in its social and political activity, exhibits virtues, and that they have a responsibility, as citizens, to promote these virtues.'[10]

There is an option remaining within the political economy Dworkin supports. The other side of the wish to proliferate life-styles within a market economy is the call to use the market as an instrument to adapt individual life-styles to the limits and impera-tives recognized by the state. These two perspectives are locked together. Each celebrates the market, one for its contribution to individual freedom and the other for its contribution to the control of individuals. And each expresses repugnance for the politics of the common good, one because it limits the alternative life-styles available to individuals and the other because it is less effective than market incentives in regulating individual behavior. Charles Schultze portrays the virtues of the market in bright colors:

Market-like arrangements not only minimize the need for coercion as a means of organizing society; they also reduce the need for compassion, patriotism, brotherly love, and cultural solidarity as motivating forces behind social improvements. Harnessing the 'base' motives of material self-interest to promote the common good is perhaps the most important social incentive mankind has yet achieved.[11]

The approach commended by Schultze is familiar enough. Pollut-ing firms, commuters contributing to traffic congestion, students training for jobs in an oversubscribed occupation, and homeowners wasting energy can be given market incentives to reduce pollution, congestion, job oversubscription, and energy waste. When the mar-ket does not automatically price these activities to absorb their socially recognized costs the state can stipulate higher prices. The market thereby becomes increasingly a visible instrument of state power.

Dworkin and Schultze together draw the circle within which liberal individualism moves. One legitimizes market processes be-cause they free the individual from ties to larger social purposes and the other discovers the individual prized loose from those social bonds to be a malleable object of control through state manipulation of market incentives. The idealism of the first produces the form the realism of the second can take. For when those who celebrate the primacy of the market and denigrate the value of civic virtue finally acknowledge the necessity for extensive social coordination by public means, the market turns out to be the most convenient and effective means of conscious social coordination left.

The somber vision of Michel Foucault, exaggerated in its expression, nonetheless points to one way in which the two arcs of individualism are drawn into a single circle of freedom and control. The most 'individualized' members of the society, he asserts, meaning those whose bureaucratic record is most highly developed and who possess the fewest social resources to resist treatment based on the findings of their files, are the most vulnerable objects of disciplinary control.

In a system of discipline, the child is more individualized than the adult, the patient more than the healthy man, the madman and delinquent more than the normal and the non-delinquent. In each case, it is toward the first of these pairs that all the individualizing mechanisms are turned in our civilization . . . The movement that saw the transition from historico-ritual mechanisms for the formation of individuality to the scientific-disciplinary mechanism . . . , that moment when the science of man became possible is the moment when a new technology of power and a new political anatomy of the body were implemented.[12]

Schultze does not believe that the historical trajectory of the processes he commends points in the direction of Foucault's vision, though he does mention the 'almost frightening efficiency' of the market approach to behavorial control.[13] He avoids this abyss by drawing into his theory elements which he initially promised to exorcize. For while Schultze believes we cannot expect civic virtue from citizens in following the laws and policies of the state, it turns out that we *must* expect it when they participate in the politics of law formation and policy choice. In daily transactions people and firms act as they do 'because their self-interest dictates doing so, given the existing set of incentives'; but as voters 'they also have some views about the public good, quite apart from immediate effects on themselves.'[14] Nonetheless, it remains difficult for Schultze to believe that people guided by narrow incentives at one level of public life will in fact express a broad concern for the public good at another level: 'Therefore, I must end rather lamely. There is no instrumental solution to the dilemma. The only available course is a steady maturing of both the electorate and political leaders.'[15]

The issue Schultze alludes to, but does not address, is this: How could an administrative state, regulating individual behavior through a complex of bureaucratic controls and market incentives, encourage the political knowledge and allegiance it needs to generate public support for the system of private incentives? Is the system of political economy he celebrates consistent with the standard of citizenship to which he must appeal? The liberalism Schultze represents stands at a critical juncture. It must either show how the preconditions of civic virtue can be realized in the political economy it seeks to perfect or sanction the further insulation of the administrative state from the electorate whose conduct it regulates.

The dialectic of dissolution

The free rider presents a paradigmatic form of evasion which the thin theory of the public interest recognizes and promises to resolve by the manipulation of market incentives. Idealistic theories of citizenship, as they would be described within this tradition, are thought neither to recognize the phenomenon of the free rider nor to devise a strategy realistic enough to cut this cowboy off at the pass. It is pertinent, in this respect, to note that Jean-Jacques Rousseau posed this same question while developing his own theory; he concluded that no individualist theory of citizenship could hope to resolve it.

In the *Geneva Manuscript* Rousseau imagines an 'independent man' of reason listening to a 'wise man' counsel him to protect his own security and welfare by agreeing to abide by laws in support of the common good. The independent man replies:

I am aware that I bring horror and confusion to the human species, but either I must be unhappy or I must cause others to be so, and no one is dearer to me than myself. I would try in vain to reconcile my interest with that of another man. Everything you tell me about the advantages of the social law would be fine if while I were scrupulously observing it toward others, I were sure that all of them would observe it toward me. But what assurance of this can you give me, and could there be a worse situation for me than to be exposed to all the ills that stronger men would want to cause me without my daring to make up for it against the weak? Furthermore it will be my business to get the strong on my side, by sharing with them the spoils from the weak. This would be better than justice for my own advantage and for my security. [16]

In a society without civic virtue the free rider will inevitably find room to roam. This is Rousseau's thesis. And I wish to argue, first, that he is quite right, and, secondly, that this phenomenon grows in conjunction with the expansion of coercive mechanisms designed to curtail it. I will do so by taking the thin theory of the public interest more seriously than its authors intend, revealing in this way the implicit background of common understandings and commitments it must draw upon to work effectively. The thin theory to be examined denies the importance of such a background. It recognizes that people have interests in their capacities as parents, workers, consumers, owners, and citizens, and it treats the public interest as that interest we share as citizens. But it draws upon a minimal conception of citizenship. When I act in my capacity as a citizen, according to this view, I think of myself as an undifferentiated member of the public: I am the *anyone* or *everyone* who might suffer if the highway accident rate increases or if pollution levels are uniformly high. The interest we share as citizens in this restricted sense exhausts the public interest, and the public interest, so defined, is to prevail only if the 'net interest' of most people in it prevails over the aggregation of particular interests people have in their other capacities.[17] Once a policy in the public interest is passed it becomes necessary to enforce it so that it does not become advantageous to some to benefit from the general policy while avoiding its particular application to themselves.

The advantage of this theory is supposed to be its realism. It does not expect people to vote or lobby for policies except when their net interests incline them to, nor does it expect the policies to be effective until they incorporate a set of incentives which incline individuals and firms to follow them in their self-interest. But it is not a realistic theory. It is a utopian theory which can only work when the polity has resources of civic virtue to draw upon not recognized within the theory itself. It is also a destructive theory, inadvertently sanctioning practices and policies which deplete the supply of civic virtue it needs.

Consider a political economy like the American in every respect except that it is drained of a shared commitment to a common good which stretches beyond those interests anyone has as an undifferentiated member of the public. The public faces health hazards from air, water and soil pollution, and threats to the health of its economy

because of the disproportion between its demand for energy resources and its control over the sources of that energy.

Affluent members of the system have both an interest in avoiding
the worst effects of environmental deterioration and the private
capacity to promote those interests. Since these effects are differentially distributed across geographic areas, urban and suburban settings, and occupational sectors, the more affluent parties can secure
work that is environmentally safe, move to suburbs where the air
is cleaner and the streets safer, locate residences away from nuclear
facilities, replace shoddy products which break or perish, use large,
safe cars to commute to work, and act in an indefinite number of
ways to minimize the extent to which the most adverse, dangerous
and uncomfortable effects of the environmental degradation impinge upon them.

But the private escape exacerbates the problem in the city left
behind. Commuting increases traffic congestion and pollution; the
city is pressed to construct urban expressways which break up further the established network of neighborhoods; the city's tax base
is eroded; and new political pressures are produced to channel a
higher proportion of state aid to suburban areas. Most importantly,
because the private escape route requires heavy expenditures by the
escapees, and because the affluence which allows them to finance
these escapes is typically connected to ecologically destructive busi-
nesses, the escapees now have a double incentive to oppose collective
responses to these public issues. To support now public policies in
favor of urban transit systems, public parks, clean air and waterways,
occupational safety, improved garbage collection and disposal systems would be to pay once again for benefits flowing primarily to
the urban area they have left behind. The net interest of the affluent
escapees in the public interest is small indeed; the private escape
erodes the *will* to support the public interest.

An inverted expression of this result emerges for many blue-collar
workers living in urban areas. If they demand too much of the firm
which employs them it may move to greener pastures; and if they
support the needed public policies their taxes will rise even further.
The availability of a private escape for some accentuates the dependent status of others, and the two positions converge to undermine
the public will to support policies in the public interest. These tendencies in turn are intensified by the Madisonian structure of the
political process; it too works in familiar ways to obstruct the

effective formation of a public will to respond collectively to these collective issues.

But suppose the public will and the political means were somehow generated (though without recourse to civic virtue). Suppose a mix of market incentives and bureaucratic regulations is introduced somehow through the political process to bring private incentives and the public interest into closer harmony. Firms are given tax incentives to produce durable and energy efficient commodities; energy prices are fixed at a higher rate to reduce unnecessary use; consumers are given tax and price incentives to adjust their private purchases to those compatible with the public interest. If the conditions we have specified are still operative, two consequences will emerge. First, some constituencies will believe themselves to be unjustly treated through these policies by comparison to other constituencies serving as a point of comparative reference, and the fact that the outcome is the visible result of conscious policy will deepen this sense of grievance. Secondly, while most segments of the populace retain some interest in the public interest, many now have a greater interest in *appearing* to abide by it, benefitting from its general application, and evading its application to them in particular.

These two conditions suffice to launch a negative dialectic with the potential for its progressive universalization. Some will organize black markets to evade official specifications of price, tax, or product quality. They will bribe officials (who themselves do not, remember, flow over with civic virtue) to cover up these practices. And those citizens who hold out will soon find themselves suffering a double disadvantage. They pay the highest price for goods and services, including a price for the bureaucracy needed to enforce this price, but the extension of evasions diminishes the benefit flowing to them from these fees. Compared to those who evade the official policy they pay a higher price and bear greater burdens.

The state can act to shore up the monitoring processes by increasing the number of public monitors and the penalties for breaking the rules. But the monitors, given our stipulations, are not different from other citizens, and the question arises: Who will monitor the monitors and how will they do it? For private firms, intensely interested in particular evasions, have the will and means to bring the net interests of some monitors in line with the particular interest of the particular firm. And once some officials and firms are implicated in schemes of evasion they share an interest with other evaders in avoiding detection, or, more specifically, they are jointly motivated to derail or debunk any public interpretation of these practices which makes them appear to be evasive or illegal. For investigations, once launched in one area, acquire a momentum of their own and may extend to others. Under these conditions it may be prudent for elected officials to appear to tighten up enforcement procedures while falling short of doing so effectively in crucial areas. They cover the alliance of the strong against the weak anticipated by Rousseau.

Inside this dialectic of dissolution is a process which extends and accentuates it. For if the private agents and public monitors are guided only by the thin conception of the public interest, they have limited resources to draw upon in interpreting the specific import of public policies in particular settings. The evasive interpretation one constellation of claimants and monitors concurs upon in one setting creates the precedent for the proliferation of legal evasions in other settings. Those who fail to receive favorable readings from public authorities will then feel unjustly treated, and their will to abide by restrictions applied specifically to them will be further weakened.

Where the *will* to abide by the public interest is weak the *knowledge* of what counts as an instance of it becomes increasingly indeterminate and contestable. Those who agree merely to follow the letter of the law – for those without civic virtue by definition ignore its spirit – now find it more difficult to locate the letter with precision. The inherently open texture of any set of rules is magnified in this setting by the dissolution of the background of prior understandings, convictions, and trust; for it previously provided the legacy of custom which allowed participants to recognize and solidify the practical import of abstract rules. The implications of this development are serious because the situation under scrutiny has already evolved to a point where those who are the target of a negative rule have an intense interest in rendering its applicability to their particular case doubtful or contestable. The intensification of the will to evade is matched by the deterioration of the ability to define evasions within a shared set of understandings and norms. The phenomenon deserves close attention.

'How should we imagine,' Wittgenstein asks in *Zettel*, 'a complete list of rules for the employment of a word? What do we mean by a complete list of rules for employment of a piece in chess? Couldn't we always construct doubtful cases, in which the normal list of rules does not decide? Thing, e.g., of such a question as : how to determine who moved last, if a doubt is raised about the reliability of the player's memories.'[18]

An unmarried male living alone is certainly a bachelor and a male legally married to a female with whom he is living is clearly not. But what about an unmarried woman? A male living with a woman for a lifetime without a marriage certificate? A male who leaves his legal spouse and sets up an independent household (for a week, seven months, seven years)? A male who contracts to live with a woman for seven days every month? For sixteen days a month? Every day every second year? If the concepts of marriage and bachelorhood play a role in our assignment of moral and legal responsibilities for child support and alimony these borderline questions can assume great importance. Purely self-interested parties, for instance, might find it advantageous to live just over the edge of a particular boundary, thus producing a social trend toward a particular kind of life-style. And if there is no settled background of common assumptions and social purposes within which to interpret the meaning of the notions 'married' and 'bachelor,' we will lack the social resources to adjust the boundaries of the concepts, or to create intermediate notions, when the terms are applied to unfamiliar and unexpected situations. The society lacks sufficient resources to adjust these notions to novel situations, and individual participants have the will to create novel arrangements which allow them to 'have it both ways.'

Consider another example. Affirmative action in American society is a creative amendment to the rules governing equal opportunity. The assumption is that women, ethnic minorities, and the disabled have been discriminated against in preparing to compete for the relatively small number of cherished careers available. Therefore, the usual rules ostensibly governing merit are to be revised enough to redress the previous imbalance but not so much that the competence of personnel in key positions is reduced. The notions of equal opportunity, merit, discrimination, and competence play an essential background role in fixing both the rules which govern affirmative action and the considerations invoked in adjudicating between competing interpretations of those rules in particular settings. And these notions themselves are interpreted within a larger framework of assumptions and purposes making up our way of life. If, for instance, the primary purpose was to locate role models for young people of different gender and ethnicity, the evolution of affirmative action would take one path; if it were primarily to enlarge the pool of talent to improve the efficiency of private and public institutions it would take another; and if each of these objectives played an approximately equal role it would take yet a third.

The white male we are now to consider moves in a setting where the dialectic of dissolution is partially developed. He is committed only to follow the letter of affirmative action policies, having no regard and little understanding of the larger purposes of these policies. Those who judge his claims, similarly, strive to conform to the letter of the law. They must decide for or against him, but the resources of knowledge and authority they can draw upon to do so have dwindled.

'I declare myself to be a woman,' announces this person with male reproductive organs. The court or the bureaucracy must rule against the eligibility of this person or face the prospect of a flood in the affirmative action pool. But the rationale they can draw upon to support this finding is weak. 'You have not been discriminated against in the way persons with female reproductive organs have,' they may say, closing off this avenue even if the rationale carries little authority with the claimant. The claimant accepts the finding, remaining committed to the letter of the law and to advancing his interest within it.

'I was treated like a girl throughout my childhood. My father thought I was a sissy. My mother made me wear dresses. Male teachers took advantage of me.' The authorities have more difficulty here. For now they must assert criteria separating closely those practices which count as discriminatory from those which do not or produce a finding which appears arbitrary and further undermines the will of those excluded by it to abide by its letter.

'I have undergone surgery to instill female reproductive organs,' our claimant may now assert. Or: 'When I was eleven my parents ordered surgery to convert me into a female.' The claimant may add, 'the only person in our society treated worse than a natural woman is a man who artificially becomes one through surgery.' The public authority can ascertain whether the claim to have submitted to surgery is true, but must *decide* then whether the true claim is relevant. And, in the conditions we have stipulated, their ability to reach *authoritative* judgments in this area will be impaired. The findings must appear arbitrary to a range of recipients who will further contest the letter of the law while remaining out of touch with its spirit.

Men, women, ethnic minorities, consumers, workers, parents, children, and owners are all encouraged to contest creatively the boundaries of explicit rules regulating their conduct once the tendency to do so acquires initial momentum. For to be left out of the process is to be deprived of the benefits of general compliance and to face the burdens of personal compliance. Employees can work 'according to rule'; owners can shift investments abroad to evade domestic regulation; parents, locked into an internal struggle over the sexual division of labor, can rear their children in conformity with the law while losing touch with the psychic economy of child development. Controversies will proliferate over the precise 'stipulations' governing tax payments, welfare allocations, equal opportunity, the rights and duties of parents and children, the discretionary use of public funds, job performance evaluation, and conflicts of interest in public life.

The dialectic of dissolution thus draws upon three sources simultaneously. The polity possesses limited resources to *will* policies in the public interest, to *sustain allegiance* to the letter of the law, and to *interpret* the letter of the law in particular cases; the members possess powerful incentives to oppose public interest laws to their private disadvantage, to evade compliance and to contest the applicability of the law to their particular case. Each of these sources feeds the development of the others, and the dialectic which unfolds progressively thins out the supply of public will, integrity and knowledge. Those who abstain initially from this process are eventually drawn into its orbit on pain of suffering the double disadvantage described by Rousseau. The extension of evasions and contested interpretations produces in turn a corollary proliferation of bureaucratic regulations, monitoring agencies, and litigious relationships. To the extent social order is maintained, it approaches the appearance of a Hobbesian system in which the sovereign defines the meaning of key words by fiat and sustains these definitions by the extensive use of incentives and penalties.

The logic of the process touches tendencies at work in advanced capitalist systems. To the extent these tendencies are modulated or muffled, the thin theory of the public interest represents a distorted reading of the actual complex of institutional ties, implicit understandings, and common purposes which persist in the order. We are not now as individualized as it construes us to be. But this general theoretical orientation, prominent once again in theories of public policy constructed with the categories of neo-classical economics, is still not innocent of social consequences. Where the imperatives of the political economy fail to speak to purposes adopted by a wide range of participants, the thin theory of the public interest interprets the discrepancy to reflect universal features of the human condition. In these circumstances, its categories celebrate the ideal of the detached individual, distract attention from the deeper sources of dissolution within the civilization of productivity, and legitimize the acceleration of administrative controls over individual conduct. The resurgence of the theory is a symptom of the phenomenon it purports to comprehend and resolve.

Politics and the common good

If Rousseau anticipates a compelling critique of the thin theory of the public interest, his own theory of the General Will is inappropriate to the conditions of modern life.[19] The participants in his polity are situated in a rural, face-to-face community; each family retains a measure of independence by owning enough land to provide its own subsistence; property is divided rather evenly among members of the polity to make it easier for the citizens to discover, will, and abide by laws which impinge upon all equally; the country is secure from the threat of invasion and minimally involved in commerce with other states; finally, the traditions which bind the polity together are protected from dissolution by censorship of the arts and by strict rules governing education and family life. Some of these preconditions are today unrealizable while the attainment of others would require political repression on a massive scale.

Situated between a politics of the General Will, which would smother individuality and self-consciousness, and a politics of the public interest, which converts individuality into social regimentation, is the politics of the common good. A theory of the common good is a necessary, if insufficient, ingredient in any account of the deeper sources of dislocation and dissolution within our political economy.

To be an individual with specific ideas, feelings, standards, principles, and interests one must first *be* within a society. The language one shares with others, acquired before the capacity to criticize it is developed, provides the medium within which our ideas, judgments, purposes, and emotions are constituted. To share this language is to share a range of criteria for making distinctions, picking out objects, reaching judgments. To inherit, for instance, the vocabulary of labor, productivity, merit, leisure, competence, job description, collective bargaining, punctuality, and efficiency is to inherit a language which turns our attention toward a particular range of distinctions and standards. The vocabulary embodies criteria of appraisal which are quite alien to some other societies. To say today that a worker has merit is to claim that he lives up to specified skills and effort which justify special recognition or rewards. The notion 'merit' describes the worker's activity from an evaluative point of view. If that point of view were to be abstracted from the concept we would lose the rationale for using it and the ability to adapt it to new circumstances.[20]

To participate in a way of life is to carry an enormous load of settled criteria of judgment, standards of appraisal, and beliefs. In sharing a language, we share, even if incompletely and imperfectly, these pre-understandings; and we bring them to bear on the specific issues and questions which arise between us. Class or generational conflict within a society embodies this general truth in a special way. The struggle assumes a more intimate quality than that between members of two alien tribes or between Martians and Earthlings because there are common points of reference from which it proceeds. The parties support a different scale of priorities in a setting where each can make intimate contact with crucial assumptions and priorities of the other. If one party to the struggle anticipates a future which breaks completely with the present, it must acknowledge its inability now to characterize that future in anything but the most abstract (that is, utopian) terms.

One can abstract from the specific pre-understandings which constitute *us* as, say, American intellectuals to those we share as Americans, to those we share as members of an advanced industrial society, to those we share simply as persons. At this last level of abstraction, unless we implicitly draw back into it historically specific characteristics, we can speak only of the most general capacities for reason, sexuality, emotion, morality, and so forth. We might acknowledge that these general capacities and orientations help to define the most general moral limits that anyone, who has some acquaintance with more than one culture, should recognize. But they could not suffice to guide practical judgment; no individual could express merely these universal capacities and maintain social relationships with members of the same society. When we confront a practical question we already acknowledge a set of pre-understandings embodied within the setting in which the question is posed. We unavoidably invoke some of these prior understandings in appraising this individual, that governing principle, those feelings, that policy, and so on. We are fated either to adopt universal principles which leave us without reason in particular settings, or to fill out the universal in particular ways by drawing upon specific beliefs, standards, and judgements within our way of life. No way of life could be neutral between alternative conceptions of the good life or in the provision of the institutional supports for recognized alternatives.

It is possible to become more self-conscious about some subset of pre-understandings. One can immerse oneself in alternative orientations, vicariously through the study of the literature from other times and places or directly by participating in an unfamiliar way of life; and this process allows one to consider more reflectively and critically judgments previously adopted unreflectively.[21]

The possibility for self-consciousness, highly developed in contemporary society, must be incorporated into any theory of the proper relation between politics and the common good.

Our concentration now, though, is on the materials from which a sense of the common good can be constructed. When we draw on the available stock of pre-understandings we are predisposed to *recognize* some distinctions and standards and to ignore others; within this framework we are further predisposed to affirm some and to deny others. Out of this background of imperfectly and implicitly shared distinctions, standards, and purposes a sense of the common good might crystallize, though there is no guarantee, first, that this will occur; secondly, that the crystallized conception will secure the allegiance of all who recognize it; thirdly, that each of its ingredients will prove to be compatible with the others; or fourthly, that its realization will be as fulfilling as anticipated by those who initially give allegiance to it.

A collective value or a good shared in common is one which

makes essential reference to a particular social complex for its realization. One depends upon some institutional setting to secure sufficient food to survive, but a collective value is implicated in institutional life in a more essential way than this. When one participates in a banquet, one, in conjunction with others, draws upon a set of pre-understandings concerning how a banquet is held. The affair requires mutual awareness among the participants, and its enjoyment includes the common understanding that this mutuality is part of the banquet itself. Ethnic jokes aimed at one's own ethnic group can be so entertaining at such affairs, for example, because they accentuate the particular spirit of collectivity which is the banquet. Old and familiar stories play a similar role, expressing the tie across generations which is often also an object of collective reference at such affairs.

If a banquet is successful, one enjoys the food. One also appreciates the ritualized expression of fellowship appropriate to that occasion, the enjoyment that others take in these rituals, and the understanding by others that all appreciate these rituals. The rituals represent and crystallize these common understandings and feelings. The banquet as an object of appreciation for me, one might say, includes its status as an object of appreciation for us. Neither the individual nor individuality are submerged at a banquet. Indeed, they flourish in a particular way. But, at a successful banquet, each person identifies himself as a participant in addition to the usual identifications as a parent, a physician, a humorist, etc. It is because the banquet is supposed to serve as a common object of value that so many things can go wrong. 'I enjoyed the food' is a joke or an insult as a parting comment at a banquet. And it is because the banquet has this status that parents and spouses so urgently press rebelling teenagers and cynical spouses to pretend they appreciate the entire affair.

Here are some possible objects of collective value which might be acknowledged by a people larger than a face-to-face community as the good it seeks to share in common. It might seek to serve God, to expand its boundaries and dominate neighboring populations, to create a civilization of productivity which brings affluence, freedom, and leisure to future generations, to support contemplation and scientific inquiry, to maintain conditions of equal citizenship, to define and adjudicate its internal conflicts within the frame of a written constitution inherited from the past and admired by contemporaries, to multiply the range of life-styles individuals may experience within one lifetime.

As soon as such a set of possible objects of the common good are stated a number of distinctions concerning the range, content, and viability of these possibilities become pertinent. A populace may share a restrictive set of collective ends and its institutions may secure them effectively; or it may identify with a broad set of ends some of which turn out to be incompatible with the realization of others; or the very realization of the collective end may expose characteristics implicit within it which weaken the allegiance of future generations to it. At another level, some segments of the populace may militantly repudiate a collective good fervently endorsed by others; or all may subscribe to it in common while doing so in a weak or attenuated way; or the populace may profess commitment to a set of practices and purposes which is belied by the commitments expressed in their actual conduct; or the ends supported may be too abstract and indeterminate to provide effective guidance in concrete situations. The impressive thing about the relation between the common good and politics is the indefinite variety of ways in which the contribution the first makes to civility in the second can be disturbed or derailed. That is why an understanding of these relations is crucial to a comprehension of the trials, struggles, aspirations, and dislocations which inspire and plague a political order.

I will speak of a *politics* of the common good, as an ideal type, when the following conditions are operative. Most citizens much of the time identify with a set of common standards and purposes; the standards are flexible enough to allow space for political conflict and dialogue over their proper deployment in particular settings, but determinate enough to play a creative role in reaching political solutions and compromise; the good appreciated and pursued in common involves reference to the interests of future generations who are to reside in the polity; and the general allegiance to the common good, though growing out of a set of pre-understandings, can be sustained even as citizens become more reflective about its institutional preconditions and the constraints imposed by these institutions on the expression of other admirable virtues, purposes, and ends.

When a common good, so construed, is operative, politics flourishes. Citizens, though with more reservations in their own case and fewer in the case of others, agree that the articulation of political claims is to be confined and limited by respect for the good we share in common; and the adjustment of competing claims is to be pursued with an eye to its bearing on these cherished institutions, purposes, and standards. Interests which fall within this framework acquire legitimacy as claims, even though a legitimate claim will not necessarily be confirmed fully in public policy. Part of the point is to *search* for common ground within shared norms which will also speak to the legitimate interests of a variety of citizens.

The common good is continuously undergoing closer specification in established contexts and in adjustment to unexpected circumstances. Its historical character thus makes it an unsuitable object for a technical analysis of the most efficient means to a fixed and sharply defined set of ends. Indeed, *one* of the criteria that a policy is well suited to the common good is the concurrence by most participants at the end of a political dialogue that it is. Politics, in this way, is intrinsic to, as well as a means toward, the common good.

Citizens understand that sometimes they will have to subordinate particular and immediate interests to the common good, but they also understand that those particular interests which harmonize well with it are to receive high priority. They have an interest in showing that such a harmony exists and in adjusting their claims to foster that harmony. In their allegiance to the common good they are thus neither simple egoists nor simple altruists. Rather, their partial identification with the larger order encourages them to define their interests within its range of tolerance, to take a longer term view of the connection between the one and the other, and to abide automatically by the spirit as well as the letter of laws which express the common good.

The politics of the common good, because of the very connections we have perceived within it, can be or become a politics of false consciousness. Participants may be confined by commitment to a good which is, unbeknownst to them, unrealizable; or the failure of some to recognize the extent to which they are held in bondage to others may be a necessary component in the retention of common allegiance to collective ends. But these possible derailments merely emphasize the precarious and problematic status of the politics of the common good; they tell us nothing about its dispensability. If the connection between politics and the common good were severed completely, politics would degenerate necessarily into the dialectic of dissolution or into the coercive imposition of order by some on a recalcitrant populace. More likely, social dissolution and coercive regimentation would occur simultaneously. The common good is a precarious *and* unavoidable pursuit for those who admire politics itself. To deny that it is precarious is to adopt a utopian posture toward civic virtue; to pretend that it is avoidable is to hold either a utopian or ruthless commitment to technocratic politics.

Examination of one particular issue from this perspective may shed more light on these general statements. Karl Marx, in an early essay critical of a proposal to relax the divorce law in Germany, argued that the proponents of this change, thinking only of the purported right of individuals to do what they want, would inadvertently help to destroy a social form, the family, whose health was essential to the formation and preservation of the bonds of social life. Those in favor of the reform, says Marx, think only of the individual taken alone, not of the ways in which we are all implicated within, and dependent upon, a common way of life.

They think only of the two individuals and forget the *family*. They forget that nearly every dissolution of a marriage is the dissolution of a family and the children and what belongs to them should not be dependent upon arbitrary whims, even from a purely legal point of view. If marriage were not the basis of the family, it would not be subject to legislation, just as friendship is not. Those opponents, therefore, take into account *only* the individual wish, or rather, the caprice of the spouses; they do not consider the will of the marriage, the ethical substance of this relationship.[22]

Marx is arguing that the institution of the family is part of the good participants seek in common. It both contributes to and helps to constitute the social ties which bind us together. Each citizen should come to understand this relationship and should then support laws and customs which protect the integrity of the family. And the citizen is obligated to do this even if in doing so the citizen realizes that anyone, including himself, might someday be adversely affected by the law. 'Nobody,' says Marx, 'is forced to enter into a marriage, but everybody must be forced to make up his mind that he will obey the laws of marriage when he enters into it.'[23] A divorce law consonant with the common good will be one in which an impartial third party judges whether the marriage is really 'dead,' that is, whether the desired separation is in the best interests of this particular family and, as a background consideration, is based upon desiderata which could be extended to other cases of a similar sort without weakening the institution of the family in important ways. If the separation is too lightly granted the cumulative effect of such decisions will work to dissolve those ties between generations which form a crucial part of civic virtue. Each citizen, comprehending these connections, should support a rather stringent divorce law, even though that law might impose onerous burdens on any one person.

The nuclear family is today, of course, an embattled institution, and I do not suggest it is either possible or appropriate to try to shore it up by such legal means. Civic virtue among citizens, though, does presuppose some intimate, stable, nurturant unit that promotes self-confidence among children, establishes ties across generations, instills an understanding of the responsibilities of citizenship, and, in general, provides a particular medium of experience which prepares its members to participate in the larger life of the society. Suppose, though, it is argued, correctly enough, that while the family as we know it today must mediate between the individual and the state, the family also serves as the medium in which women are forced into a subordinate and demeaning position. The commitment to the first good would limit the ways in which we could respond legitimately to the second evil. Remedies which further detached parents from their children would have to be rejected in favor of those which helped to equalize the burdens inside and outside the family. And the latter orientation, to succeed, would surely require changes in the occupational career patterns prevailing in our society, making it less disadvantageous for each spouse to work part-time over the large part of a career. The obstacles to change in this latter area are great – that is one of the reasons the politics of the common good is unattractive to particular constituencies in a setting where it tends to be ignored by others – but if it were true that the family as an institution were central to the common good, this course would be the preferable one to follow.[24] The politics of the common good sets limits within which recognized evils are to be considered and remedied. Without such limits, without the idea that certain possible remedies are unthinkable, this mode of politics disappears.

The idea to be drawn out of the idealized image is not one in which each individual voluntarily, unilaterally, and thoroughly subordinates private interests to the common good. It is one in which particular claims are articulated and contested within a frame of reference established by the good we seek in common. The process by which a settlement of these claims is reached is essentially political, first, because there is no single criterion or fixed set of criteria to which the plurality of common ends can be reduced and, secondly, because politics is essential to the further specification and acceptance of the common good by the populace. If the public interest, thinly conceived, contributes to a dialectic of dissolution, corruption, and coercion, the politics of the common good, when the setting is propitious, tends to reverse that dialectic. The understanding that the good we seek in common limits and confines the claims legitimately pressed by other constituencies makes it easier for me to adjust my own claims to conform to its limits. Knowing that others generally will abide by the spirit of the laws, I know that it is not necessary for me to evade it in order to escape the double disadvantage identified by Rousseau. Knowing that other disinterested parties will publicize evasions they perceive, it no longer seems so fruitless for me to expose such evasions on occasion. Knowing that those aspects of my private interest which are most congruent with the common good legitimately have high priority in our politics I am more willing and able to abide by those policies which require a sacrifice of my particular interest. And knowing, if I have children, that the pursuit of the common good involves collective concern for the welfare of future generations I no longer have to concentrate exclusively on the interests of my own family in appraising policy alternatives. The politics of civic virtue, once established, acquires an affirmative momentum of its own. When *civitas* is firmly entrenched, one does not have to be a hero to do one's part. It is enough to be a citizen.

This idea of the politics of the common good, it will inevitably be charged, exudes an air of unreality; it floats above the political life we recognize or could hope to realize in our society. I wish to concur in this contention while insisting that it is improperly expressed. The unreality resides more in the image of politics many have come to accept as a norm. For that image, if fully operative, could not sustain democratic politics at all. In our society the idea of the common good serves both as a lens through which to detect otherwise invisible features of contemporary politics and as a touchstone against which to delineate the preconditions of a more viable politics. Several considerations are particularly pertinent.

First, if the imperative to coordinate social conduct by public means has intensified in advanced capitalist societies, if market processes and internalized tradition decreasingly serve as media through which coordination is achieved automatically, then a deficit in the supply of civic virtue generates pressure for an enlarged investment in the state's use of market incentives, legal discipline, and bureaucratic regulations to control behavior.

Secondly, if the ideas of individual rights, freedom, and equal opportunity, which play a role in the most progressive aspects of our politics, require implicit reference to a common good in order to be specified sufficiently and to be acknowledged by broader constituencies against whom the claims are made, the eclipse of the politics of the common good would involve the deterioration of these values as well. They would either perish in the proliferation of unlimited demands made in their name or dissipate into a light mist of rhetoric hovering over the more brutal and ruthless struggle for hegemony.

Thirdly, if appeals to the common good are today received with cynicism because those in the lower reaches of the stratified society realize that they are asked to carry a disproportionate share of the collective burden, this cynicism is a symptom of the internal relation between a reduction in inequality and the politics of the common good. In an order which is highly politicized *and* highly stratified, an appeal to the common good must always receive the same reply: 'If we are all in this together, why do some of us enjoy so many privileges while others suffer so many burdens?' The appeal will then be converted by state authorities into a program of selective incentives and controls designed to bring the conduct of the most vulnerable constituencies quietly into line. The relative absence of a politics of the common good can be explained in part by an absence of the will and the ability within the political economy of advanced capitalism to foster the egalitarian preconditions for its realization. Much of the impetus within the dialectic of dissolution is captured within Rousseau's dictum: 'Laws are equally powerless against the treasures of the rich and the indigency of the poor; the first eludes them, the second escapes them; one breaks the net and the other slips through.'[25]

Fourthly, if the politics of the common good is both indispensable and unrealistic today, it is imperative to ascertain whether its unreality resides more in the failure of a variety of constituencies to acknowledge the good life realizable within the established political economy, or in the inconsistency between the imperatives generated by the political economy and the ends to which a modern populace might give its reflective allegiance.

The wish to avoid these issues forms the controlling impulse behind the resurgence of the thin theory of the public interest, along with the theories of 'rational choice,' 'public goods,' and 'economic models of democracy' to which it bears a close family resemblance. These utilitarian theories, in their minimal reference to civic virtue and the common good, would be realistic theories within the political economy of advanced capitalism if only they were true.

5

Some theories of state crisis

The priority of the state

In a variety of intellectual traditions the compelling importance and priority of the state is thought to reside in its unique responsibility to promote social justice and the public interest through conscious and purposive action. The authority of the state, its legitimate use of coercion, its war-making power, its accountability to citizens, the structure of its constitution, the loyalty and patriotism of its citizens, the protection of citizens' rights against it – all these prerogatives, concerns, practices, and limits take on overriding importance because the state is supposed to promote common purposes not by accident (as the market was thought to do), not habitually (as established tradition does at its best), but consciously through policies supported by binding law. Because the prerogatives invested in the state to carry out these essential functions are so susceptible to conversion into instruments of domination the state becomes the single most important object of public attention and inquiry in the social order.

Nonetheless, the problematic of the state receded into the background of American political inquiry in the period between World War II and the early stages of the Vietnam War. Theorists of pluralism concentrated on the inner workings of the bargaining system. Critics of pluralist theory sought to extend the categories of power, interests, freedom, and politics through which the bargaining processes were understood, but they too avoided the problematic of the state. C. Wright Mills' text, *The Power Elite*, for instance, launched an offensive against the pluralist image of politics, but the text makes no reference at all to the state as an institutional complex having a special relation to citizens, the public interest, justice, legitimacy, and authority.[1]

This neglect, or what appears to us retrospectively as neglect, seems to have two principal sources. The first source reflected the hegemony of behavioralism during this period. Advocates of this view treated the categories of the state, legitimacy, authority, citizen, and public interest as legal notions which referred more to norms of how politics ought to proceed and less to the actual behavior of people in political settings. Only if inquiry escaped these legalistic categories could it reach real political behavior. The second source was a widespread optimism about the ability of the civilization of productivity to promote its chosen purposes and the readiness of the populace to endorse these achievements. The end of ideology meant an end to basic debates over the proper role of the state in the economy and its legitimacy. Since the larger system seemed to take care of itself it was more intriguing to examine the multiplicity of ways in which groups jostled for marginal advantage within it.

The re-emergence of the problematic of the state occurs in a setting where the behavioralist agenda has lost much of its credibility, the state's ability to monitor the privately incorporated economy is increasingly a point of contention and the long-term ability of the welfare state to retain the reflective allegiance of new generations is in doubt.

The resurgence of theorizing about the state within the Marxist tradition is organized through the concepts of class struggle, the state's role in capital accumulation, its role in the reproduction of labor, and the displacement of economic contradictions to state arenas. The focus within the liberal and conservative traditions is on the eclipse of citizenship, defects in the state's ability to plan, the institutional inhibitions to the protection of the public interest, and the decline in the legitimacy of the welfare state. But the most interesting studies in each tradition find themselves drawing, if selectively, upon concepts and insights central to the others.[2]

The texts we shall examine, written respectively by Theodore Lowi, James O'Connor, and Daniel Bell, share a tendency to incorporate elements drawn from alien traditions into the theoretical framework to which the author is oriented. They thus provide fertile ground for the cultivation of further comparisons, additional insights, and internal critiques. Each author constructs a theory of state crisis, though not necessarily presenting it as the claim that the state now faces, or soon will face, a crisis. But each seeks to identify the sources, structural location, and probable outcomes of a crisis were it to occur; and the remedies proposed in each theory flow out of the diagnosis presented. All of these texts converge in concluding that the ability of the state to retain its legitimacy in the eyes of its populace is in jeopardy, that this deficit in legitimacy increases the burdens imposed on the state, and that it reduces the resources it can draw upon in responding to them. It is the differences within this very general framework of shared concerns which will receive our attention.

Reform of the welfare state

Consider first the interpretation advanced by Theodore Lowi in *The End of Liberalism*.[3] Early reviews of the book emphasized, as the author himself did, the distance between Lowi's interpretation and the prevailing pluralist account of American politics. But for our purposes, more basic commonalities (or commonplaces) deserve attention as well. Lowi contends, with pluralists in the Dahl–Lindblom tradition, with 'economic' theorists of politics in the Downs–Riker tradition, and with neo-classical economists such as Schultze and Samuelson, that the established relationship between the corporate economy and the welfare state is basically sound. The privately incorporated economy, with its characteristic systems of private ownership, instrumental work, managerial control of work processes, material incentives through graded incomes, labor mobility, restricted competition between units, and collective bargaining between labor and management, is seen to be a rather efficient mode of production and distribution. But the system, left to itself, inevitably generates undesirable effects, side effects that would undermine its very integrity if they were allowed to accumulate. Unemployment, inflation, poverty, corporate concentration and collusion, ecological devastation, neglect of the elderly, and urban deterioration are some of the side effects discussed by Lowi. Lowi states the problem quite explicitly:

the capitalist principles alone will only guarantee that production will be maximal and that prices will tend toward their lowest levels . . . that says nothing about the society except that its average members will probably enjoy improved comfort and choices.[4]

Modern society must become capable of controlling and absorbing market forces or the market becomes a menace rather than a good provider.[5]

Here Lowi is at one with the liberal consensus: the justification and task of the welfare state is to rectify the evils flowing out of the market economy; and it must do so without tampering with the basic structure of the economic system itself. The limits posed by the imperatives of corporate capitalism are, for Lowi, limits within which the welfare state's pursuit of the public interest must proceed.

It is within this liberal framework that Lowi's revision of liberal ideology is developed. For the ideology and practice of interest-group liberalism, he contends, renders the welfare state impotent and creates a crisis of legitimacy. Because the formation of public policy is pushed to the interior of public bureaucracies, because Congress passes laws in which broad objectives are unaccompanied by precise laws to guide the administering agencies, and because the expanding responsibilities of urban areas are not matched by expansion in the size of metropolitan government, the modern welfare state cannot plan effectively. It is unable to promote the public interest in ecology, public transporation, public education, or the reversal of urban deterioration. Since its policies emerge through *ad hoc* agreements with client corporations, since they are seldom given the form of law, and since they therefore are formulated and implemented without public debate, knowledge and accountability, the policies themselves can neither be challenged effectively nor provide the definite, cumulative experience through which to assess the rationality of such challenges. Lowi puts it this way :

The group process is dynamic and cumulative when groups have institutional structure against which to compete. Without that formal structure the group process is not truly pluralistic at all. It is merely co-optive. And it is ineffective. Worse, it converts mere ineffectiveness into illegitimacy ... The interest group method ... has proved itself unequal to the task of planning and achieving justice.[6]

Lowi's prescriptions flow neatly from his diagnosis. We must institute juridical democracy. Public policies must be defined precisely through law; an independent civil service must be created which is not dependent on client corporations; the process of law-making must, in most cases, be pushed up from bureaucracies to Congress where issues and debate are more visible and where the public-interest dimension of these issues will thereby receive more attention. Lowi adds: 'Centralizing through law and formalizing through administrative recruitment would only centralize the places where groups must seek access.'[7]

The key to a politics of the public interest, Lowi believes, is a policy process which screens out particular interests and collects those citizens have in common. A policy in the public interest affects either *each* of us in his capacity as a citizen (e.g. traffic regulation) or might affect *any* of us in that capacity (e.g., laws against crime). The special responsibility of the state in promoting the public interest through law flows from the fact that particular constituencies will not often act unilaterally and voluntarily in support of it unless they are assured that all other constituencies are bound by law to do so. To act in support of the public interest unilaterally would be irrational from the point of view of any particular individual or group, for others would reap the benefits of my sacrifice while their inaction would make my own positive action less effective. Practices in the public interest, then, must usually have the force of law, and the needed laws will not normally emerge from compromises between particular groups reached silently within the 'interior' reaches of the system.

Lowi's acceptance of this perspective is intimated when he says that juridical democracy relates to people 'through their citizenship . . . rather than according to their location in a group, a class, or a race.'[8] Thus crime control, pollution control, public transportation, alleviation of urban blight, might (arguably might) be to the advantage of anyone as a citizen – everyone when he or she thinks of the conditions needed to sustain a secure, comfortable life for *anyone* – even though particular individuals and groups, when thinking in terms of advantages and disadvantages particular to them in their capacities as owners, workers, wives, husbands, or students, might find some reason to oppose these policies. The politics of juridical democracy, in intention at least, reduces the pressure points available to particular interests while exposing public officials to pressure from broader constituencies whose net interests are more likely to coincide with the public interest. It encourages citizens' pressure for laws in the public interest, and this support comes from the same citizens who would not act in its support in the absence of such laws. It also encourages public officials to respond to that pressure affirmatively.

Some of the ideas in Lowi's theory of juridical democracy are pertinent to the pursuit of the public interest in any modern industrial society. But it can be argued, first, that there are flaws in his prescriptions even if his explanatory theory is broadly correct, and, secondly, that the explanatory framework itself is defective. We shall now consider possible defects within the framework, delaying more fundamental criticisms until we have access to an alternative theory.

1. Even if juridical democracy would promote a politics of the public interest, it is not clear that it would, as Lowi supposes, also promote greater social justice. Nothing in Lowi's argument ensures more effective political leverage for oppressed and unorganized minorities. Lowi to some extent acknowledges this claim, though interpreting it differently. For since the capitalist system, as he correctly perceives it, is incompatible with significant reductions in economic inequality, the welfare state must redress these distributive outcomes only at the margin.

2. Lowi stakes his hopes on the Supreme Court to initiate the needed impetus toward juridical democracy. It must require Congress to enact only precise and clear laws, thereby limiting bureaucratic discretion and reducing the space for enclaves of private, unaccountable power. But there is little reason to suppose that the court will proceed in this direction. Perhaps Lowi hopes (every theorist does) that widespread acceptance of his theory will generate sufficient public pressure to inspire the appropriate judicial action.

3. Most importantly, Lowi's analysis concludes just where the fundamental issues facing the civilization of productivity commence. Political support for the procedural reforms he proposes would require the civic virtue he thinks has been eroded by interest-group liberalism. His dilemma, though it is not his alone, is to ascertain how these civic energies and loyalties could be regenerated once they have been broken by a crisis of credibility and allegiance. The issue is not squarely confronted. Why would we, in our capacities as citizens, support procedures and laws which will treat all *citizens* alike, when in all of our other social capacities we are so unevenly and unequally treated? Can the politics of a stratified society embody civic virtue, whereby each assumes a share of the collective burden willingly, when the highly visible and politicized areas of social and economic life reinforce such an uneven imposition of sacrifices? It could, perhaps, if the uneven sacrifices were justified as necessary to a set of common purposes shared by most members

of the civilization. But this is exactly the question Lowi refuses to pose even while examining the 'crisis of legitimacy.'

Lowi might have penetrated more deeply into the legitimacy deficit facing the welfare state if he had interpreted the porous political process, loosely defined laws, and administrative protection from political accountability (the structure he calls interest-group liberalism) to be functional supports of an order which requires an extremely uneven distribution of incentives and sacrifices, but lacks sufficient ideological resources to justify them. The arrangements he deplores render invisible potentially illegitimate features of the larger system he admires while they themselves contribute to a decline of allegiance to the welfare state. The reforms needed to support system rationality may pose a threat to citizen allegiance. Failing to discern this possibility, Lowi fails to probe beneath the surface manifestations of the legitimacy deficit.

Lowi does give reasons for confining his inquiry. He concedes, in the revised version of the text, the possibility that interest-group liberalism may express more fundamental 'weaknesses of mature capitalism and of the inabilities of capitalism to survive without massive, systematic, and authoritative efforts to shore it up.'[9] But he rejects the socialist alternative lurking within such a critique because of its dismal performance in the twentieth century in protecting civil liberties and sustaining human dignity. He opts instead for reforms moving in the opposite direction. He aspires to a 'neo-laissez-faire' regime in which there will be a 'substantial deflation of government in general with a strengthening of certain aspects of government in particular.'[10]

But the argument against socialism, even if correct, does not establish the case for the sufficiency of Lowi's own diagnosis or for the remedy of juridical democracy and economic deregulation. It simply does not follow that a 'political party capable of bringing about the transition to socialism' would also and necessarily possess sufficient resources 'to deal with capitalism within the existing constitutional scheme.'[11] The possibility of protecting constitutional rights while sustaining the performance of the privately incorporated economy is not established in Lowi's text; it is the premise from which the argument for procedural reform of the welfare state proceeds. It is one thing to conclude that *revolutionary* socialism must produce an authoritarian regime if it succeeds and an authoritarian reaction if it is defeated. It is another to suppose that a negative answer to these questions ensures an affirmative one to the possibility of maintaining together a neo-laissez-faire economy, juridical democracy, and the legitimacy of the state. The answer to that question turns upon a set of issues Lowi has not explored, including the extent to which the welfare state could sustain the allegiance of subordinate constituencies, promote productivity in the private economy, and still promote justice and the public interest.

Whatever answer we propose eventually to these questions, there are certain strengths in Lowi's argument which must be retained. First, the protection of political democracy and accountability do require a reconstitution of the internal politics of bureaucracy, greater simplicity in legal enactments, and an improved public capacity to hold public officials responsible for policy decisions. If, as I shall argue, the civil society Lowi endorses progressively tends to dissolve the institutional supports for his political agenda, then concern with perfecting democratic politics in these ways will require closer attention to its social preconditions of existence. Secondly, I read in Lowi's comprehension of the relation between the citizen and the state the understanding that the bond is reducible neither to a communal tie nor to an instrumental connection. Attempts to institutionalize the first conception would submerge the individual while the second would deny the state essential resources to coordinate social life without recourse to extensive coercion. The delicate balance of identification and independence which must be retained between the citizen and the state in a democracy is insufficiently appreciated in many traditions of inquiry. Lowi, I think, does appreciate its importance.

The fiscal crisis of the state

An alternative view of the established relations between the welfare state and the privately incorporated economy is provided by James O'Connor in *The Fiscal Crisis of the State*.[12] The state, according to O'Connor, is compelled to respond to contradictory imperatives within advanced capitalism; the effort to meet either one inevitably undercuts its ability to fulfill the other.

O'Connor contends that a class analysis of the political economy is necessary, but it must be qualified by a sectoral account. The three sectors of the economy – the monopoly (or corporate) sector, the competitive (or market) sector, and the state sector – stand in complex relationships to each other. The different priorities and differential distribution of strategic resources between these sectors produce a set of opposing pressures to which the state must somehow respond.

The relations between the monopoly and competitive sectors favour the former. The monopoly corporation has some control over its costs of production and the prices of the goods it sells; it is thereby in a better position to secure a favorable profit margin for itself. Also, since the performance of the monopoly sector is crucial to the health of the general economy, the state is eager to support the economic performance of these firms. Since their privileged market position and ability to improve productivity levels allow them, first, to increase the wages of labor and, secondly, to pass these costs on to market firms and consumers, they are able to maintain a degree of peace in their labor force. Market firms absorb these higher prices as higher costs of production. And workers in the market sector, finding themselves relatively disadvantaged by comparison to counterparts in the monopoly sector, then find it impossible to win similar gains from the market firm. They are in competition with workers in the monopoly sector. These internal divisions, within capital and within labor, play a prominent role in O'Connor's interpretation.

The monopoly sector cannot sustain its growth unless the state subsidizes it in a variety of ways. And the state cannot secure the tax revenues it needs unless it provides such subsidies. The state thus moves into areas that are essential to the production of private profit but are not themselves privately profitable. The expansion of the economy itself progressively extends the dependence of the corporate system on socially established supports for continued expansion. State expenditures for technical education, research subsidies, industrial parks, convention centers, military production, transportation subsidies, development of energy resources, and the maintenance of a military apparatus to protect needed markets and resources abroad become essential props to the performance of monopoly firms.

But the state does not support merely the *accumulation* of private capital; it must protect its own *legitimacy* while doing so. The escalating 'side effects' of capitalist production nudge the state into more and more areas to maintain the allegiance, or at least the acquiescence, of those constituencies disrupted by the effects and excluded from the benefits of the expansionary process. If new patterns of transportation and mobility erode neighborhoods and kinship ties the state must move in to care for the elderly, the infirm, the insane, the children of working parents. If private production processes foul the air, pollute waterways, impoverish the soil, the state is expected to move in with programs to rectify these evils. If the system generates unemployment and inflation, if crime syndicates take over areas of the economy, if violent crime increases, if millionaires evade taxes, the state's legitimacy depends on its ability to rectify, or appear to rectify, these evils.

To meet these *performance* and *legitimacy* imperatives the state, at least theoretically, has three options. It can itself develop and run profit-making enterprises; it can engage in deficit spending; and it can tax. The first option is illegitimate in the American system; the second is constrained by the inflation it creates; the third is thus the most acceptable option available. But the state is thereby caught in a bind. It loses legitimacy if its expenditures and policies are insufficient to relieve these social burdens and it loses legitimacy if it continues to impose high taxes. The result is a persistent tendency toward fiscal crisis in which the gap between the state's revenues and its expenses is closed by inflation. O'Connor states the 'contradiction' in these terms:

The state must try to maintain or create the conditions in which profitable capital accumulation is possible. However, the state must also try to maintain or create the conditions of social harmony. A capitalist state that openly uses its coercive force to help one class accumulate capital at the expense of other claims loses its legitimacy. But a state that ignores the necessity of assisting the process of capital accumulation risks drying up the source of its own power, the economy's productive capacity, and the taxes drawn from this surplus. The state must involve itself in the accumulation process but it must either mystify its policies by calling them something that they are not or it must conceal them (e.g., by making them into administrative, not political, issues).[13]

The state, striving to meet these two imperatives, contributes to the appearance of fiscal crisis. But the appearance is misleading. What presents itself to the populace as a fiscal crisis of the state, potentially subject to technical management, is really a deeper crisis in the terms of relation between the state and the economy. In

O'Connor's language, the contradiction between the expanding socialization of the costs of production through the medium of the state and the private appropriation of profit is manifested as the fiscal crisis of the state.

The fiscal crisis is exacerbated by the very growth of the state sector. Since the state is supposed to move into economic areas that are socially necessary and privately unprofitable, the areas taken over by the state are exactly those least subject to productivity increases (e.g., education, welfare, the creation of new weapons systems). Employees in the expanding state sector strive to keep pace with those of comparable training and status in the private sector. If they do keep pace without achieving comparable productivity increases, they fuel inflation. And they eventually turn highly taxed employees in the private sector against them. The expansion of the state, necessary to support economic performance and political legitimacy, eventually threatens the legitimacy of the state.

This summary of O'Connor's thesis is sufficient for our purposes. I will now consider some of its themes more closely and critically, with the intention of assimilating them to a broader critique of the defining institutions and purposes of the civilization of productivity.

It is essential to O'Connor's thesis that inflation is endemic to advanced American capitalism; state expenditures are not its only source. The state contributes to a dynamic which is developed inside the economy. O'Connor's argument here can be extended in two directions. There is, first, a range of production processes and commodity forms which are rational from the vantage point of private profit creation within the existing political economy but irrational from the point of view of a collective effort to control inflation with a minimum of state coercion. The private automobile, for instance, produces more profit than the production of buses and trains, in part because the state subsidizes the costs of driving through the construction of a national network of highways. Once the automobile becomes the principal means of transportation the necessity to use it imposes a whole series of costs on the private user and the state. The private expenses are eventually transmitted to the corporate system as demands for higher wages, and the social costs are transmitted to the state as new imperatives for public expenditure. And once the automobile has acquired such a prominent place, a whole set of political interests emerges to ensure that it does not lose it. Workers and owners in automobile, oil, tire, and steel industries converge with those in road construction, tourism, and shopping malls to protect the dominance of this mode of transport.

The case of the automobile merely exemplifies the way in which the pursuit of profit through the proliferation of products for individual consumption generates persistent inflationary pressures. New production processes, labor mobility, and prevailing commodity forms constantly expand the sphere of goods which must be bought through market expenditures. Peace and quiet, pleasant scenery, clean air and water, safe neighborhoods, food free of carcinogenic additives, baby-sitters, facilities for the care of the elderly or the sick, access to a university education for one's children, recreation – all of these goods progressively become necessary items of expenditure. Some of them previously had been free; others had been provided by family and neighborhood; still others had not yet been produced as skills or resources needed to participate effectively in the economy in an earlier era. The new necessities flow from the 'side effects' of production processes and established forms of consumption, and from the ways in which these market processes undermine established social units of support and sustenance at the micro level of social life. In these ways the common pursuit of private affluence progressively introduces new barriers to the realization of the satisfactions it promises, and those with the strategic resources to do so then demand higher wages to cross each new set of barriers.

A complementary movement accelerates the pace of the entire process. If the civilization of productivity persistently generates within the subordinate population demands it cannot meet, and imposes disciplines it cannot justify, growing segments of the populace eventually will tend to withdraw their allegiance from the defining practices and purposes of the civilization. The withdrawal, even if it does not find a direct political expression, can exacerbate inflationary pressures in several ways. If one's job is recognized to be unavoidable even though it now seems to serve no larger social purpose worthy of pride and commitment, the performance of the employee will deteriorate while the demand for higher wages to bear these increased burdens will intensify. The loss of significance is compensated by the demand for more of what the employer can give: money. If one invests no psychic commitment into a declining neighborhood or a struggling community, a wage increase becomes important; it allows one to purchase recreational facilities, entertainment, and access to commercial sites for meeting and conversing with people. A color TV is a psychic necessity in a broken-down neighbourhood as are two cars in a suburban area deserted during the day. The decline in the ability of the defining institutions to sustain performance and allegiance also accelerates state expenditures to buy off, coerce, neutralize, or intimidate the reluctant role-bearers. The state compensates for the deflation of meaning with an inflation of expenditures. The expansion of expenditures on welfare, mental hospitals, juvenile centers, police surveillance, prisons, job corps programs, and daycare centers embodies, to some degree, a response to the contraction of identification by marginal constituencies with the role requirements and social purposes available to them.[14]

These two sources of inflation, the first anchored in the pursuit of private affluence through private production and the second in the declining identification with the means necessary to that pursuit, do not contradict but complement one another. The struggle for affluence is located within a historical dynamic which progressively erodes the social preconditions for other pursuits, especially for constituencies located in the middle and lower levels of the income and security hierarchy. The progressive disenchantment with the discipline required to pursue these ends, caused in part by the growing recognition that the promise of affluence necessarily recedes as the apparent means to its realization is acquired by a larger percentage of the populace, converges with the recognition that these pursuits have now become the principal ones available. The inflationary spiral is fueled, then, by the demand for more money to acquire the limited range of 'goods' available, by subversion, absenteeism, and malingering on the job, by the production of durable goods which do not last and the delivery of services which do not serve, by increasing state expenditures to meet the social costs of production and consumption and to maintain social discipline, by expansion in the size of the tax bill facing citizens, and by the corollary intensification of pressure by strategically located constituencies to evade taxes and disciplines imposed upon them.

O'Connor examines how dislocations in the privately incorporated economy generate specific forms of state intervention. One can distinguish several levels at which such a conversion process operates. There is, first, the generalized motive of state officials to maintain

the tax capacity they need by protecting and fostering the preconditions of private profit realization. State officials, recognizing this
imperative, actively seek ways to provide corporations with incentives, and dependent workers with disciplines needed to expand
productivity. Interest-group pressure or corporate manipulation are
often unnecessary to motivate such action. There is, secondly, a set
of more specific considerations which shape the scope and form of
state intervention. The absolute size of the needed investment, the
lag time between investment and its expected return, the degree
of risk that the investment will not bring a return – all of these
factors help to discriminate state expenditures from those left to the
resources of the privately incorporated economy. There are, thirdly,
considerations, reflecting more than O'Connor acknowledges, the
norms of legitimacy prevailing in American society. It is legitimate,
for instance, to support the creation of private profit through state
activity, but illegitimate for the state to produce for public profit.
Similarly, if it were legitimate to indenture trainees for life it would
be profitable for corporations to provide technical education for
their own employees. But since such a system would contradict a
widely held ideal of individual freedom, corporate needs for technical education are met primarily through a public/private university
system. And this location, with its partial autonomy, limits the
extent to which the commodity form has been allowed to prevail in
higher education. In a similar way, welfare, police functions, and
care for the elderly and the sick are deemed too important to be
located entirely in the market. If the ranks in these categories are
swollen, the size of the state will thus be swollen too. The prevailing
norms of legitimacy in the system powerfully shape and limit the
terms of relation between the state and the privately incorporated
economy, though they too are the crystallized result of previous
political struggles. If the legitimacy deficit facing the welfare state
grows into a legitimation crisis, the opposition between those who
seek to legitimize the universalization of the commodity form and
those who would legitimize its contraction will provide the cutting
edge of political struggle.

The final impetus directing state intervention is provided by a
variety of power constellations organized to shape state priorities.
When O'Connor discusses forces at this level, his argument re-
sembles Lowi's. But he telescopes the range of power constellations
more narrowly than Lowi does. He sees corporate capital, organized

labor in the corporate or monopoly sector, and capital in the market sector as respectively the most powerful constituencies.

O'Connor underplays the role of the American electoral system. It in fact establishes broad parameters within which these strategically located constituencies operate, even while the reach of the electoral system itself is confined by the terms of relation between the state and the economy.

The incentive for the broader electorate to define grievances which fall within the reach of legitimate state policy is provided by the location of the corporate economy outside the orbit of electoral accountability and the location of the state within it. State officials are motivated to respond, or, sometimes, to appear to respond, to pressure from subordinate constituencies because of the necessity of standing for public election. The electoral system is not simply a ritual covering the real relations of power; it does process grievances to the state; it does help to constitute those relations. But because of the irrational relationship between the state and the economy, the processing is distorted. The result is a politics of *displacement* in which the state is held accountable for dislocations more deeply rooted in the basic institutions and priorities of the civilization of productivity, and in which the state response to these displaced pressures often lays the groundwork for future dislocations in the economy.

Thus victims of spiralling inflation, unable to curb the style changes, advertising budgets, shoddy products, product priorities and price mark-ups in the corporate sector, demand cuts in school budgets and welfare expenditures to ease these proximate sources of taxes and inflation which are subject to some degree of political accountability. Unemployed workers, unable to hold corporate owners responsible, press the state to subsidize new jobs in the private sector or to expand unemployment insurance. Workers in the corporate sector, unable to alter the structure and authority of work or to create local communities capable of converting many private consumer costs into less expensive community services, resist state efforts to limit the monetary rewards the corporate system can give them. Blacks and whites, men and women, unable to expand the limited supply of decent jobs, collide over the issues of affirmative action. Pressures and policies that appear rational within the established system often do not speak to collective needs; and state policies justified in the name of the public interest bear upon those with the least political resources in ways which provoke the further withdrawal of allegiance to the defining institutions.

Attention to the political dimensions of this conversion process brings out a further implication in O'Connor's theory. In the initial stages of his text O'Connor appears to present a structural thesis whereby the state must respond to the opposing imperatives of accumulation and legitimation, and must create a fiscal crisis in doing so. But the structural argument is eventually qualified by references to a more open and uncertain political process. The qualification is implicitly acknowledged in the last sections of the text when O'Connor states that the potentiality for fiscal crisis may or may not be realized depending upon the form which the political struggle assumes. Here, again, the legitimacy dimension of the argument assumes a status more prominent than that acknowledged in the formal summary of the theory. For before the latent crisis becomes manifest members of the subordinate population must resist actively the sacrifices and disciplines the state seeks to impose upon them. If they acquiesce, the fiscal crisis will be averted at their expense. O'Connor says, 'Budget needs may remain unsatisfied and human needs may go unfulfilled, but if those who are dependent on the state do not engage in political struggle to protect or advance their well being, the fiscal crisis will remain relatively dormant.'[15]

Both the realization of fiscal crisis and the direction its resolution assumes depend crucially upon the political will and capacity of the most dependent segments of the populace. Moreover, the exertion of their will and effective capacity for action turn to some degree on the legitimacy of their claims in their own eyes and the eyes of potential allies. The relation between fiscal crisis and the politics of legitimation is more intimate than the early sections of O'Connor's text would lead one to expect.

O'Connor dedicates his book to 'the workers, the unemployed, the poor, the students and others whose struggles against the state have made this work possible.'[16] This is the constituency he hopes will press the state to maintain its legitimacy in their eyes even while it strives to support the preconditions of capital accumulation. They will bring the fiscal crisis into the open. But the sectoral analysis O'Connor deploys to uncover conflicts within the working class speaks against the political strategy he anticipates. That portion of the potential constituency with the greatest leverage – organized workers in the corporate sector who can disrupt the production process through strikes – can also reach accords with corporate and state officials which exclude the other constituencies. Similarly, the segment with the most motivation to press for class unity has the fewest political resources to bring to that quest. O'Connor is not alone in failing to identify a strategic orientation corresponding to his diagnosis of the system's ills; indeed one of the strengths of his argument is its ability to detect structural barriers to political effectiveness. But attention to the strategic dilemmas which flow from the intersection of sectoral and class divisions highlights the importance of established norms of legitimacy in deflating the demands of the marginal segments of the populace and inflating those of others. Those norms enter into political strife; they are implicitly among the objects of political contestation.

The weaknesses, or, better, areas of underdevelopment we have identified so far in O'Connor's argument point to a central affinity between O'Connor and Lowi. While one author works within a neo-liberal and the other in a neo-Marxian framework, they share a thin theory of legitimacy, a theory which fits well with the thin conceptions of citizenship and the public interest examined earlier. A thin theory of legitimacy tends to treat the state as the principal object of allegiance or disaffection; it construes the means by which the state retains allegiance to be confined largely to policies which place money in the hands of welfare recipients, or subsidize the costs of production, or manipulate tax incentives; and it tends to equate the *belief* by participants that a practice is legitimate with its actual legitimacy.

A revised conception of legitimacy allows us to probe more deeply into the pre-understandings which help to constitute the political economy. It looks to the presence or absence of allegiance to a whole set of institutions in which the participants are implicated; it connects the increasing state dependence on monetary incentives and punitive discipline to the loss of identification by role-bearers with the defining ends and purposes served by the practices of work, consumption, and education; and it examines the means by which overt belief in the legitimacy of established institutions is maintained even while covert behavior expresses subversive beliefs. Both O'Connor and Lowi underplay, though the tendency is unevenly distributed between them, the extent to which citizens in a variety of positions quietly obstruct the performance of the political economy even while calling upon the welfare state to support its general performance and to discipline a particular set of obstructionists. The thin theory of legitimacy endorsed by each impairs their ability to penetrate these appearances.

Where Lowi tends to construe the interdependent practices of instrumental work, individualized consumption, labor stratification and mobility, bureaucratic rationality, economic growth, and private profit as rational institutions and goals properly left outside the sphere of politics and political theory, where O'Connor tends to construe many of these same arrangements as coercive forms imposed upon a subordinate populace, they can be more fully comprehended as practices essentially bound up with the self-interpretations of the participants implicated within them. These social relations are partially constituted by the intersubjective understandings of the participants; they are energized, when they work well, by the collective aspirations of those whose identities are interwoven with the understandings they encourage and the purposes they serve. The rationality and efficiency Lowi detects in them embodies, to the extent that it exists, a self-interpretation by participants which coheres with the ends supported by the institutional structure. And the discipline and control O'Connor detects would be accompanied by a corollary web of evasions and escapes unless a broad range of participants tacitly believed that these constraints were a means to the good life they pursue. The relationship between an institutional structure and the self-interpretation of those who bear its roles is variable and complex, as we have already seen. But to adopt an explanatory account which obscures the intersubjective dimension of institutional life in either of these two ways is to ensure that any historical shifts in the infrastructure of the political economy operating below the level of external appearance will remain in the shadows of the theory as well. And this is exactly what has occurred in the accounts offered by Lowi and O'Connor.

Allegiance to the civilization of productivity flowed in earlier generations from the common belief, accepted to varying degrees by different constituencies, that these institutions would promote a common good for future generations, that they would produce an affluent society providing freedom, leisure, security, and happiness to its industrious members. The daily activities and public struggles of the participants, though all were oriented to the protection of particular interests within the larger setting, expressed tacit allegiance to the dream embedded in the order, even when pressing for specific institutional reforms. The dominant forces in the American labor movement, for instance, affirmed these general expectations and hopes while trying to contain excessive corporate power. Many sought to unionize, not too many to socialize. And even those who dreamed of socialism thought of it as a more rational and just way to achieve the society of abundance. Many role assignments seemed natural to many of these constituencies, even when they were burdensome; and many of the burdens were lightened by the hope that they would disappear in the future. This was a period of building the new world; the completed structure was to be enjoyed at a later date. Even the depression spurred hope for recovery more than for reconstitution of the ends of the civilization.

The established institutions of work, markets, profit, and bureaucracy were treated as instruments to these desirable social ends. Criticism would call for reform of the instrumentalities because the ends could be promoted more effectively. But when doubts eventually began to emerge about the viability of the collective ends pursued a more pervasive shadow was cast over the legitimacy of the institutional means as well. This tacit withdrawal of identification can have an implicit rationale, even before it receives a clear political expression. Participants come to sense, through progressive historical experience, that the ends pursued entail intractable consequences unexpected by the early dreamers and increasingly intolerable to a range of contemporary participants. The realization spreads that the collective pursuit of private affluence has a self-defeating character, that the continual expansion of productivity depletes resources needed by future generations, destroys ties of kinship and neighborhood through its rapid pace of change and mobility, denies dignity to the old through the recurrent obsolescence of old skills and old workers, damages the natural environment through the shape of its production processes and consumption forms, condemns a large miscellany of constituencies to a marginal existence because they are unneeded by the productive system, and perpetuates the risk of nuclear war through its extensive dependence on resources and markets in foreign countries. The ends of the civilization of productivity, as these implications emerge progressively to view, eventually assume a different appearance to the participants, even to those who have privileges to protect in the established order. What had once appeared as eliminable side effects to worthy pursuits now emerge as intrinsic components of the pursuits themselves. The question becomes: What *is* the point of these pursuits then? And the growing sense of pointlessness in the common life eventually infects the sense of purpose in private life. The class conflicts of one era assume new expressions in the next because of this implicit, generalized erosion of confidence in the future realizable within the existing institutional structure.

The realization may fail to receive a clear political expression, and we shall try to account more fully for that failure in the next chapter. But it does find space for covert expression within the institutional infrastructure, within the instrumentalities which continue to support the old purposes. It is expressed in growing divorce rates, the decline in public trust of public and private officials, the growth of theft and sabotage in the workplace, the troubles bosses have in motivating workers and teachers in motivating students, the emergence of the litigious personality who sees no higher purpose in the law than its instrumental use in jockeying for private advantage, the withdrawal into fundamentalist religion, and the retreat to various cults of communalism and hedonism. These reactions, though each has causes and characteristics peculiar to itself, embody a common characteristic. They together express the dialectic of dissolution which sets in when large segments of a populace find themselves caught in institutional arrangements which now seem pointless or unworthy of reflective allegiance. One implicit strategy to maintain the appearance of allegiance, and therefore of personal integrity, in circumstances where other collective possibilities do not appear credible, is to find ways to avoid or resist reflection into the historical course we are on. And several of the reactions listed above can usefully be viewed as alternative strategies of evasion. They present the appearance of mindlessness among those who wish not to become too mindful of the course we are on.

It is a moot question how deeply these processes are entrenched in our society or how far they must proceed. But they surely are operative to some significant extent, and any contemporary theory of the state which ignores them cannot account satisfactorily for the phenomenon it seeks to explain. Understanding this background to contemporary political conflicts, we can expect each constituency to call upon the state in general to promote growth, eliminate waste, and increase the efficiency of other segments of society; and we can also expect each constituency to resist and evade, to the extent of its political capacity, the specific sacrifices imposed on it by the state. Such discrepancies between abstract demands and specific compliance exist, of course, in every society. But they are more highly developed in a society whose members have begun to lose faith in the historical trajectory it is on.

This deeper legitimacy deficit does not contradict O'Connor's central contentions. The two accounts are complementary. What emerges at one level as the discrepancy between the state's ability to generate tax revenues and the performance–legitimacy expenditures it must make is absorbed as part of a more pervasive discrepancy between the ends the state must serve and the growing disaffection from the ends and the instrumentalities which serve them. The amended interpretation identifies new blockages facing the state, and it will eventually help us to explain why the welfare state is set up to be the primary target of a disaffection really rooted in the civilization of productivity itself.

We can now consolidate these findings, formulating a summary of the interpretation which emerges from this series of revisions in O'Connor's argument.

The welfare state must look in two directions at the same time. First, dependent on the performance of the privately incorporated economy for the production of the tax revenues it needs, it must support, protect and subsidize the preconditions of private profitability in an environment where those preconditions are increasingly difficult to maintain. Secondly, because it is formally accountable to the general populace through public elections, the state, to retain legitimacy, is expected to relieve the most onerous burdens imposed upon citizens by the 'side effects' of the accumulation process. The strain on its capacity in responding to this double set of pressures is accentuated by (1) the economic effects of its own growth in size, (2) the proliferation of claims pressed upon it by a variety of specific claimants through the porous processes of interest-group liberalism, and (3) the public consequences flowing from the implicit withdrawal of allegiance from the defining institutions of the civilization of productivity.

Since these imperatives pull it in opposing directions, since it becomes the depository for functions and clientele which are unprofitable to private corporations, since it visibly contributes to the inflationary spirals it seeks to control, and since the ends it is constrained to serve no longer sustain the full allegiance of those asked to sacrifice in their name, the welfare state has a declining supply of civic virtue to draw upon to carry out an expanded set of functions. Its officials are thus progressively attracted to technocratic solutions such as an expansion of disciplinary mechanisms and the political manipulation of market incentives. These mechanisms are attractive because they seem to work without drawing upon the scarce supply of civic virtue. But these tools themselves are difficult to introduce coherently because of the many points of access in the political system, allowing some constituencies to veto or displace the more onerous burdens to be placed on them. The decline of civic virtue intensifies the will of particular constituencies to press their particular cases, as long as they retain the capacity to do so. The welfare state is caught in a bind.

Lowi's theory, seen from this perspective, remains at the level of appearance. It locates the source of state ineffectiveness entirely within the organization of the state when it is really rooted in more basic characteristics of the civilization of productivity *and* the structure of the state. Through his reforms, Lowi intends to increase the accountability of the state to the general public and to decrease its particular accountability to groups with special access to strategic points in the national legislature, the bureaucracy, and state and local governments. But in the setting we are really in, Lowi's prescriptions will actually produce consequences he neither anticipates nor desires. The closure of space within which political constituencies can lobby, the rationalization of bureaucracy to bring it under more centralized control, and the sharper specification of laws to regulate conduct more closely will help to convert the mechanisms of public accountability into more effective conduits for identifying the necessary preconditions of corporate expansion; and the procedural reforms will help to generate the political coalition needed to support the identified policies. Lowi's proposals, remember, are designed to support the public interest over particular interests within the capitalist economy as presently structured. In this context the very concentration of points of access is likely to encourage alliances between organized workers in the corporate sector, corporate capital, and the highest level technicians and managers in the state sector. And the priorities of that alliance are not likely to appear attractive to other constituencies.

When the background structure of the economy remains outside the terms of political discourse, when the imperatives of capital accumulation and labor discipline become more sharply defined, when the bureaucracy is more highly rationalized, when the enclaves for less strategically located constituencies are cleared away, will not the most convenient and effective alliance be one which imposes the harshest burdens upon those least essential to the performance of the corporate system? In the midst of persistent fiscal crisis, especially one which appears to many as the product of unnecessary state expenditures for those who refuse to help themselves, we can expect the state to apply new *incentives* to corporate capital, wage and benefit *pay offs* to labor in the corporate sector, and new *sacrifices* and *discipline* to low level public employees, laborers in the market sector, welfare recipients, the unemployed, the sick, the psychologically immobilized, and the old. Lowi's proposals, some of which would be salutary in combination with other institutional changes, will crystallize economic imperatives, solidify oppressive coalitions, and dislodge subordinate minorities from the political enclaves previously susceptible to their limited influence. The more complete rationalization of the state in advanced capitalism enhances its capacity to subjugate those segments of the populace located in vulnerable sectors of the economy, and the motive to do so will be intensified by the clear signs of disaffection and apparent lack of self-discipline among the targets of this attack.

The cultural contradictions of capitalism

The interpretation sketched in the previous section makes apparent contact with themes recently advanced by Daniel Bell.[17] I shall differentiate the two accounts, trying to establish the superiority of the former.

Bell agrees that the dislocations facing the contemporary welfare state are entrenched within the civilization over which the state presides. He highlights ways in which the decline in the legitimacy of dominant institutions impairs their performance and limits the potential effectiveness of state policy. The basic contradiction resides in the conjunction of a set of imperatives within the workplace, the market, and the bureaucracy and the emergence of a hedonistic populace. The institutions require self-discipline, responsibility, industriousness, attention to the civic consequences of activities, while the personal orientation encourages self-indulgence, withdrawal of allegiance from larger institutions and purposes, the concentration on new objects of desire and consumption, sexual permissiveness, personal display, conspiratorial images of politics, and contempt for intellectual life. The hedonist culture was produced by the industrial system it jeopardizes: the expansion of consumption possibilities, modernistic art, advertising technologies which aggrandize the self, the cultivation of diverse experiences through new media and opportunities for travel – all these contribute to the culture of hedonism. Its paradigm is California, where one of Bell's anthropological sources reports

the good godless, gregarious pursuit of pleasure is what California is all about. The citizens of lotus land seem forever to be lolling around swimming pools, sauteing in the sun, packing across the Sierra, frolicking nude on the beaches, getting taller each year, plucking money off trees, romping around topless, tramping through the redwoods and . . . preening themselves on camera before the rest of the envious world.[18]

The contradiction between the culture of hedonism encouraged in the sphere of consumption and the continuing imperative of discipline within the spheres of production and politics is summarized succinctly by Bell:

The characteristic style of industrialism is based on the principle of economism and economy: on efficiency, least cost, maximization, optimization, and functional rationality. Yet it is this style that is in conflict with the advanced cultural trends of the western world, for modernist culture emphasizes anti-cognitive and anti-intellectual modes which look longingly toward a return to instinctual sources of expression. The one emphasizes functional rationality, technocratic decision making and meritocratic rewards; the other apocalyptic moods and anti-rational modes of behaviour.[19]

Bell then explores possible routes to the resolution or alleviation of this contradiction. He is convinced that 'new purposes have to be established' and 'new assumptions have to be laid down' to restore loyalty, allegiance, and performance within the society. But then he seals off a variety of conceivable avenues. A reduction in equality might sustain greater commonality of purpose but it would require too much bureaucratization. One might look to a shift away from the priority of economic growth because of the adverse social consequences which accompany it. But it is the most important solvent of conflict in a modern, *stratified* society, and the defining institutions and expectations of the society are built around the assumption of its continuation. Finally, no form of socialism bears close scrutiny: the history of the twentieth century reveals it to be the inevitable parent of regimentation and repression.

As the historical options are reduced, even before considerations of their political feasibility are invoked, Bell's hopes become fastened upon the possibility that a new political maturity will emerge among citizens. The very trials through which the civilization is going, joined to a new self-consciousness about the self-defeating character of the modernist response to these trials, may spawn a new mood of reconciliation to the nature of things and a new appreciation for the civil liberties and sense of dignity our society is able to sustain. 'This basis,' Bell asserts in the penultimate paragraph of the text, 'must be created by conjoining three actions: the reaffirmation of the past – for only if we know the inheritance from the past can we become aware of the obligation to our posterity; recognition of the limits of resources and the priority of *needs*, individual and social, over wants; and agreement upon a conception of equity which gives all persons a sense of fairness and inclusion in the society.'[20]

Bell is certainly correct in his contention that any way of life must recognize certain limits, must acknowledge that there are admirable virtues, pursuits, relationships which *it* cannot exemplify if it is to nourish the particular set of worthy possibilities residing within its own institutional structure. Political maturity does involve reconciliation to such limits. But Bell does not really tell us what these limits are in our society, except that we must promote growth, resist the temptation to reduce inequality significantly, and transcend hedonism. He does not have space in the last paragraph to fill out the content of the formal requirements summarized in the preceding one, nor to show how the fleshed-out requirements could be achieved and accepted within the order as he understands it. What aspects of our inheritance are most crucially relevant today? What conceptions of merit and equity will sustain the society of productivity and give all citizens a sense of inclusion? Bell slides away from these questions because the institutional arrangements to which he would reconcile us are mobilized around collective purposes which, first, cannot be realized and, secondly, cannot sustain reflective allegiance once their full content is revealed through progressive historical experience. The culture of hedonism, to the extent it exists, helps to deflect public attention from this deeper disjunction. It simultaneously reflects, obstructs, and protects the civilization of productivity.

Why must the conjunction of the disciplinary imperative within the economy and the cultural disposition for hedonism be contradictory? Why can't I work hard during the day and play joyfully at night? Raise my family with care and consume products with abandon? Be mature in politics and immature in recreation? These two orientations could indeed coalesce if the first imperative was widely acknowledged and honored in its sphere *because* it created space for the second in its sphere. The first would then be viewed as the necessary means to the second, and the second would be viewed as the sufficient reward for the first. But the hedonism perceived by Bell — we leave aside the exaggerations within the perception — breaks out of this confinement. It appears to him as a way of life which is rather satisfying to its beneficiaries, while the collective consequences of its extension into the practices of production and politics jeopardize the rationality and civility required in those spheres. Why, then, does it slide into these latter spheres?

There is another interpretation of hedonism, developed by Hegel, which can help to answer this question.[21] Hedonism is best understood as an expression of despair and desperation. The breakdown of micro-institutions of sustenance and support, the loss of the sense of a social future which *we* can identify with and help to establish, encourage the individual to concentrate on the narrowly conceived *I*. The focus is on those satisfactions which are immediate and minimally dependent upon persisting relationships with others. Instead of dreaming of another while masturbating, one treats sex with another as a form of masturbation. The alienation from existing norms, limits, and ideals is now intensified, for they are now experienced as barriers or obstacles to the only pleasures attainable. Hedonism 'plunges therefore into life and indulges to the full the pure individuality in which it appears.'[22] Since the emergence of hedonism already signifies rejection of a larger way of life, the pure hedonist is likely to do only what is absolutely necessary at home, at work, and in politics to protect the means to these pleasures. But the dialectic of hedonism eventually erodes further the commitment to these role assignments.

The hedonist's withdrawal from the means which sustain hedonism as a collective good soon acquires a momentum of its own. For hedonism, as a way of life, can only appear to resolve the loss occasioned by disenchantment with the larger society; and its own development soon explodes this appearance. If my own pleasure is my end, then my death would mean the end of everything important to me. No children or record of achievement or contribution to higher principles is available to reconcile me to my unavoidable fate. If nothing touching me, recorded in the memories of others, lives on after me, death is the end of everything. Death is necessarily *for* nothing. The hedonist might court death carelessly for a while, but such hedonists do not last long. The ones who remain are likely, especially as they age and contemplate death, to treat the avoidance of death as the highest priority of life. But having avoided entangling relationships, obligations, and commitments in the name of hedonism, the hedonist must now strive to avoid new perils produced by this very orientation. A potential sexual partner, for instance, may have syphilis; moreover the hedonistic partner has no interest in telling me about it, for that might detract from the momentary pleasure available. Suspicions thereby proliferate. And each hedonist is surrounded by risks, obstacles, and dangers to the pursuit of pleasures, produced in part by the hedonist's own avoidance of a larger web of ties, obligations, and commitments. The enlarged fear of danger and death, and the expanded sense of their probability, takes all the pleasure out of hedonism. To avoid death one withdraws further from life. Surely, as this dialectic proceeds, the aging hedonist's willinginess to accept sacrifices in the name of hedonism must disappear. Hedonism is already sacrifice enough in itself. Hedonism as an overriding end thus cannot sustain voluntary commitment to the institutional means for its realization. It is not satisfying enough to justify those means. But the cautious, uprooted and fearful hedonist does become an easy target for the institutional manipulation of penalties and incentives designed to produce the behavior needed in the order. The agent reduced to the pursuit of momentary pleasure becomes the perfect object of official control through the manipulation of incentives and penalties.

Hedonism is thus an expression of disenchantment with the ends and prospects of the larger way of life, and it sets up its bearers to be the recipients of new modes of discipline. Advertising techniques and the expansion of consumption opportunities may accelerate its development, but they could not suffice to explain its origins and persistence. Attention to the rationale implicit within it is necessary to an understanding of the phenomenon. It may be, as it is in our society, an impoverished reaction to the implicit recognition that the ends sustained by established institutions can no longer attract the reflective allegiance of a populace. It has a measure ('a moment') of rationality in it even if the dialectic it launches is self-defeating.

Bell avoids the social bearing of the phenomenon he portrays. He needs to do so, given his conviction that the defining institutions and objectives of American society must not be touched by socialist hands. For acknowledgement of the sources and implications of hedonism must lead to despair among those who repudiate the possibility of reconstituting the priorities of the civilization of productivity. If the theorist can interpret hedonism as a relatively superficial phenomenon reversible by an enlarged self-consciousness about the imperatives of the established order, hedonism could be transcended within it. But I will argue that the new politics of maturity and reconciliation sought by Bell cannot emerge without a more serious reconstitution of established institutions. Bell's solution, though not intentionally, is likely to foster and legitimize the selective extension of repression within the old order.

If rapid economic growth historically has contained social conflict and confined the reach of disciplinary mechanisms, how will the same institutional practices sustain social peace as the growth dividend dwindles? If work is organized around the incentive of private affluence, how will motivation be maintained as the supply of the old incentives is depleted? If the attainment of private affluence is a defining justification of the civilization of productivity, what is to attract the allegiance of those who see themselves permanently excluded from the circle of affluence? One answer, as we have seen, is the extension of coercive controls over those located in the most vulnerable and inessential positions within the political economy.

Bell appears to believe that another agenda can be realized. His faith seems to rest upon the assumption, first, that the persistent demand for increased levels of consumption is shaped primarily by the experience of relative deprivation on the part of lower income strata and, secondly, that the necessary sacrifices could be equitably distributed and acknowledged as equitable by those asked to bear them. Political maturity involves the willingness to contract consumption expectations, to divert scarce social resources to subsidize

147

the system of productivity, and to acknowledge an equitable allocation of sacrifices when it appears.

But these hopes are likely to be dashed. The political preconditions for an equitable allocation are precarious. The sectoral structure of the economy, the dependency of the welfare state on the economic performance of the corporate sector, and the weak political and market position of those constituencies living on the margins of society coalesce to undermine them. An aggregate reduction in real income, if it is to occur, will be drawn primarily from those with the fewest power resources and the greatest needs.

Even this fate might be tolerable to the recipients, tolerable because it is thought to be unavoidable within the established order, if they agree that their previous demands for higher levels of consumption rested more upon a sense of relative deprivation than the objective inability to make ends meet. Perhaps as the participants come to see that they have helped to fuel a process whereby 'past luxuries are constantly redefined as necessities'[23] they may be more willing to slow down the pace of redefinition. This assessment, familiar enough in neo-conservative prescriptions to reduce consumption levels and to debunk proposals to reduce inequality, overlooks continuous shifts in the social infrastructure of consumption generated by previous patterns of economic growth.

We have seen how changing technologies and production processes progressively convert free goods into necessary items of expenditure, how the established system of transportation and shopping malls makes the automobile a necessity to the individual, how the weakening of ties of local community and kinship accelerates the need to convert a number of services into the commodity form. Items can be added to this list indefinitely. If the iceman no longer brings ice around and the local grocery store has given way to the distant supermarket, one must buy a refrigerator and pay the electric bill for running it; if laws covering zoning, construction, and insurance obligations introduce new expenses, the expenses must be paid to use those facilities; if 'durable' appliances have a shorter life, one must replace them more often; if the complexity of the machinery in cars and appliances is increased enough and the tools become too specialized, the possibility of doing the maintenance and repairs oneself disappears; if a high percentage of the cost of such repairs includes unneeded work, the deskilled consumer must usually pay the cost anyway; if expensive higher education is now necessary to ensure that one's children have career possibilities today equivalent to those available in the past without this training, one must try to finance one's children through college; if one's job is unhealthy or one's life depressing, one must pay the bill for medical care or therapy to relieve the suffering; if the advertising bill for products increases as a proportion of their cost or if the central distributor now holds a strategic market position, one must incorporate these new expenses into old objects of consumption; if taxes rise to cover the expanding costs of crime control, official corruption, public monitoring of private corruption, environmental destruction, and military expenditures (all flowing, to some degree from the prevailing system of production, consumption, and distribution), then one must pay these additional costs as well.

Initial changes in the conventional package of consumption goods reflect both new luxury choices by affluent consumers and the persistent effort by capital to extend the commodity form into new areas of life. But once these changes have been installed corollary alterations in the infrastructure of the consumption system convert them into needed expenditures for less affluent consumers. Some new items of consumption serve as compensation for the loss of social meaning, and others become needs or necessities in the changing social framework within which consumption proceeds.

Bell's call to leave the prevailing forms of work, politics, profit, consumption, and community intact while reducing the aggregate level of consumption carries repressive implications. Those who are called upon to curtail their greed when they are in fact trying to make ends meet, and those striving to compensate for the deflation of social meaning through the inflation of private expenditures will evade and resist the sacrifices to be imposed. Those with sufficient political and market resources are then likely to protect their more favorable position by shifting the heaviest burden on those without these resources. They will be tempted to support a right wing regime which promises to deliver the goods once again to those who are deserving and which defines the undeserving as those who cannot make a go of it in the current structure of things.

Bell's hope to see a mature populace reconciled to new limits – even while the civilization of productivity is built around the aspiration to surpass them – cannot succeed. As the anticipated maturation fails to emerge, the basic assumptions of the theory will push its theorists to conclude that the populace is irrevocably immature. The next step is to compel the immature hedonists to become more mature in behavior if not in judgment and responsibility. The state will have to be protected from too much democracy so that it can impose restraints unacceptable to its least industrious constituencies. The repressive import of the theory flows from its tendency to explain the source of current dislocations too much in terms of greed, immaturity, hedonism and relative deprivation, and not enough in terms of global shifts in the self-understanding of a populace implicit within these appearances. The case for the exploration of possibilities Bell repudiates without close argument is supported by the implications of the case he supports explicitly. The first interpretation fails to detect the element of rationality in the tendencies he deplores, and its adherents may eventually conclude that the irrational populace must have reason imposed upon it from above.

6

Personal identity, citizenship, and the state

The quest for personal identity

The problem of personal identity, as it is construed within Anglo-American philosophy, is really a series of problems. By what criteria do we properly decide that the person we are engaged with now is the same person we knew three days or three decades ago? How do we distinguish the class of beings called persons from other objects such as computers, corpses, monkeys, and corporations who resemble persons in some respects? And what is there about the self which makes it possible, if it is, to say that 'I' have a unified personality, a set of ideals, or a problem of identity? We might call these respectively the problems of individuation, species identity, and the unity of the person.

The problem of identity, as it is construed in social theory, seems to assume a different shape. To have an identity, in this sense, is to identify with a set of beliefs, norms, and purposes, to accept as one's own a set of standards exhibited in one's conduct.

There is a double edge to this second concept of identity. For if the identity people seek to sustain is not confirmed to some degree by roles and norms available in the social order, the role-players can become disoriented and demoralized. *But* if that connection were total, and unmediated by the critical consciousness of the participants – if I achieved no distance at all from my role performances – then it would be difficult to speak of 'my' identity at all. The conception of personal identity we are striving to characterize, one might say, involves an identification with a set of established practices, tempered or qualified by a certain individuation and critical reflection into the nature of the roles adopted. It is, then, a precarious achievement, for it can be attacked from two directions.

These two sets of questions about personal identity, as they are defined in the philosophical and sociological literature respectively, are certainly connected. The recent proliferation of literature on the philosophical issues coincides with the proliferation of constituencies whose identification with the roles they are expected to play is visibly corroded. If Wittgenstein is right in his view that the conventional criteria by which we decide questions of identity normally suffice because 'the many characteristics which we use as the criteria for identity coincide in the vast majority of cases,'[1] the philosophical problem of identity will be accentuated in importance as the *fracturing* of social roles and the development of new medical technologies proceeds. Some of the conventional criteria will point in one direction while others point in another. New advances in brain surgery make it possible, for instance, that the continuity of one body will coincide with sharp discontinuities in the memory or character of its inhabitant. And the multiple roles a single person might play in contemporary society – as a citizen, a member of a particular political lobby, a worker, a union member, a parent, a friend, a male or female, a member of a particular religious and ethnic group – will support divergent sets of priorities, principles, and character traits with which the role-bearers are expected to identify. A certain degree of such pluralism is essential to the very consciousness of self as a unity not exhausted by any particular role within which it is implicated, but this self-unity amidst a plurality of self-expressions, if stretched too thin, can contribute to a variety of identity problems.

One 'puzzle case,' a case anyway which is puzzling to a group of Anglo-American philosophers, might give us some sense of this connection between the philosophical issues of identity and the practical issue of self-identification in contemporary society. In this case a patient emerged from a brain operation with one hemisphere exerting control over part of the body and another exerting control over other parts. The patient, it is reported, 'would sometimes find himself pulling down his pants with one hand and pulling them up with the other. Once he grabbed his wife with his left hand and shook her violently, while with the right trying to come to his wife's aid in bringing the left, belligerent hand under control.'[2]

From the vantage point of the philosophical tradition we are characterizing the question here is : Is one person doing two contradictory things or are two persons struggling for primacy within the same body? The answer depends on what we treat as the controlling criteria of personal identity. But whichever answer is given to that question, this one person has, or those two people have, an identity problem in our second sense, of the first magnitude. Anyone who wears pants or has a spouse would recognize its symptoms immediately.

I will consider the idea of identity in its broad sense, partly because attention to these concerns will eventually push us to the first set of issues and might even cast some illumination on them, more pertinently because clarity about this larger idea is surely crucial to an understanding of the political self-interpretations which prevail in our society.

We might gain a preliminary view of the sort of problem to be explored by considering briefly the connection between personal identity and self-interpretation in a primitive tribe, as that tribe has been portrayed by Mary Douglas in *Purity and Danger*.[3]

The Lele of the Congo yearn for an order in the universe which can be grasped with a set of clearly demarcated and mutually exclusive concepts. Their identity as tribal members is closely bound up with their cosmology. They construe anomalous elements in nature as dirt – as matter out of place. Such dirt is not simply a threat to cleanliness; it jeopardizes the purity of the spirit and the transparency of the world order. It is thus a pollution to be avoided, or, sometimes, a holy object to be incorporated into a religious ritual. Each reaction is designed to ward off disquiet and danger. Animals, for instance, which do not fit neatly into the classification scheme are treated as unsuitable for ordinary human consumption. Since the classification scheme separates flying animals from land animals, flying squirrels, displaying characteristics that cut across these categories, are never to be eaten. The pangolin, or scaly ant-eater, however, defies all the usual criteria of classification.

It is scaly like a fish but it climbs trees. It is more like an egg-laying lizard than a mammal, yet it suckles its young. And most significant of all, unlike other small mammals its young are born singly. Instead of running away or attacking it, it curls in a modest ball and waits for the hunter to pass.[4]

The pangolin is eaten solemnly during fertility rites by a select group of tribe members. The tribe confronts the categories through which it lives by endowing with special significance an animal which defies its categorical scheme; and the ritual reconfirms the validity of this scheme. If the members became conscious of the ritual in exactly these terms, the ploy would no longer ward off disquiet and anxiety. Yet, paradoxically, failure to see through such a ritual can also have catastrophic results in some circumstances. To take the most obvious example, changes in the natural environment might deplete the supply of acceptable food leaving only those animals too pure or too polluted to serve as food. The attempt to retain the relation to nature required by this classification scheme could contribute to the tribe's disappearance.

To forestall the claim that there is *no* connection between the identity of a primitive tribe and the identity of a modern populace, no connection because we are so self-conscious about the ideas and customs which sustain us, let me, with apologies, pose one counter-example. If I began nonchalantly to pick the nose of my intimate lover, she (or he) would surely react with horror. This limit, not quite treated as a taboo in our society because few are tempted to break it, forms an implicit ingredient in our conceptions of self and privacy. When we ask why one is normally quite willing to ride in a car with a casual acquaintance but quite reluctant to share a bed with the same person if the primary purpose of that sharing is to sleep (an inhibition not recognized in inns in the middle ages), or why we conventionally treat food recently eaten as garbage, or why it is more acceptable to speak obnoxiously during a social event than to burp during one, we are asking a series of questions about conventions which help to constitute our sense of personal privacy and integrity. They help to sustain distance between oneself and others. The commitment to the private self finds expression in our insistence on not having our bodily integrity or personal space violated in particular ways, and in our wish to limit some of the public expressions of the private self. Recent challenges to previous notions of personal privacy and integrity take the form of flouting these 'taboos' to expose their purported irrationality.

To characterize adequately the identity that people in our society seek to sustain would be to elaborate our experiential relationships to nature, work, members of the opposite sex, death, the state, the past and the future. One would need as well to show in what respects an orientation in each of these areas tends to limit the possible range of orientations in others. For instance, the idea of instrumental work fits well with the view of nature as a deposit of exploitable resources; these two orientations, in turn, cohere nicely with our scientific view of nature as an objective system of lawful regularities susceptible to our understanding and control. And that whole set meshes with our historical aspiration to establish a civilization of productivity which can provide all its members with private afflu-ence, security, and leisure. We define ourselves as free agents capable of acting purposively partly by contrast to this view of nature as an objective system of regularities amenable to our control; and we see ourselves as exercising self-discipline when we work today so that our progeny can enjoy the fruits of that work tomorrow. The modern idea of love, as a union of two partners who have freely chosen each other unencumbered by considerations of family expectation or ethnic difference, further expresses this concept of self and fits nicely with the practice of labor mobility and the organization of households around the nuclear family. The notions of agency and responsibility implicit in these practices coheres with the ideal of equal opportunity to attain lower or higher positions in society through one's own efforts. To the extent that we believe the principle to be operative and valid, we feel justified in holding people res-ponsible not only for, say, their integrity as neighbors, but also for the amount of money they earn, the kind of job they have, the sort of school they send their children to, and so on. The idea of being personally responsible for the self one becomes and the principle of equal opportunity are so closely intertwined that it is hard to visualize shifts in our perceptions of the latter practice which would not carry important implications for the commitment to treat people as significantly responsible for their own character and lives. Finally, the practice of competitive elections in which each person has one vote equal in importance to all others reflects and crystallizes at the public level these ideas of personal choice, in-tegrity, rights, and responsibility.

My point in delineating some of the internal connections among these conceptions and practices is not to suggest that these relation-ships and those identifications are now quite intact. As a descrip-tion of contemporary life this characterization is already rather quaint and anachronistic; it overlooks a whole series of develop-ments in relations between the sexes, within the family, between the family and larger bureaucracies, inside occupational life, and between the citizen and the state. The point of the characterization is to intimate how a deep and persistent shift in one of these self-conceptions would necessarily be bound up with shifts in the practices to which it is connected. Moreover, to reconstitute successfully and significantly any of the practices of production, science, consumption, politics, family or mobility which embody and express these self-conceptions it would also be necessary to reconstitute the other practices with which it is articulated.

If the identity a society can confirm through its defining practices is limited by the range within which its institutional structure can vary, then one of the potential dilemmas such a society can face is the emergence historically of a disconnection between the vague identity aspirations of broad segments of its populace and the limits posed to their articulation and realization by the institutional structure. This disconnection between the identity sought and the identity confirmed within the established structure can contribute to a profound disorientation. Its surface manifestations might assume the shape of a decline in the legitimacy of prevailing institutions and a deterioration in their performance.

I believe that such a disconnection, characterized experientially as cynicism about, or disillusionment with, established practices and aspirations, is now well entrenched in our society. It is difficult to discern just how deeply it reaches or to extrapolate from its current manifestations to its future direction and consequences. Indeed if the underlying structural bind is quite intractable we must expect each of its surface manifestations to have a rather short life-cycle, as each new set of dissidents 'sees through' the redemptive projects upon which their immediate predecessors had pinned such high hopes.

Since I am not ready to characterize all of the sources and manifestations of this disillusionment I will concentrate here on one relation, the relation of the citizen to the state as it is manifested in the electoral process. For the conception of citizenship which citizens themselves seek to sustain within the electoral system screens political perceptions and confines the legitimate range of policies to a set which eventually encourages a further withdrawal of allegiance by some constituencies and a willingness by others to expand disciplinary controls over the surplus population. The effort to sustain the role of citizen in these circumstances contributes to the erosion of citizenship.

Citizens and looters

On 13 July 1977, early in the evening, the lights went out in New York City, and soon thereafter scattered areas in the city were looted by gangs of youthful minorities drawn from the lower end of the stratification system. The looting contrasted dramatically with the reaction ten years earlier when the lights had also gone out. And the more recent reaction was frightening to residents. It was, as Midge Decter put it in a *Commentary* essay, as if each middle-class resident had 'been given a glimpse into the foundations of one's house and seen with horror, that it was utterly infected and rotting away.'[5]

Decter herself mocks the 'instant analysis' of liberals who explained the looting in terms of the society's failure to provide hope and sustenance to those stuck at the bottom; she insists that a decade of liberal programs and apologies actually licensed the looting this time around. The spree reflects a decline of responsibility and civility among young people in the ghettoes; and liberals who find excuses for such conduct hold in contempt, she says, those whose conduct they would explain: 'The message they (the looters) are given, in short, is that they are not fully human enough to be held morally responsible for their own behavior' . . . 'It is, to be blunt, the message of liberal racism.'[6]

Decter rejects the view that the looting was an expression of resentment against a social order which closes the under-class out of good jobs, decent housing, and a solid education. Rather, the looters consisted of those who refuse to take advantage of the real opportunities available to them partly because they have been encouraged to believe that what others have earned they are entitled to receive without effort or sacrifice.

The response by many to Decter's interpretation was highly favorable. The next edition of *Commentary* included a rash of congratulatory letters; polls taken by the media revealed that a large proportion of the populace concurred in this interpretation. Most of those polled agreed, for instance, that the looters were 'those who steal if they think they can get away with it' and seventy per cent of the respondents rejected the contention that most of the looters were 'poor and needy.'[7] Press reports in the New York newspaper were also highly supportive of this thesis.

But a closer examination of the available evidence, provided by

Robert Curvin and Bruce Porter in *Blackout Looting*, reveals serious distortions and exaggerations in this general perception. Participants did treat the blackout as an opportunity to get some loot to which they felt they were entitled. 'It was like a gift,' one looter confessed to a sympathetic interviewer, 'somebody was just saying, when the lights are out you all just get what you can before the lights come on.'[8] And the same looter acknowledged that it was not hunger which drove him to the streets: 'I wanted sneakers; I wanted the gold, the diamonds and what not; I wanted money in my pocket . . .; you know, it wasn't necessities; it was just things I wanted for myself . . . I mean, everybody wants a color television, a stereo.'[9]

This self-report is so far consonant with Decter's account. Respect for the property of store owners and for the work ethic had deteriorated prior to the incident, and the first wave of looters did consist primarily of professional crooks and street people. But the background to this explosion diverges from that implied in Decter's account. Each of the areas in which looting was widespread had recently experienced either a large influx of new and uprooted minorities or a significant decrease in its employment and income levels. Most districts had experienced both.[10] High rates of inflation, unemployment, and marginal employment left a large proportion of residents in these areas in worse economic shape than they had been in 1967, and the rate of marginal employment and unemployment for those arrested was three times higher than for those arrested in the more overtly political riots of the 1960s.

Against this background, the widespread participation in the looting, and the tendency by an even larger number of residents within these districts to sanction it, must be interpreted as an expression of rage and hostility by those who are officially called upon to live according to standards of work, self-restraint, and responsibility which do not correspond to their actual conditions of existence. The collective disdain for these expectations is accentuated by the daily visibility of store owners, police, and other public officials who flout the very standards they seek to see enforced on the minorities. The common message within the collective act was, 'we abide by your rules and standards, not because we accept the negative picture they necessarily present of us, but because it is usually prudent to do so when the lights are on.'

The sense of exhilaration and release experienced by participants reveals another dimension in the action. For many of the participants much of the time are ambivalent about the negative light in which they are placed when the dominant conceptions of identity and responsibility are applied to them. They partly accept the conception of self prevailing in the larger society even while feeling that it unfairly projects a negative image of them. Their daily behavior, at least, often *seems* to acknowledge this view, and that appearance takes its toll in one's self-concept. The split between the professed view of self and that often manifest in conduct (think of relations with police, store owners, welfare workers) jeopardizes the sense of integrity attained when one says what he thinks and does what he says. This act provided participants with a rare occasion to express complete disdain for this negative portrait, to free themselves completely of this negative self-image. The sense of exhilaration and the carnival atmosphere flowed from the nice consistency, on this occasion, between the image they wished to project of themselves as people with deep grievances ignored by the larger populace and the action which expressed these sentiments so clearly. The ambiguities of daily life could be resolved in the dark. Some things become more visible when the lights go out. One participant expressed these sentiments in quite direct language. 'The lights was out, you know; we was gonna see what we can do. Like I was really charged up.'[11]

But the message sent did not find a large audience ready to receive it. Decter's translation is more congenial to the recipients. For it kills three doubts with one stone. It reaffirms the idea of responsibility for one's own position in society by holding the looters accountable for their actions as well as their more generalized plight. It casts a portion of blame for the explosion on liberals who had inadvertently challenged the claims of working- and middle-class people to respect for their achievements and self-discipline by construing the minorities to be caught within forces beyond their own control. And it relieves the white majority from the felt obligation to support a renewal of expensive, ineffective liberal programs to help those who refuse to help themselves. The white majority, understandably frightened by the threat of further violence by the looters, were thus relieved of public responsibility for inaction, supported in their hostility to the looters and liberal idealists, and vindicated in their wish to see themselves as responsible agents. For only if the losers are responsible for their own defeats can the others easily see themselves as responsible for their modest success;

only if the losers are held responsible for failing to live up to a reasonable standard of conduct during the period of looting can those in more secure positions claim merit for abiding by that standard; only if the looters are punished for their deeds will the looters themselves be treated with the respect they deserve as free, responsible agents; and only if this justice is done can the hard-earned achievements of one constituency remain secure from the threats posed by the other. The first judgment in this list, needed to sustain the self-identity of the threatened constituencies, can be held most confidently if the next three are affirmed too. Efforts to protect the identity of the first constituency thereby contribute (terms such as 'produce' or 'cause' are too imprecise to capture the loose texture of the relationship) to the repression of the second.

Decter correctly portrayed the liberal interpretation and remedy as 'completely familiar.' She failed to note, however, that her own response was equally familiar. Indeed, in recent history, the life cycle of each interpretation correlates nicely, if inversely, with that of the other. They are locked together in a persistent adversarial relation, and the very persistence of that debate leads one to suspect that shared assumptions implicit in the terms of debate themselves play an important role in sustaining a cherished view of the citizen's relation to the state.

Important clues about the nature of this relationship are provided by Marx in an essay written in 1844 entitled 'Critical Notes on the Article "The King of Prussia and Social Reform".'[12]

The most advanced political society of the time, Marx claimed, was England. It had public elections and a two-party system. But just because this advanced political democracy was connected to an economic system which was not susceptible to public control, the English were in a particularly unpromising position either to discern the sources of pauperism or to devise an effective remedy. Two approaches competed for public acceptance, each taking its turn as the program pursued by the government. The first found pauperism to be caused by the defective administration of the Poor Laws. The condition of paupers could be improved by reforming the administration of those laws. But as each new series of reforms failed to eliminate pauperism, the opposition party would argue that it was due to the indolence and laziness of the poor themselves. Pauperism was not 'to be regarded as a misfortune to be prevented but as a crime to be suppressed and punished.'[13] And, Marx prophecied, the two parties in England would remain locked in this debate indefinitely. Each time the new administrative program favored by one party failed the other party would be elected to impose new penalties and controls on the paupers. The rationale for this prophecy is briefly – too briefly – stated in three passages from the text.

1. Wherever there are political parties each party will attribute *every* defect of society to the fact that its rival is at the helm of the state instead of itself.

2. Insofar as the state acknowledges the evidence of social grievances it locates their origin either in the laws of nature over which no human agency has control, or in private life which is independent of the state, or else in a malfunction of the administration which is dependent upon it.

3. If the modern state decided to abolish the impotence of its administration it would have to abolish contemporary private life. However, no living person believes the defects of his existence to be based on the principle, the essential nature of his own life; they must be grounded in circumstances outside his own life.[14]

Transposing Marx's prophecy to our own setting, Decter's argument treats welfare state clients as responsible for their own plight, and the liberal alternative blames that plight on defects in the administration of the welfare state. Each contention is the familiar counterpoint to the other. And the electorate tends to shuffle between supporting programs which promise to provide state aid to the poor more effectively and those which promise to crack down on the poor. Why does each option present itself repeatedly as the only viable alternative every time the opposing option fails? Why does the electorate not see through the options themselves? Assuming, as I will, that neither option suffices to cope with contemporary dislocations, I will try to show that the answer involves the continuing attempt of large segments of the populace to see themselves as free citizens in a free state.

Personal identity, electoral politics, and the state

In earlier chapters I have contended that the ends of affluence and leisure which helped to justify the defining institutions of the civilization of productivity are today declining in their ability to retain the reflective allegiance of people who continue to work, consume, raise children, politic, and bargain within that civilization. These ends, once the achievements and burdens implicitly built into their actual attainment are revealed through progressive historical experience, can lose their normative hold on new generations trying to shape meaningful lives for themselves. The word eventually seeps out that the constant expansion of consumption opportunities increases the proportion of consumption expenditures which serve as means to gratifications rather than as gratifications themselves; that the labor mobility which promises to improve the standard of living for some must also damage cherished ties of kinship and neighborhood; that the system of work incentives through graded pay persistently excludes some segments of the society from the circle of affluence; that the accelerating exploitation of natural resources constantly deepens the state's dependence on resources located in foreign countries and generates a huge war machinery to protect these essential resources; that the prevailing processes of production and forms of consumption render the natural environment increasingly unfit for human habitation; that the rehabilitation of the environment would require a massive diversion of resources away from the forms of consumption which justify the civilization of productivity; and that the rapid pace of technological change required to increase productivity renders each new generation of workers obsolescent just when they have reached the age when they are most in need of the respect and dignity bestowed on those functionally important to the society. The suspicion arises that these consquences are not dispensable side effects to a pursuit which can be carried on without them, but that these consequences are intrinsic to the civilization of productivity itself. Since these suspicions are not incorporated into the wider political dialogue they remain cloudy and inchoate. They take their toll more indirectly, as in the withdrawal of identification from many of the roles available to people, the deterioration of performance within established roles, the decline in the legitimacy of institutions which are supposed to articulate and respond to public grievances, the proliferation of litigious activity, and the hostile repudiation of political movements which articulate these doubts without revealing practical ways to resolve the issues defined.

In such circumstances, we must expect those who are strategically located within the civilization to escalate their demands for a larger share of the rewards available within the order. The deflation of identification with the order, with, say, the project of perfecting it for future generations, is correlated with the inflation of demands for a larger share of the fruits of affluence. This correlation emerges because the decline in identification with the institutions of family, work, and school enlarges the experience of sacrifice in carrying out assigned tasks: the participants then demand more rewards to compensate for the enlarged sense of sacrifice. Performance deteriorates while the demand for the paradigmatic rewards available accelerates.

But two apparent anomalies must now be accounted for. First, the withdrawal of allegiance on the part of the more secure and affluent constituencies does not tend to find the same expression as it does among those shuffled to the margins of the system. Rather, the different modes this common withdrawal of affection takes helps to shape and extend the adversarial relations between these constituencies. Secondly, in neither constituency does the political expression of disaffection assume the form it might if the constituencies concurred explicitly in the interpretation offered here. The expressions tend to be symptomatic rather than self-conscious, private rather than public, public rather than political, sporadic rather than organized, factionalizing rather than unifying. The credibility of this interpretation requires that it assimilate these two apparent anomalies in ways which cohere with the larger reading. We have already gone some distance toward accounting for the first; the largest share of our attention will now be concentrated on the second.

The quest to confirm personal identity under unfavorable circumstances, the corollary desire to see oneself as a free citizen in a free state, and the dynamics of two-party competition within the welfare state provide the elements from which such an account can be constructed.

To see oneself as a free, responsible agent, as a person whose position in life is merited by the skills, energy, and self-discipline exercised at home and at work, one must identify with some of the practices within which one is implicated. In identifying with the purposes and standards embodied within these practices one experiences the activities within them as expressions of oneself, as projects, goals, and norms that are one's own. If these identifications were to dissolve, some of the same practices and norms would be experienced as limits and obstacles to one's freedom. In the most extreme circumstances one's identification might recede so far that one approximated the condition of the underground man in Dostoevski's novel. Not just the imperatives of work, or the criteria of promotion, or the norms of politeness, but the very rules of reason would then be treated as external, as impediments to one's self-expression. But, certainly, in this extreme condition, it would be impossible to identify a subject richly textured enough to act freely. Even if all these external impediments were removed one of the preconditions for free action would be absent. To refuse to identify with the most pervasive standards, norms, and expectations in one's society in the name of authenticity and autonomy is to render one's identity marginal. It is to invite hypocrisy in which one's professed repudiation is belied by one's practical affirmations. But if the professed repudiation is *rationally grounded* – resting upon a correct perception of inner contradictions or unresolvable tensions within the established practices – while those practices seem thoroughly resistant to change, the agent who would be free and rational is locked into a paradoxical situation. Neither affirmation nor repudiation could secure the identity desired.

In less extreme conditions, closer to those in which we actually live, these contradictory pressures will still take their toll. But their recognition can be more readily evaded. One can struggle to save appearances, to convey to self and others through behavior and statement that no deep discrepancy exists between the convictions expressed in one's role performances and those worthy of one's rational support. One affirms the practices by suppressing evidence and arguments which would display their irrationality. The struggle to suppress is itself a perverse sign of how important the values of freedom and reason are to the identities of those involved.

If the quest for personal identity under unfavorable circumstances encourages one to maintain the appearance of an agent whose outer performances express inner commitments, to affirm publicly that which makes up the center of one's life activity, politics provides an appropriate medium for this expression to make its appearance. The internal pressure to affirm the larger way of life through the political process is accentuated if the prospect of restructuring prevailing institutions by public means seems dim.

This preliminary posture of identification on the part of many participants renders them amenable (no stronger connection can be detected) to a political dialogue which confines the definition of public grievances and political objectives to those falling within the scope of the state's apparent capacity for effective action.

The charge that a ruling class manipulates mass perceptions and political commitments misfires, not only because no ruling class be identified which is sufficiently self-conscious, united, or organized, but also because such a theory ignores this preliminary orientation to perception and interpretation on the part of the ostensible objects of manipulation. The dual accountability of the welfare state, as we shall see, then coalesces with the dynamics of two-party competition to translate this preliminary self-orientation into a politics which obscures the implicit disaffection from the civilization of productivity. The oscillation between attributing recognized blemishes to defects in the administration of the welfare state and to defects in the character of marginal constituencies operates to deflect public discourse consistently from the identification of deeper dislocations in the order.

The modern welfare state, as we have seen, looks in two directions at the same time. It is the agency of public accountability and it is dependent upon the successful performance of the private economy to generate the tax dividend it needs to meet that accountability. It is both accountable to us through elections and limited in its effective accountability. But its continued legitimacy in our eyes depends significantly upon the visibility of its accountability and the invisibility of the ways in which that accountability is circumscribed by the need to subsidize the accumulation of private capital.

As the agency of accountability through competitive elections, as the one institution which can claim to promote justice and the public interest through the conscious creation of public policy, as, ideally, the repository of common values, the state, when it is healthy, attracts the patriotic allegiance of its citizens. I can see myself as free if the roles I play are congruent with the purposes I adopt upon reflection. *We* can see ourselves as free, free as a people, if the central institution of electoral accountability and public action is widely believed to have sufficient resources to act with effectiveness in the pursuit of collective ends. The internal connection between my sense of individual freedom and my belief that the state is the locus of effective, collective action is this: If I find certain role requirements to be both conventional and unjustifiably restrictive, if I can neither reconstitute them by myself nor adopt others, *my freedom is still potentially intact if we can collectively reconstitute them should others come to agree with my assessment.* Unless the state could (if it would) alter such conventions then its unfreedom contributes to mine. Thus our very identity as free agents is bound up with our belief in the state's capacity to promote publicly defined purposes; further, my identity as a member of a free society is bound up with the effective accountability of the state to its electorate, with its ability to promote the common good as we understand it. This is the basis – the rational basis – of that emotional bond between the citizen and the state we call patriotism.

The patriotic tie is extended to a larger set of public practices if the participants believe that the basic state constitution symbolizes the collective identity they acknowledge, sustains their ability to forge a public will, and protects the most basic rights of those who participate in the formation of that will. The constitution constitutes their political relations insofar as it is thought to embody public dimensions of the identity they seek to sustain.

This deep tie between the citizen and the constitutional order is often misrepresented in radical and liberal theories. The former tend to see patriotism as an inauthentic sentiment propagated by the ruling class which benefits from it. The latter sometimes treat patriotism as an unnecessary and irrational emotion generated by people who are too insecure to stand on their own two feet. Both of these interpretations, because they miss the rational element in the patriotic tie and the indispensable role it plays in sustaining the civic virtue a healthy state requires, also tend to ignore the institutional preconditions for its rational expression and containment. Underestimating the tenacity with which a populace will cling to patriotism, the extremes to which it may go under adverse conditions to retain identification with the larger order, these theories thereby each underplay, though in different ways, the potential participation of a populace in the construction of an ideology which misrepresents their own conditions of existence. To ignore the inner rationality of patriotism is to misconstrue both its importance as a binding agent and its potential power as a catalyst of public repression.

The visibility of the state's accountability to its electorate solidifies the patriotic relation between the citizen and the state. But if the state also stands in a relation of close dependence to the privately incorporated economy, if its public accountability depends upon its ability to subsidize economic expansion, then it cannot speak effectively to the disaffection from the civilization of productivity. The duality in the relation between the state and the society discourages public articulation of that disaffection. For if we articulate those grievances and it is powerless to act, not only it, but we must be seen to be unfree. And our experience of disenchantment and closure would be magnified.

The duality I refer to, again, is lodged, at one level, in the beliefs needed to sustain the patrioic bond to the state and the connection between that tie and the self-identification of the participants as free agents. At the second level those beliefs and ties are threatened by the state's dependence on, and its necessarily large role in, the corporate economy. The first relation encourages us to see it as capable of acting effectively and the second diminishes its ability to reconstitute institutions of work, consumption, and community. The duality itself is thereby shrouded in ambiguity, and we participate in a public dialogue which redefines our grievances so that they do fall within the ambit of legitimate state activity. We define political issues which do not speak directly to the deeper disaffection from the civilization of productivity. We define our grievances and policy agendas as falling within the limits of action available to the welfare state so that we can see the state, and ourselves, as free. And the electoral system works to channel the public dialogue within these banks while it screens the electorate from awareness of the confines within which its exploration of alternatives is defined.

Thus one of our parties (or one faction within it) will contend that the market is an efficient means of setting prices, maintaining employment, ensuring that consumer needs are matched by production priorities, and providing workers and owners with the independence needed to organize and press claims upon the state. But the market, these welfare state proponents will insist, is not effective in pricing public goods such as clean air, good education, and the needs of future generations. Its distributional consequences also deviate somewhat from our standards of justice. It fails to provide adequately for those who are too old, too young, or too sick to provide for themselves, and it generates cycles of unemployment and inflation which expose people able of mind and body to insecurities for which they are not personally responsible. The welfare state, within this public philosophy, is legitimate; it deserves our allegiance because it redresses imperfections in the market without defeating the virtues of the market.

Proponents of this position increasingly acknowledge today the signs of declining allegiance to public and private institutions as it is reflected in low voting turnouts, widespread cynicism about public officials, the apparent increase in crime and corruption, the emergence of tax revolts, the periodic popularity of maverick candidates for the Presidency, and the retreat from public life manifested in the resurgence of fundamental religion and hedonism. But these reactions, they contend, reflect, first, public misunderstandings of the constraints within which any large industrial society must operate and, secondly, the inefficient and ineffective procedures which hamper the performance of the welfare state bureaucracy. Public allegiance, they claim, can be restored by improving political education to promote public awareness of the limits facing industrial society as such and, most importantly, by further rationalization of state bureaucracies to bring them under the control of state officials who are accountable to the electorate.

Advocates of this welfare state philosophy understand that the expansion of the system of productivity, and the progressive concentration of economic units accompanying it, necessitates an interventionist state. The state must support the conditions of private capital accumulation, regulate the behavior of large corporate units, and redress the least acceptable side effects of market transactions. But the very ascendancy of this perspective has bloated the size of the welfare state, and the visibly enlarged state is thus progressively caught in a bind.

The welfare state gradually emerges as the depository, first, for projects which are privately unprofitable but supportive of private profit creation and, secondly, for clients who are inessential to the productive process. Taking on tasks that are not readily amenable to the productivity increases operative in the private sector (compare education and automobile production, or crime control and the production of electronic instruments) the state is then held responsible for failing to meet standards of efficiency and cost effectiveness ostensibly met in the private sector. And the dependent clients it accumulates further set it up as a screen upon which a wider, less articulate, disaffection can be projected.

Consider the charges levelled against the welfare state by those with sufficient job security to provide the state with a steady flow of tax revenues but with insufficient income to participate fully or securely in the good life sanctioned by the order. The state gives handouts to welfare freeloaders and taxes workers; it coddles criminals and mocks thereby the self-restraint of the working poor; it offers special opportunities to young women and minorities and thus implies that older white males in poor jobs failed to take advantage of the real opportunities offered them; it inflates the economy and deflates the spending power of consumers on relatively fixed incomes; it protects the right of educated people to criticize the system and ignores the deepest grievances of common people loyal to it; it buses blacks into white neighborhood schools and disrupts the vestiges of neighborhood life to which the latter cling; it calls for sacrifice from some and rewards self-indulgence in others; it expands in size and declines in effectiveness.

The state is the depository for those projects and clients which pose threats to the personal identity a broad range of constituencies strive to sustain within the civilization of productivity. To support welfare state policies and clientele enthusiastically would be to jeopardize the self-identity of the supporters. This decline in allegiance, this evasion of the spirit of the laws, expands the regulatory assignments of the state and depletes the resources of civic virtue it can draw upon in carrying out its expanded role. The role imposed on the state in the contemporary order weakens its ability to carry it out.

There is great ambivalence within this withdrawal of allegiance from the welfare state. For many of the critical constituencies face the potential perils of illness, unemployment, divorce, and hardship which state programs are designed to cushion; and most depend on a good public educational system to provide their children with the skills needed to escape the condition they themselves are in. The critical dimension of this ambivalence will be crystallized in one set of circumstances while the supportive aspects will achieve greater prominence in others. But, amidst this ebb and flow of explicit commitment, the political conflict between constituencies is carried on persistently within the individual.

When defects in the administration of the welfare state are most transparent, following, perhaps, the failure of a well publicized program to eliminate poverty, repair the cities, or break stagflation, there is internal pressure within the electorate to identify an alternative agenda which also falls within the sphere of activity legitimately available to the state. Unless such an alternative appears to be credible, those who have lost confidence in welfare state priorities cannot see themselves as free citizens in a free state. Unless existing state officials are seen to be unnecessarily incompetent – lacking in leadership or the right policy priorities – we cannot see the state as the potential sphere of collective freedom. Its unfreedom will contribute to ours and our unfreedom will contribute to mine.

The periodic predominance of one public philosophy, based on some version of the idea that 'defects in the administration of the state' are responsible for the most blatant public ills, is followed periodically by the idea that the cause is rooted in the refusal to use punitive instruments available to the state. The opposing party (or factions within both parties) will insist that the welfare free-loaders and the crooks are responsible for their own plight. When we dismantle large parts of the welfare state, the market will assume its former role effectively. And the state can concentrate on using its legal powers to discipline and control those unwilling to abide by the rules of the free enterprise system. The reduction of the welfare state bureaucracy will increase the disposable income of workers by reducing taxes; it will also improve the self-regulatory capacity of the market and remove some of the false incentives subsidized clients have to evade work.

Proponents of the modified market philosophy would continue to subsidize the performance of the privately incorporated economy because it is the provider of jobs, but they would dismantle the *welfare* apparatus of the state because it encourages the losers to construe themselves as victims and to believe that they are entitled to state handouts. If those who have the ability to work choose not to do so, then they must be disciplined and controlled. The loafers bring these punishments upon themselves and the punishments enhance the security of those willing to exercise self-discipline.

Our political dialogue tends to be frozen within this stereotyped set of alternatives because each contender for office must claim that *he can use resources now available to the state but ignored or misused by his most recent predecessor.* It is always 'time for a change,' but the change commended is either a newly polished version of the agenda pursued prior to the previous change or a new promise to exercise the leadership missing in the last administration.

The shuffle between a focus on flaws in the administration of the state and flaws in the character of the losers does not have to be distributed evenly between parties or constituencies. Each party contains some constituencies which emphasize one of these perspectives over the other and many constituencies within each faction feel the pull of both orientations. But the dynamics of party competition, where each candidate must promise to pursue a program which diverges from the one most recently tried within a context where the range of acceptable alternatives is limited by the collective wish to see the state as the agency of collective freedom, works to crystallize one option at one moment and the other at the next. For each party is pressed to identify policies which allow the state to deploy the tools legitimately available to it. The debate between the parties thus rests upon the common conviction that existing state resources suffice to cope with the most important issues. The challenging party concurs with the wider electorate in the implicit assumption that we are potentially free because existing state officials are unnecessarily inept.

I do not claim to have demonstrated that the resources available to the state, given the existing relation between the state and the corporate economy, are insufficient in principle to cope with the issues of inflation, unemployment, insecurity, worker motivation, energy dependence, the decline of civic virtue, the expansion of corruption, and so on, though I do think that the considerations advanced in previous chapters support the suspicion that it is not. Nor am I, certainly, suggesting that one-party rule is preferable to two-party politics. I do claim to have shown how the quest for personal identity, in a setting where the implicit allegiance to the defining institutions of the civilization of productivity has diminished, generates a political dialogue which obfuscates this disaffection and projects its most hostile expression onto the one institution which is formally accountable to the electorate. The resulting ambivalence and demoralization in the body politic accentuates cleavages in the system, intensifies general hostility against the victims of the civilization, concentrates patriotic sentiments on an abstract idea of the American state rather than on the concrete institutions through which the state operates, and depletes the supply of civic virtue available to the state in carrying out its inflated tasks of social coordination. This combination provides some support for the identity of many who wish to see themselves as free, responsible and dignified, but it also threatens to sanction the extension of a repressive politics.

If people repeatedly exposed to the established terms of debate eventually conclude, first, that the existing dialogue exhausts the range of conceivable remedies, secondly, that neither remedy alone, nor both in conjunction, can succeed while remaining within the bounds of civility and justice, and thirdly, that a less just and more ruthless order is better than no order at all, the cumulative impact would license an expansion of cynicism and opportunism among the well located, increase the willingness of relatively secure constituencies to ignore the claims of those pushed to the margins of the system, and sanction expanded state intimidation of those who lack a strategically powerful location within the system of productivity. The United States is not readily prone to such a reaction, since its constitutional limits are internalized as norms by large sections of the populace, and since its competitive party system usually encourages one party to pick up constituencies dropped by the other. But it is not immune to it either. Competitive elections provide a bulwark against repression when the institutional order allows a variety of constituencies to sustain their identity in general harmony, but it becomes a conduit for selective repression when the programs available to one constituency severely threaten the dignity available to others. This possibility is signaled by the Decter interpretation and by the willingness of many to accept its general assumptions and tone.

The quest for personal identity can be threatened institutionally in at least two ways: When the historical aspirations of a populace begin to depart from the possibilities of achievement within the institutional structure, and when a range of participants seeks to ward off the disquiet and anxiety accompanying such a rupture by covering up its most vocal and vociferous expressions. The first response undermines the needed identification with a larger order; the second retains the appearance of identification by closing off essential preconditions to private and public freedom. Those who wish to avoid the first of these outcomes must be alert to the extent to which their political priorities and orientations unwittingly make a contribution to the second.

7

Socialism and freedom

Socialist ideals and political strategies

Socialist theory presents many faces to capitalist practice. One version criticizes the exploitation, alienation, and domination inside capitalist institutions of productivity, while promising an alternative system of productivity and abundance which will eliminate these evils. If capitalism produces needs it cannot satisfy, socialism will satisfy the needs it creates. This version of socialist theory (or this strand within prevailing socialist theory) can usefully be seen as the last affirmation of capitalist idealism. It promises to reorder institutions and people so that historical priorities of capitalism can be met without generating the destructive relationships inherent in the present order.

One prominent American Marxist, Bertell Ollman, looks to a realizable communist society in which there is social ownership of production, elimination of bureaucracy, a marvelous expansion of productivity, making material goods 'as abundant as water is today,' social and economic equality, and freedom for everyone from 'external rules and . . . all forms of coercion.'[1] The citizen in this society appears as 'someone who is interested in and skillful in carrying out a variety of tasks, who is highly and consistently cooperative, who conceives of all objects in terms of "ours", who shares with others a masterful control over the forces of nature, who regulates his/her activities without the help of externally imposed rules, and who is indistinguishable from other persons when viewed from the perspective of existing social divisions.'[2]

In this society without shadows, productivity, abundance, freedom, and social coordination all reach their highest level. The capitalist aspiration to maximize freedom and productivity together is achieved to a degree unimaginable to capitalists because those capitalist institutions which impair the possibilities for social co-operation and productivity are transcended.

Let us ignore for now the suspicious absence of those shadows and hues which provide any picture with definition. For the sketch itself cannot be drawn by those who believe that institutions organized around the primacy of productivity must eventually generate consequences which impair reflective allegiance to the order. In this study the phrase 'civilization of productivity' has been used to identify particular dimensions of the institutions and priorities which mark American society and, more generally, to refer to *any* developed political economy in which productivity, growth, and material abundance assume overriding importance. A socialist society mobilized around these objectives will eventually generate its own dialectic of dissolution and disaffection, and the socialist state will then be under pressure to discipline those lacking the self-discipline required by the order.

The idea of socialism, on this alternative reading, deserves close examination not because it will be the perfect system of productivity. Rather, while contemporary capitalist and socialist systems are now mobilized around the pursuit of productivity, this priority is a systematic imperative of capitalism, and it may not emerge as such a compelling imperative within a well ordered socialist society. In the first system, the private appropriation of profit, market competition, the social infrastructure of consumption, and the dependence of the welfare state on the performance of the privately incorporated economy combine to produce awesome pressures in support of continued economic expansion. When austerity becomes necessary, it must be implemented in ways which do not undermine the engine of economic growth. It is thus imposed primarily on those least essential to the system of production.

These imperatives, if not breakable completely, might be tamed and moderated significantly in a society which sharply reduced the role of private profit and market competition, and which revised through public policy the established social infrastructure of consumption. But, given the crude vocabulary available to us in public discourse, such a political economy, because it is non-capitalist, is bound to be labelled socialist by its supporters and adversaries. There is no good reason to reject the label and one excellent reason to endorse it: the endorsement immediately raises questions about freedom which must be addressed by any socialist theory which hopes to be convincing.

My judgment is that while the trajectory of contemporary capitalist societies threatens to restrict freedom increasingly, and while contemporary socialist societies have already suffocated some of its essential expressions, there is a version of socialism not now instituted in practice which holds promise for the supporters of freedom. And inside that general thesis is a particular contention: while capitalist systems will necessarily institute programs of austerity in the coming decades to fulfill the growth imperative under adverse conditions, no capitalist system can do so without accelerating simultaneously the dialectic of dissolution and disciplinary controls. A capitalist economy on the road to socialism might be able to moderate these tendencies. It may be able to institute austerity equitably without expanding domination. The intuition and contention together provide the rationale for a reappraisal of the relation between socialism and freedom.

The first version of socialist theory, then, the one which promises to unite abundance, freedom, and cooperation, deflects attention from the distinctive advantage socialist theory may have in the last part of the twentieth century. Another version acknowledges indirectly the thesis to be explored here, even though it too diverts attention from it. Much of the attraction of the structural version of Marxist theory resides in its apparent ability to dissolve dilemmas which beset socialists in the humanist tradition. First, by placing agency at the level of structure and displacing the idea of the subject, it bypasses the issue of securing personal freedom in a socialist polity. If there are no agents capable of acting freely it is not necessary to appraise an order in terms of its support for the principle of freedom. Secondly, if the behavior of role-bearers is structurally determined in all orders, including the socialist order, the theorist does not have to worry too much about motivating people to bear new roles once the new mode of production is intact. The role-bearers, once the structure is in place, become the 'supports' of the structure. The problem of legitimacy (along with the associated issues of consent, allegiance, freedom, justice, and rationality) can be left to those humanists who have not escaped the subjective categories of bourgeois theory. Thirdly, if it appears that the constraints of the present order can be broken through revolutionary means, the advocates of structural theory are released from the burden of humanist objections to the human costs of such a break-through.

To a proponent of interpretive theory, construing the free subject to be an achievement possible only within the medium of inter-subjectively shared concepts, beliefs, and ideas, this technocratic theory of the Left must present a utopian and ruthless appearance. It is utopian in its understanding of the basis of social order and ruthless in the means it is willing to sanction to secure it. Within the particular interpretation offered in this text, the priorities of structural theory appear defective in another respect. For its theorists support the pursuit of productivity as an overriding objective of socialist society, failing to see how continued concentration on that pursuit in an advanced industrial society eventually accelerates dis-affection among a variety of role-bearers. If the first vision of socialism expresses a version of capitalist idealism, the structural theory of Marxism takes capitalist realism to its extreme point by eliminating moral objections to the introduction of social controls in the pursuit of productivity.

The strategic import of structural theory must be opposed from this alternative perspective. If revolution, defined as the violent, rapid, and wholesale transformation of a social order, succeeds, it destroys the settled background of common understandings and expectations within which citizens form intentions, respond to ex-pectations, reach agreements, and resolve conflicts. The rapid and thorough displacement of established social relations and norms of social coordination must thoroughly disorient participants and open them to coordination through authoritarian means. A critical theory with democratic aspirations, in acknowledging the intersubjective constitution of social relations, sets moral limits to the pace of change; the pace and scope of change must be adjusted to the imperative to maintain the medium of public understanding through which democratic politics proceeds. Similarly, if a serious revolu-tionary effort were to fail, it would release the potential within the present order for an escalation of repression and disciplinary con-trols from the Right. Althusser was correct in his assessment of humanists on the Left. They are not faithful and reliable members of the revolutionary movement.[3] But if the social epistemology of intersubjective theory is correct he was wrong nonetheless in his repudiation of humanism. Within this latter framework revolution must be viewed as the political expression of tragedy: it may be necessary to support revolution in the most extreme circumstances, but it cannot, in the short term, serve the ideals of humanists who endorse it. And the modes of social control revolutionary success and failure generate in the short term also discourage optimism about the long term.

Erik Olin Wright, writing broadly within the frame of structural theory, has recently examined the obstacles to a successful transition from capitalism to socialism.[4] He assumes that the immediate question is not how to achieve socialism but how to put socialism on the political agenda.

Wright identifies two sorts of obstacles. The first involves the hegemony of the capitalist class, its capacity 'to define ideologically what kinds of social alternatives are possible at a given moment.'[5] The second refers to the domination by that class, meaning its 'capacity to enforce a certain range of social alternatives regardless of whether people believe other alternatives are possible or not.'[6] Although the account of these two obstacles is often perceptive, the discussion of hegemony is deficient. It is not merely that Wright underplays the active involvement of the participants in the construction and defense of their own political interpretation, he also ignores the rationale within their active repudiation of the socialist alternative. Formally endorsing a theory which denies the capacity for freedom and reason to the human objects of inquiry, Wright slides over constitutive elements inside the obstacles he would comprehend.

Wright believes that a socialist movement should identify defects in programs developed within the limits of the established order; and these flaws must be linked publicly to structural limits unacknowledged by the proponents. The hope is that the eventual recognition of these limits by those asked to bear a disproportionate share of burdens will help to mobilize new support for a socialist movement. But such a demonstration, even if convincingly made, could not produce the political dividends sought by Wright. For if those so convinced continue to believe that socialism is an anthill – that a socialist economy must destroy the freedom, dignity, and diversity they prize – the demonstration will merely accelerate the dialectic of cynicism and corruption already in motion.

There is an uneven development in contemporary critical thought which generates adverse political consequences. While socialist critics deflate the pretensions of the advanced capitalist system, while they identify constraints, imperatives, and burdens unacknowledged by mainstream publicists, a growing body of citizens assimilates much of this critical understanding and rejects the affirmation of socialism to which it is connected. Constituencies which become resigned to a status quo they no longer believe can live up to humane standards embodied in its justifying rhetoric, will endorse an expansion of corruption, intimidation, and repression within the order. We have already seen that the commitment to freedom among these constituencies is so deep that they will struggle to save its appearance even when that forces them to obscure other features of their social condition. If these new impositions are thought to be necessary to maintain the order, and if the only known alternative is thought to suffocate more completely the freedom and dignity of ordinary people, the desire to preserve the only order we have will legitimize the escalation of repression within it. It is the rationale within this reaction which structural theorists fail to grasp, which they treat as merely the result of (structurally) limited experience and elite indoctrination. They therefore fail to grapple with the most potent forces sustaining belief in the priorities of the established order.

If the belief that socialism must expunge freedom could be challenged successfully many of the obstacles identified by Wright would still be operative. But the expanded sense of the possible would also encourage a series of progressive responses to political actualities.

First, intermediate programs, otherwise attractive, could no longer be frozen out of the established political agenda because they were said to represent another step on the slippery road to socialism. A party might call, for instance, for the nationalization of the major energy industries, promising to plow the profits back into research and the development of new forms of energy, thereby weakening the hold of a few companies and a few foreign countries on the domestic economy. It might develop a long-term program to revise the social infrastructure of consumption so as to break the inflationary cycle without imposing the worst effects of that break on the poorest and most insecure sections of the populace. Such intermediate programs could attract a broad constituency if they could be disconnected from the long-term spectre of socialist regimentation.

Secondly, a democratic socialist movement could help to define the moral limits of the tolerable within mainstream politics. To the extent that its intermediate proposals acquired initial credibility, official policies to expand disciplinary controls or to enforce austerity on the subordinate populace would face more serious resistance. A socialist movement which helped to define the limits of the acceptable in this way would make an impressive contribution indeed to contemporary politics.

Thirdly, a credible socialist movement could weaken the legitimacy of American military and intelligence interventions against socialist movements abroad. Because America is the military center of the western world, this internal limitation on foreign adventures could have world-wide significance. And the success of democratic socialism in another advanced capitalist system could mobilize new energies in the United States.

If a socialist movement achieved some success in these three ways it could hope to assume a more impressive role in American politics. Yet a necessary (though quite insufficient) condition of its success in these areas rests on the ability of socialists to establish a credible case for the compatibility between socialism and freedom. Such a case cannot be established merely through theoretical analysis. But that is an appropriate place to start. A preliminary task is to consider more sympathetically popular arguments against the compatibility of socialism and freedom. Perhaps inside the defects in these arguments we shall find a moment of truth which helps to explain their persuasive power. And perhaps that discovery will encourage us to adjust the ideal of socialism to incorporate this moment of truth.

The inquiry launched here is exploratory and incomplete. For one thing, it rests upon an assumption which will be taken for granted: Since there is no heaven on earth, every system of political economy will contain a particular set of limits inherent to it; every system will limit the freedom of the populace in some respects. An advanced capitalist system, for instance, (depending on the degree to which it is qualified by a positive state) will impose job insecurity on a class of workers, making them unfree to secure the work and self-respect they may desire. It supports a particular infrastructure of consumption which confines the range of consumer choices available. These are restraints on freedom because they significantly impair the ability to act on reflective choices, and because the impairments are the result of institutional priorities which could be reconstituted.[7] Similarly, a socialist system (depending on the degree to which it is qualified by market principles and private profit) will limit freedom to invest for private profit, to attain an income significantly higher than the average level, and to consume certain products which might be readily available in another system. The difficult and absorbing questions arise in assessing, first, the extent to which the structural limits of a particular system are justified by the freedoms and other worthy ends it supports and, secondly, the extent to which its attainable combination of virtues and limitations compares favorably with that attainable in other systems. Even John Locke appears to acknowledge this unavoidable characteristic of assessments of comparative freedom when he says, 'that ill deserves the name of confinement which hedges us in only from bogs and precipices.'[8]

The classical debate reconsidered

The criticisms of socialism advanced by classical liberals such as Milton Friedman and Frederick Hayek are quite familiar.[9] The central contention is as follows: since socialism goes against the grain of human nature, and since it requires binding policy decisions in areas where consensus is unlikely, any form that could work would necessarily undermine human freedom and any form that sought to institutionalize freedom could not work. Neither socialist theory nor socialist practice, they claim, has shown how this nexus between socialism and oppression could be broken. Milton Friedman is characteristically blunt in his charge:

None of the people who have been in favor of socialism and also in favor of freedom have made even a respectable attempt at developing the institutional arrangements that would permit freedom under socialism.[10]

Unfortunately for socialists, Frank Parkin, a sociologist with socialist commitments, has recently reached a similar conclusion after completing a comparative study of inequality in capitalist and Soviet bloc countries. His statement of the issues deserves close attention. First, commenting on the political obstacles to economic equality in a capitalist system, he says,

A political system which guarantees constitutional rights for groups to organize in defense of their interest is almost bound to favor the privileged at the expense of the disprivileged. The former will always have greater organizing capacities and facilities than the latter, such that the competition for rewards between different classes of persons is never an equal contest. . . . Given this fundamental class inequality in the social and political order, a pluralist or democratic structure works to the advantage of the dominant class.[11]

Parkin's critique of pluralism within a privately incorporated economy is familiar enough. But the other side of his argument is less comforting to the Left.

Egalitarianism seems to *require* a political system in which the state is able continually to hold in check those social and occupational groups which, by virtue of their skills or education or personal attributes, might otherwise attempt to stake claims to a disproportionate share of society's rewards. The most effective way of holding such groups in check is by denying them the right to organize politically or in other ways to undermine social equality.[12]

Equality requires socialism and egalitarian socialism seems to require the suppression of civil liberties. That is Parkin's conclusion. The challenge to socialist thought and practice, he intimates, is to show how these connections could be broken. But Parkin himself offers no further suggestions.

The two most common rejoinders to Parkin's challenge, each perceptive in its own way, fail nevertheless to face the issue squarely:

(1) The Soviet bloc states were constructed out of quasifeudal systems. The population was unprepared for modern life; the new experiment was threatened first by capitalist encirclement, then by fascist invasion. It continues to be confined by the imperatives of the cold war and by the heavy weight of institutions initially shaped in the most unfavorable circumstances. These arguments (and others like them) are of course quite true, but they are also inadequate. They do not suffice to establish the required counterfactual claim, namely that in the absence of these historically specific constraints the Soviet bloc countries could and would effectively institute and maintain equality and freedom within a socialist system.

(2) Parkin unreflectively accepts a defective ideal of freedom, an atomistic, individual ideal appropriate to classical libertarians such as Friedman and Hayek, but inappropriate to a socialist's understanding of human relationships. Once one adopts a social ideal of freedom the theoretical contradiction between freedom and equality will dissolve.

There is an important insight in this rejoinder. It is intimated by Marx in *On the Jewish Question*. The (classical) liberal, he says, thinks only of freedom for abstract individuals, of individuals emotionally separated from a complex web of community ties. The liberal's defining image is the individual 'separated from the community, withdrawn into himself, wholly preoccupied with his private interest, and acting in accordance with his private caprice.'[13] Against this conception of freedom for the abstract individual, Marx juxtaposes a communal ideal of freedom:

Human emancipation will only be complete when the real individual has absorbed into himself the abstract citizen; when . . . , in his everyday life, in his work, and in his relationships he has become a species being, and when he has recognized his own powers as social powers, so that he no longer separates his social abilitities from himself.[14]

Those who pretend that such a notion of freedom is completely alien to the American mind should consider the formulation of G. H. Mead who speaks of the person 'who takes over the institutions of the community into his own conduct' and of social institutions 'in which each individual would carry just the response in himself that he calls out in the community.'[15] My interpretation of conduct and practices in American society such as the ideology of sacrifice, patriotism, and the confinement of public debate to options currently available to the state, draws upon a theory of the relation between freedom and identification similar to this one in some respects and, as we shall see, dissimilar in others. If that interpretation is on the right track, it means that this conception of freedom makes contact with ideas implicit in American practices, ideas which have not been comprehended by formal, individualist readings of freedom.

The idea conveyed by the aphorisms of Marx and Mead is difficult to state precisely, but the central point is clear enough. Many of the laws, rules, competitive pressures, and conventional expectations encountered by individuals in capitalist (or individualist, or bourgeois) society as obstacles to be resisted, defeated or resigned to, can, when reconstituted within a communal setting, emerge as a set of norms and ideals internalized by the participants themselves. The community norms, because they embody mutual respect and reciprocity (equality), can become goals and projects voluntarily accepted by the individual. Through identification they become premises of action rather than obstacles to its success. They become one's own.

Even those remaining norms that individuals continue to see as posing limits to their conduct become different in texture from the constraints of bourgeois society. They become rules voluntarily accepted by individuals who correctly understand them to be essential to the community life they prize. The citizen exercises self-restraint with respect to these directives.

A society in which these two orientations to established norms was thoroughly developed, would, in this view, be perfectly free and fully legitimate: its individual citizens would identify freely and rationally with its rules and collective aspirations.

In this light, we can see more clearly how the socialist redefinition of freedom is thought to dissolve Parkin's dilemma. In Soviet society, it will be said, work is still instrumental and alien to the worker: he is still coerced to work. But in socialism as it can be, work relations will be embedded in social relations; work will be less an imposition externally imposed on each worker and more a voluntary (even though arduous) project launched with others in pursuit of collective goals. Similar arguments could be advanced for other dimensions of economic and political life in a socialist society.

This attempt to dissolve the theoretical problem, though penetrating in its recasting of the individualist idea of freedom, is still unsuccessful. It is almost as if those who had once been captured by the individualist notion of freedom are now dazzled by the alternative view and blinded to other dimensions and limits internal to that idea itself. And by failing to explore the limits of the alternative conception, they lend credibility to the critique of positive freedom already articulated by Isaiah Berlin: if the leaders in a collectivist society were to believe that 'the ends of all rational beings must of necessity fit into a single, universal, harmonious pattern, which some men may be able to discern more clearly than others,' then when recalcitrant groups resisted, the leaders would be tempted to coerce, manipulate, and terrorize them in the interests of 'educating' them to accept the established ends of the state.[16]

Marx was trying to perfect Rousseau's conception of freedom, but the attempt, while progressive in one respect, was implicitly regressive in another. Rousseau does speak of an ideal society – not likely to be realized – in which 'each associate though he becomes a member of the group, nevertheless obeys only himself, and remains as free as before.'[17] But he insists that the acceptance of community standards could not be treated as free acceptance unless the participants retained sufficient independence to ensure that they did not accept the standards out of weakness and dependence rather than strength and independence. Each of Rousseau's families (though the unit is notoriously unfree internally) possesses enough property to provide it with subsistence, not so much that it can buy the will of another. And this economic precondition of public life is essential to the *free* identification of the members with the standards of the community.[18] Marx, in seeing correctly the sphere of independence as one which impairs the individual's full identification with the collectivity, underestimated the importance of providing the institutional supports which would allow partial identification to be reflective. He saw the tension between independence and free identification but not the essential connection between them. He tried to dissolve, thereby, a tension within the theory and practice of freedom which is indissoluble.

Consider the slave who interprets himself as the master does, who agrees that he lacks the ability to make rational decisions or to live up to reasonable standards of conduct without external control, and who believes that he properly serves another who is naturally superior. One who thoroughly internalizes the slave mentality is thoroughly unfree, and any socialist would concur in that finding. But because the socialist articulation of the ideal of freedom in a socialist society pays insufficient attention to the difference between reflective and unreflective identification, the conception of freedom formally celebrated provides no warrant for this judgment. The ideal of freedom nullifies itself because it fails to articulate elements implicit within it. To correct itself it must either support a series of institutional preconditions for independent judgment and action, and explicitly give up the ideal of total identification with the order, or retain the latter ideal and lose the theoretical power to distinguish between indoctrination and reflective allegiance.[19]

There are at least three dimensions in an ideal of freedom appropriate to socialist aspirations. Each constitutes a part of, and a limit to, the others.[20] They stand together necessarily in a relation of interdependence and tension.

First, the social relations in the home, the workplace, and the community must embody, insofar as possible, that mutual respect and reciprocity that encourages people to develop as social beings, that allows each, if not always, at least often, to 'obey oneself' while responding to shared norms and objectives.

Secondly, the citizen must have a number of options available, options which allow each space to carve out a life in accordance with his own considered judgment.

Thirdly, the attainment by each of self-consciousness must be encouraged and fostered. For without self-consciousness, the selection of projects (as in 2 above) is impulsive rather than reflective, and the adaptation to collective norms (as in 1 above) assumes the form of passive acquiescence rather than considered acceptance.

The self-conscious person compares intentions embedded in previous actions to their actual consequences and then forms new purposes and goals in the light of that expanded knowledge. But since the assumptions and concepts within which one habitually thinks might limit that self-awareness, and since the assumptions readily available to the agent are likely to be those prevailing in the society, *self-consciousness requires access to alternative interpretive systems. That is how one becomes more fully aware of the possible limits to thought and action posed by one's own ideas.* Moreover, access to alternative interpretive systems requires an institutional setting that encourages free and open exploration of a variety of ideas. This space for exploratory thinking and open discourse necessarily places a strain upon the individual's natural (unreflective) identification with prevailing community norms.

Self-consciousness, not required in the more extreme formulations of an individualistic idea of freedom, gives life to the socialist idea. But it also sets limits to the socialist quest for consensus. It requires, for instance, educational institutions with some degree of autonomy in which alternatives to the established ways are explored actively, and it requires a set of protections for those who may pose challenges to established ways. We shall return to these requirements shortly.

It may seem unnecessary to remind Marxists of the importance of self-consciousness in the idea and practice of freedom, since Marx aspired to bring self-consciousness to the exploited and alienated members of capitalist society. But this appreciation of self-consciousness is not emphasized by Marxists when appraising actual socialist societies or discussing the ideal of socialism itelf; and this equivocation is most apparent in the failure to explore the institutional preconditions of self-consciousness in a socialist polity. When the idea is placed explicitly at the center of the ideal of freedom that equivocation can no longer persist. The disappearance of equivocation at this definitional level eventually generates the appearance of a liberal dimension in socialist theory.

The assumption of indefinite community

So far we have treated community and communal relations as though these forms could stretch indefinitely across political space. Those who think that socialism and freedom easily or spontaneously coalesce seem to assume too that the creation of community at the local level and the resolution of alienation in the workplace would thoroughly transform the relations between communities and between productive units within the same nation. On this reading, to use Marx's language, the communal bond would absorb the political tie; the abstract citizen would disappear and the real (communal) individual emerge.

The Assumption of the Indefinite Community, seldom stated explicitly, but forming the background of optimistic statements about the full and free identification of the citizen with the socialist polity, does not stand up to critical scrutiny. To see why it does not is to clarify the relationship between the citizen and the state in a socialist society; it is also to show why *institutional protection* of freedom for citizens within the socialist state is an imperative for any conception of socialism that would include a place for freedom.

We shall run a short thought experiment in the following pages in which the relevant variables are controlled in the direction of socialist aspirations. The purpose of controlling the variables in this direction is not to pretend that we could arrive there, but to show that even under highly favorable conditions, the assumption of indefinite community has to be modified significantly. Assume, then, that alienation is resolved in the workplace and that community relations are securely established within the localities that make up the state. Assume too, that the citizens are morally awakened and educated by the relationships nourished in the workplaces and communities. Our question: What then would be the nature of the tie across communities and between the citizen and the state? What bearing might the form taken by these political relations have on the problem of promoting freedom in a socialist polity?

In a socialist polity as large as a modern nation, the role of the state is expanded. It represents the society in foreign affairs; it replaces the market as the coordinator of relations among economic units; it is the agency that promotes those common objectives that no particular unit can pursue by itself alone. The activities of the socialist state are potentially more transparent to the citizens than are those of the welfare state in a capitalist system. The citizens know, for instance, that the prevailing distribution of burdens and benefits is subject, not to the impersonal imperatives of the market, but to priorities politically established by the state. If inequality prevails, it must now be justified, not as caused by events outside of the state's purview, but as the result of decisions and priorities consciously adopted by state officials. One side of the relation between the socialist state and its citizens, then, is this: since the state is the repository of collective aspirations and the preeminent medium through which collective goals can be crystallized and pursued consciously, the citizens tend to identify with each other through it. It is that part of us which acts upon history. It is the manifestation, the embodiment, of our collective freedom. The socialist citizen (in these circumstances) will surely be a patriot.[21]

But the bond between the citizen and the socialist state exhibits another side as well. The relations between communities, mediated by the state, and between the citizen and the state, are necessarily abstract. They are impersonal, distant, detached from direct and concrete experience. Though a patriot, the socialist person will necessarily display some of the features that Marx identified and criticized as characteristic of the abstract citizen.

Communal relations (at their best) are intimate, concrete, and transparent. The individual's understanding of local issues is derived from direct experience, his obligations are to others he knows or could readily know; the benefits of collective wisdom and the burdens of collective mistakes are shared concretely with others. But the political tie, across communities, is, at its best, indirect and distant; it is forged through elections, representation, and the play of group pressure within a shared set of aspirations. Just as the love relation cools when the intimate couple decides to spread its warmth around, so the bonds of community weaken as the space across which they stretch is extended.

Because the interests of a particular community (or group within it) are sometimes at odds with the public interest or justice, the citizen's concrete ties to work and living units will conflict sometimes with the more abstract tie to the entire system through the state. And yet, since the citizen's loyalty to the state is intense, even if abstract, the claims of other groups against it will sometimes be viewed with suspicion and distrust. The citizen will be tempted to identify with the state against the claims of others and with his community against the claims of the state. And the distant, abstract tie between the citizen and the state will make it more difficult to decide just when the weight of evidence and argument supports or overrides those inclinations. The citizen, as the recipient of opposing pressures, will often feel ambivalent, and the different relationship he bears to the sources of that pressure will make it difficult to resolve that ambivalence in a reasonable way.

The civic virtue nourished by the community, and encouraged by the state as the sphere of collective freedom, faces a continuing strain : within each person there is a conflict between the abstract responsibility of the citizen and the concrete obligations of the parent, worker, spouse, and neighbor. As Rousseau saw, only if the state were as small as the local community could these internal tensions be minimized. But that solution, if it ever was feasible, is not available today.

In summary, because the state is needed to promote the public interest and justice, because citizens will identify with it as the repository of collective aspirations and as the agent of collective freedom, because the bond between the citizen and the state is abstract and cannot be absorbed into the local, communal bond, and because the material resources and civic virtue the state requires to perform its legitimate tasks are great, the problematic of the state remains even in a well formed socialist polity. How can state officials retain enough space, skills, and patriotic support to accomplish just goals, while stopping them from converting these resources into instruments of selective repression? How can citizen judgment be informed and the state held accountable? How can the freedom of citizens be secured in a socialist state?

Some institutional revisions

My purpose has been to show how and why the interwoven problems of citizenship, the state, and freedom will not disappear in a socialist polity – even in a polity that escapes a series of specific constraints plaguing actual socialist states, and even when we revise the individualistic and egoistic assumptions about human nature that have informed mainstream criticisms of the socialist ideal. To establish that is to show that the American citizen's wariness of received socialist ideology, a wariness that persists even when the citizen has lost confidence in the old ways, has some basis in reason. It also supports the case for a reformulation of the socialist ideal to provide institutional support for the idea of freedom celebrated in its justificatory rhetoric. For unless the advocates of socialism revise its ideals to provide secure space for freedom, for freedom as socialists should conceive it, socialist criticisms of the prevailing order will merely contribute to wider acceptance of corrupted forms of the capitalist state.

There is no guarantee that a theoretically correct account could be made politically convincing to a wider public constituency, no certainty, to put it mildly, that those convinced could acquire sufficient political leverage to push the welfare state toward a socialist polity. But these uncertainties do not count against the theoretic project itself. If, for instance, socialists proved unable to convince themselves that these internal issues could in principle be resolved, that failure would provide a compelling reason to recast radical critiques of corporate capitalism.

I propose to offer some preliminary ideas about the terrain to be explored. My proposals assume that the space within which the needed institutional arrangements could be lodged and protected is to be provided by the partial autonomy retained by work units and local communities within the state, and by the state's corollary need to gain the voluntary assent of wide numbers of citizens if it is to generate sufficient civic virtue to define and pursue collective objectives. If this space seems insecure, it arguably need be no more so than its functional equivalents – the institutions of local government and private property – were in the heyday of capitalism. In each instance, the resilience of the requisite legal protections depends to some extent upon the belief, widely shared among participants, in the propriety of these institutions and upon the ability to limit economic growth sufficiently to allow them to remain intact. And in each case the institutions would wither if this complex of beliefs and abilities were to disappear.

A socialist polity in which the citizens were modestly self-conscious, in which their commitment to economic growth was tempered by a concern for decentralization, could be one favorable to the other institutional protections needed. Indeed, once (or if) the system was properly launched, the two forces would complement and strengthen one another: citizen self-consciousness would provide support for the needed institutional arrangements and the institutional arrangements would nourish citizen self-consciousness. The central problem, though not one unique to socialism, is how to set this affirmative dialectic into motion:

In order for a people still aborning to cherish sound principles of politics and consistently follow the basic rules deriving from reason of state, *effect would need to be capable of becoming cause*, and the social spirit that the laws are to produce would need to preside over their giving.[22]

The following sorts of institutional arrangements, then, seem to me to provide support for freedom within a socialist society possessing the general characteristics we have described. None of them could be very effective unless it operated in conjunction with the others.

(1) Every adult member must be guaranteed the right to a job with an income level sufficient to make ends meet, regardless of the particular political views the person holds.

(2) Educational institutions must be subject less to state control and more to the control of local communities and teachers. It is here that alien ideas will find expression if anywhere, and such ideas are required if the tacit assumptions and concepts internalized by children are to be rendered more explicit and amenable to critical scrutiny as young adults prepare to participate in public life.

(3) Since the abstract, political relation is one in which misinformation and manipulation can gain a foothold, especially if citizens already have a deep commitment to the state, it is imperative that publishing houses, the press, and other media retain some independence from direct state control. It may be best to preserve a modest market sector here, not in the name of economic efficiency but in the interests of freedom, allowing journals and books to escape direct state and community control. Indeed the market sector might be extended into other areas on similar grounds. The issue to be resolved in practice is: How far should market principles, which support inequality, be allowed in the interests of diversity?

(4) The difference between Stalinism and Nixonism turns less on the intentions of the two executives than on the fact that the

latter faced a judiciary that, with all its biases and limits, was relatively immune from direct executive control. An independent judiciary with constitutional protections is imperative in a socialist polity as well.

(5) The right of workers to strike must remain in a socialist polity. The state and local communities should be placed in a position where they must apply a mixture of pressure and persuasion to workers asked to accept new income or production policies. The right to organize and strike, even for workers who legally have the right to participate in the governance of production relationships, helps to ensure that the mix of state persuasion and pressure will incline in the direction of the former.

One could also explore other institutional supports. Electoral arrangements, the training and accountability of civil servants, modes of participation in economic and local political units – each of these practices, under the appropriate conditions, would deserve the closest attention. But unless and until socialism attains a place on the political agenda, detailed exploration of these questions remains premature; it would be too disconnected from specific historical constraints and opportunities to be illuminating. The initial task is to demonstrate *how and why the best historically imaginable socialist system as large as a nation would inevitably threaten freedom unless a range of institutional limits and corresponding revisions in the self-understanding of socialist citizens were introduced*. It is to encourage socialists to bring their critiques, strategies, and ideals closer to the experience of those who are to be served by these efforts.

Liberalism and socialism

The question can reasonably be posed: Is it possible, even at the level of theoretic speculation, to achieve such a synthesis of socialist and liberal ideals? My response will be tentative, concentrating more on the importance of the project and less on the probability of its success.

First, a socialist movement which does not draw selective sustenance from the liberal heritage internalized by some of the constituencies it must hope to engage is not only unpolitical, it has failed to grasp limits internal to the socialist idea itself. It is true that the constitutional protections of freedom in a socialist state would delay and limit the pursuit of other socialist priorities such as work reorganization, equality, environmental integrity, and the restoration of a measure of community life at the local level. Constitutionalism necessarily displays two sides: the arrangements that protect freedom and dissent also provide leverage to resist and delay progressive change. But to reject the negative side of constitutionalism is to affirm, and not just temporarily, an ideal of socialism which is intrinsically authoritarian.[23]

Secondly, the increasingly irrational relation between the welfare state and the privately incorporated economy promises to squeeze the space in which the most salutary elements within the liberal agenda can be pursued. The liberal who remains uncritical of the prevailing relation between the state and the economy must surely find little leverage to press for the effective protection of dissent, full employment, the reduction of inequality, and significant alterations in the infrastructure of consumption. The most worthy ideals of liberalism are jeopardized by a dialectic of dissolution and disciplinary control which progressively disconnects those ideals from the institutional means of their realization.

Liberalism is pulled by two sets of priorities, and the liberal strives to retain coherence between them. It seeks to support justice and freedom and to advance policy proposals which appear practical within the current order. But the commitment to practicality can, in some circumstances, be at odds with the commitment to freedom and justice; the two priorities can pull in opposing directions. Such a tension within liberalism is posed today by the growing disconnection between liberal ideals and the institutional means for their approximation. In these circumstances, the pull of practicality is likely to remain compelling to liberals who see no viable alternative worthy of their conviction. In the name of practicality, they will support programs to discipline those inessential to the political economy of productivity and to give new incentives to key constituencies strategically located within it. Once launched on this course they will eventually support institutional reforms to reduce the public accountability of the state administrative apparatus. For it would not be reasonable to expect state officials to be closely accountable to the same constituencies they must control. Liberals who see no promise in a reconstituted vision of socialism will increasingly be under pressure to interpret the proliferation of troubles and dislocations within the present order as symptoms of excessive democracy. The pull of practicality will weaken the commitment to democracy.

But as the nature of the options within liberalism becomes increasingly apparent, some liberals may be attracted to a version of socialism which takes liberal ideals seriously even while it reconstitutes them. They may be willing, because they recognize it to be unavoidable, to sacrifice a measure of immediate practicality to the pursuit of these more fundamental interests. One does not have to be optimistic about the prospects for a convergence of liberalism and socialism to believe that it represents the most rational course today for the advocates of democracy and freedom.

Shortly after escaping the barbarism of German fascism, Theodore Adorno commented on the ironic relation in which radicals stand to liberals in advanced capitalist democracies :

We owe our life to the difference between the economic framework of late capitalism and its political facade. To theoretic criticism the discrepancy is slight, everywhere the sham character of supposed public opinion, the primacy of the economy in real decisions, can be demonstrated. For countless individuals, however, the thin, ephemeral veil is the basis for their entire existence. . . . But is not the whole construction of essence and appearance thereby affected?[24]

This earlier assessment is pertinent to the different circumstances in which we now live. The defect in liberalism resides in its failure to see how thin democratic appearances can become and how the pursuit of liberal practicality in the existing system of political economy can help to thin them out. The defect in socialist criticism resides in its tendency to understate the importance of preserving these fragile appearances, in its hesitancy to acknowledge how they offer some protection for dissent and the most viable medium for efforts to make the real order more worthy of the reflective allegiance of its citizens. Each of these orientations, moreover, has something to say to the other concerning the idea of freedom and its institutional preconditions of existence. Implicit in the opposition between liberalism and socialism is the potential for constructive engagement. For each contains a moment of truth in need of acknowledgment by the other.

Notes to the text

Notes to chapter 1, 'The politics of political explanation',
pp. 7–40

1. This intellectual strategy of reversal is a constant theme in the work of Michel Foucault. Its point, usually, is to politicize a relationship which has not been construed through political categories. See, especially, *Madness and Civilization* (New York: Vintage Books, 1973) and *Discipline and Punish: The Birth of the Prison*, trans. Alan Sheridan (New York: Pantheon Books, 1977). Michael Shapiro, in *Language and Politics* (New Haven: Yale University Press, forthcoming), elucidates this aspect of Foucault's thought very cogently. My presentation of the politicization of disability is adapted from an example developed in detail by Shapiro.

2. In exploring the relation between political explanation and politics one might pay attention to: (1) the problematic relationship between theory and evidence; (2) the ways in which the concepts employed and the dimensions of variation recognized in a theory generate normative conclusions; and (3) the ways in which alternative social epistemologies, supporting different readings of human agency, differentially concentrate the attention of the theorist in explanation. These three concerns are interconnected, but in this essay I will concentrate on (3). Charles Taylor, 'Neutrality in Political Science' in Peter Laslett and W. G. Runciman (eds.), *Philosophy, Politics and Society* (Oxford: Basil Blackwell and Mott, 1967), has examined (2) closely. Two of my previous studies, *Political Science and Ideology* (New York: Atherton Press, 1967) and *The Terms of Political Discourse* (Lexington: D. C. Heath, 1974), represent attempts to come to grips with (2) and (1) respectively.

3. In exploring the *politics* of political explanation one need not limit oneself to implications which are necessary in one framework and not possible in another. Differences of degree are very significant in politics. If one theory clearly supports the view that a person guilty of a crime has the right to punishment while another theory is compatible with more than one finding in this area, this difference may carry important implications for political life.

4. Maurice Duverger, *Political Parties: Their Organization and Activity in the Modern State* (New York: John Wiley and Sons, 1954), p. 217.

5. Douglas Rae, *The Political Consequences of Electoral Laws* (New Haven: Yale University Press, 1967), p. 147. Rae says that a 'causal interpretation of the association falls upon several exceptions, the clearest of which are Canada and Austria. . . . Nevertheless, . . . the single member district is likely to contribute to the development and sustenance of two party systems. Other factors, such as regional minorities may reverse the condition as is the case in Canada,' (p. 143).

6. Jean K. Kirkpatrick, 'Changing Patterns of Electoral Competition' in Anthony King (ed.), *The New American Political System* (Washington, D.C.: American Enterprise Institute, 1978), pp. 284–5.

7. An excellent, brief account of the conceptual connection between the law-like model of explanation and the practice of technocratic politics is provided by Brian Fay, *Social Theory and Political Practice* (London: George Allen and Unwin, 1975). The discussion by Charles Taylor, 'The Explanation of Purposive Behavior' in Robert Borger and Frank Cioffi (eds.), *Explanation in the Behavioral Sciences* (Cambridge University Press, 1970), is pertinent in this respect and with respect to issues we shall discuss later. Taylor examines how the covering law model supports technical control by explaining 'correlations on one level' by those on a deeper level in a way which shows their relations to other possible outcomes' (p. 53).

8. Since it is part of my thesis, to be developed later, that most social scientists who adopt the law-like model as a guide are not fully aware of the structure and import of the ideal, it will be useful to review the positions of one of the philosophical authors of this model in the relevant areas. Karl Hempel, 'Rational Action in Norman S. Care and Charles Landesman (eds.), *Readings in the Theory of Action* (Bloomington: Indiana University Press, 1968), outlines positions on several key issues. (1) He says that 'to attribute to someone a particular belief or end in view is to imply that under certain circumstances he will tend to behave in certain ways which are indicative or symptomatic of his belief or end in view' (p. 293). A belief is 'basically dispositional in character,' though we now lack the precise theoretical system in which to specify its behavioral expression precisely. (2) To judge that an action is rational is to judge that '*in the light of the agent's beliefs*, his action constituted a reasonable or appropriate choice of means for the attainment of his ends' (my emphasis, p. 281). There is no reference here to appraisal of the rationality of the beliefs themselves. (3) 'To say that someone is rational is to attribute to him a complex bundle of dispositions' (p. 292). (4) 'In order to explain an action in terms of the agent's reasons, we need to know what the agent believed, but not necessarily on what grounds' (p. 283). In this sentence, and in some qualifications he later introduces to a dispositional analysis of 'rational,' Hempel opens the door to an account of belief, intention, rationality, and desire at odds with the requirements of the covering law model. That is perhaps the reason he closes the essay by looking toward a future explanatory framework for human behavior in which these concepts are displaced. 'I think it likely that the vague general procedure of explanation by reasons will gradually be replaced, at least in some areas, by the use of more specific explanatory hypotheses in which our standard notions of rationality play a less important role. . . . If such theoretical developments show that the explanatory power of the concept of rational action is in fact rather limited, we will have to accept this philosophically' (p. 304). Why? I suppose because that would be the rational thing to do.

9. My discussion of 'belief' is indebted to Stuart Hampshire who explores the relations between 'belief,' 'prejudice,' and 'thought' with the subtlety they require and who links this discussion to exploration of a variety of conative states such as desiring, craving, wanting, wishing, hoping, etc. See Stuart Hampshire, *Freedom of the Individual* (Princeton: Princeton University Press, 1965), especially ch. III. See also Bernard Williams, *Problems of the Self* (Cambridge: Cambridge University Press, 1973), ch. IX.

10. The first premise is defended in chs. 3 and 6.

11. Evidence to support this view is found in those conceptual analyses of 'power' geared to its use within the covering law model. They deflate distinctions among various ways of getting another to do what the other would otherwise not do. Distinctions between persuasion, manipulation, unconscious identification, coercion and conditioning are minimized in such analyses, and where they are made, the rationale for doing so is not clearly provided. For a debate which exhibits the contrasting tendencies in this respect between interpretive and covering law theorists see Felix Oppenheim, 'Power Revisited,' *Journal of Politics* (Fall, 1978), pp. 589–608, with a response by Terence Ball, *ibid.*, pp. 609–19 and a reply by Oppenheim, *ibid.*, pp. 620–1.

12. See Wilson Bryan Key, *Media Sexploitation* (New York: The New American Library, 1976). The title of the book is a symptom of the disease it diagnoses.

13. A superb account of how many notions shared by participants in our society describe from a moral point of view, and how acceptance of the particular rules governing these concepts implicitly endorses a particular moral point of view, can be found in Julius Kovesi, *Moral Notions* (London: Routledge and Kegan Paul, 1967). An application of these themes to political vocabularies is provided in William E. Connolly, *The Terms of Political Discourse* (Lexington: D. C. Heath, 1974). Chapter 3 of that text examines the specific set of concepts noted here.

14. For an account of the relation between universal laws and probabilistic laws which is consistent with that given here see Fay, *Social Theory and Political Practice*, ch. II, Alasdair MacIntyre, 'Is a Comparative Science of Politics Possible?' in his *Against the Self Images of the Age* (New York: Schocken Books, 1971), and May Brodbeck, 'Explanation, Prediction, and Imperfect Knowledge' in her *Readings in the Philosophy of the Social Sciences* (New York: Harcourt Brace, 1968).

15. According to findings reported in a British journal, *Nature*, this protein was found in 64.3% of a sample of people with depressive diseases, a much larger proportion than found in a control group. *New York Times*, 7 January 1979, p. E7.

16. See Wilfred Sellars, 'Philosophy and the Scientific Image of Man,' in his *Science, Perception and Reality* (New York: Humanities Press, 1963), p. 25. A less favorable reading is to be found in Donald Davidson, 'Philosophy and Psychology' in Jonathan Glover (ed.), *The Philosophy of Mind* (London: Oxford University Press, 1976). A valuable summary of Sellars' argument, especially of its implications for social science, is available in Richard J. Bernstein, *The Restructuring of Social and Political Theory* (New York: Harcourt Brace Jovanovich, 1976). Compelling rebuttals of the view that such a doctrine must undermine the foundations of an interpretive social science are to be found in Stuart Hampshire, 'A Kind of Materialism' in his *Freedom of Mind* (Princeton: Princeton University Press, 1971) and Charles Taylor, 'The Explanation of Purposive Behavior,' in Borger and Cioffi, *Explanation in the Behavioral Sciences*.

17. Hampshire, 'A Kind of Materialism' p. 21. Hampshire goes on to argue, persuasively, I believe, that any self-consistent materialism will necessarily include the very capacities for reflexivity and rationality which its traditional supporters are out to eliminate. Otherwise the materialist doctrine itself could not be understood as a claim to knowledge rather than a mere effect of deeper causes. Hampshire constructs *a kind of* materialism materialists traditionally have striven to repudiate.

18. In juxtaposing these cases it is not my purpose to examine the issues surrounding the relations between conscious and unconscious desires or beliefs. It is

probably true that the results of primary repression, occurring before the child has complex concepts, are in principle less available to consciousness than are the ingredients of secondary repression. Moreover, a 'structural' reading of unconscious processes, whereby the repressed material (or the material originally located in the unconscious) is governed by rules inconsonant with the rules of conscious thought (e.g., suspension of the law of non-contradiction, timelessness), renders unconscious materials less available in principle to consciousness. But this theoretical assumption of insulation between the two levels, if highly developed, bears other theoretical implications too. For now it is difficult to see how the unconscious can have specific effects, mediated by *particular* ideas, at the conscious level. Finally, Freud did not expect the mere recognition of unconscious motives, in most cases, to dissolve the motive and the conduct attached to it, but he did think that such recognition could justify further therapeutic efforts to reduce the previous control of the unconscious in some ways. Reflexivity makes some difference, even if it is, in some cases, reconciliation to aspects of the self not susceptible to further alteration. Otherwise therapy would not be a form of healing.

19. Peter Winch, 'Understanding a Primitive Society' in Bryan Wilson (ed.), *Rationality* (Oxford: Oxford University Press, 1970).
20. I. C. Jarvie, 'Understanding and Explanation in Sociology and Social Anthropology,' in Borger and Cioffi, *Explanation in the Behavioral Sciences*, p. 237, my emphasis.
21. *Ibid.*, p. 237.
22. *Ibid.*
23. *Ibid.*, p. 238.
24. Winch, 'Understanding a Primitive Society,' p. 91, my emphasis.
25. *Ibid.*, p. 100.
26. *Ibid.*, p. 100, my emphasis.
27. So much for the view that Winch refuses to criticize a way of life. He sometimes does criticize ours. I read Winch to be prepared to appraise a practice as irrational once we have understood the point of view from which it is formed. And, in an essay reviewing earlier criticisms of his work, Winch himself sanctions such a reading. His argument, he says, 'is not *absurdly*, that ways in which men live together can never be criticized, nor even that a way of living can never be characterized as in any sense "irrational"; still less do I argue . . . that men who belong to one culture can "never understand" lives in another culture.' Peter Winch, *Ethics and Action* London: Routledge and Kegan Paul, 1972), p. 3.
28. Among the extensive literature on Winch's thesis I find the following to be most helpful: Martin Hollis, 'Reason and Ritual,' Steven Lukes, 'Some Problems about Rationality,' and Alasdair MacIntyre, 'The Idea of a Social Science,' all in Bryan Wilson (ed.), *Rationality*; MacIntyre, 'Rationality and the Explanation of Action,' in his *Against the Self Images of the Age*; and Kai Nielson, 'Rationality and Relativism,' in *Philosophy of Social Sciences* (1974), pp. 313–31. The essays by Hollis, Lukes, and MacIntyre make points against Winch, but they also, in my judgment, misinterpret his argument to some degree. They treat him as repudiating universal criteria of rationality, when I think he accepts some such set of criteria and finds them, taken alone, insufficient to guide conduct and judgments of rationality. Nielson's interpretation of Winch is closest to my own, though he does not ask how Winch would or should *explain* the irrationalities recognizable within his version of interpretative theory.

29. My reading of Hegel is influenced by accounts which emphasize the affinities to more recent versions of interpretive theory; the authors seem to me to make a very powerful case. See Richard Norman, *Hegel's Phenomenology: A Philosophical Introduction* (Sussex: Sussex University Press, 1975); Charles Taylor, *Hegel* (Cambridge: Cambridge University Press, 1975); Taylor, 'The Opening Arguments of the Phenomenology,' in Alasdair MacIntyre (ed.), *Hegel* (New York: Anchor Books, 1972). Jurgen Habermas provides some extremely interesting arguments along similar lines, along with the judgment that Hegel does not escape the dilemma of epistemology he himself identifies. See *Knowledge and Human Interests*, trans. Jeremy Shapiro (Boston: Beacon Press, 1971).

30. Pertinent here is Martin Hollis' reminder of what we must presuppose if we are to communicate with 'Other Minds' in other societies with sufficient specificity to allow us to understand, justify, or criticize their way of life 'internally.' The interpreter says to himself, 'I assume the Other Mind to be a rational man. I take it that his beliefs are, on the whole, rationally connected and that, usually, his utterances express his beliefs. I take it that he uses words as tokens governed by the rules of their type and that literal sense informs the stock from which the richest patterns are wrought. I take it that he seeks to make himself understood, recognizing that verbal arabesques are mere sound, if they destroy the sense of stock. So, when I hit on an apparent translation which would show him not to be a rational man *überhaupt*, I reject the translation. Language . . . is a way of uttering thoughts, with the intention of being understood. To grasp the rules, I must break the circle only by imputing rationality.' Martin Hollis, *Models of Man* (Cambridge: Cambridge University Press, 1977), pp. 152–3.

31. G. W. F. Hegel, *The Phenomenology of Spirit*, trans. A. V. Miller (Oxford: Clarendon Press, 1977), p. 124.

32. *Ibid.*, p. 125.

33. The specific arguments provided by Winch are certainly more subtle, but the structure of the argument fits this distillation. Sometimes the discrepancy is between presuppositions X makes about oneself and formal explanations at odds with them; sometimes it is between the formal characterization of concepts employed in inquiry and the rules actually followed in the deployment of those concepts. The sense of Winch's overall strategy is captured in this statement: 'I want to show that the notion of a human society involves a scheme of concepts which is logically incompatible with the kinds of explanation offered in the natural sciences.' Peter Winch, *The Idea of a Social Science* (London: Routledge and Kegan Paul, 1958), p. 72.

34. My argument does not imply that we can always be certain that the charge of irrationality (or illegitimacy, unjustifiability, etc.) is correct. For there are many occasions where the available arguments and counter-arguments leave space for two or more contenders. One must recognize that, while recognizing as well that each of the contenders, including oneself, must make some judgments of rationality/irrationality in social inquiry, even if they are held with more or less confidence depending on the array of arguments available. I have argued, in *The Terms of Political Discourse*, that such judgments are unavoidable in social theory and that once made they set the agenda of questions in need of further explanation within that framework. Recognition that the claims in one's theory outstrip the evidence and argument in support of them should affect the *way* one holds a theory, but not the *extent* to which it is developed. Failure to develop its full implications because it is uncertain simply increases the extent to which it

remains unsusceptible to critical scrutiny. Some forms of tolerance and judiciousness, and some ways of expressing uncertainty, cover more insidious forms of dogmatism and intolerance. The problematic relationship between theory and evidence in interpretive theory is discussed in ch. 3 of this volume, in the context of appraising a particular interpretation of American politics.

35. This shift from understanding to explanation, because of irrationalities in the established understandings of participants, is examined by Alasdair MacIntyre, in 'Rationality and the Explanation of Action,' in his *Against the Self Images of the Age*, pp. 244–59.

36. They are also reached, as earlier discussed, each time we have access to relevant knowledge not available to the participants, e.g., that lead pans, because of chemical reactions unknown to the populace, poison their food.

Notes to chapter 2, 'The underdetermination of subjects by structures', pp. 41–62

1. The target of much of this discontent is not merely capitalism but a set of priorities and imperatives attached to any civilization of productivity. That point is explored in chapters 3 and 7.

2. I use the phrase 'structural theory' to distinguish this mode of theory from the structuralism of Claude Levi-Strauss. For a thoughtful discussion, to which I am indebted, of various interpretations of the idea of a structure in social theory see Steven Lukes, 'Structure and Power' in his *Essays in Social Theory* (Cambridge: Cambridge University Press, 1977).

3. Louis Althusser, *Essays in Self Criticism*, trans. Ben Brewster (London: New Left Books, 1976), p. 173.

4. I refer to such works as Andre Gorz, *Socialism and Revolution* (Garden City, New York: Anchor Books, 1973), essays by Jurgen Habermas, T. A. McCarthy, and Charles Taylor in Paul Connerton (ed.), *Critical Sociology* (New York: Penguin Books, 1976), and Jean-Paul Sartre, *Search for a Method*, trans. Hazel Barnes (New York: Vintage Books, 1963). An introduction to the intersubjectivist form of explanation can be found in Brian Fay, *Social Theory and Political Practice* (London: George Allen and Unwin, 1975).

5. Louis Althusser and Etienne Balibar, *Reading Capital*, trans. Ben Brewster (London: New Left Books, 1970), p. 180, Althusser's emphasis.

6. *Ibid.*, p. 180, Althusser's emphasis.

7. *Ibid.*, p. 218, Balibar's emphasis.

8. Althusser, *Essays in Self Criticism*, p. 86, Althusser's emphasis.

9. *Ibid.*, pp. 87–8, Althusser's emphasis.

10. Neither the list of elements nor the connections is always consistent. Althusser's list of elements shifts from personal activity, object of labor and means of labor (*Reading Capital*, p. 170) to object of labor, means of labor and labor power (*ibid.*, p. 173) as to labor power, direct laborers, masters, objects of production, instruments of production, etc. (*ibid.*, p. 176). The connections are comprised once by the labor process and the social relations of production (*ibid.*, p. 170) and in another place by property, possession, disposition, enjoyment, community, etc,' (*ibid.*, p. 176). Althusser defers to Balibar for a theoretical analysis of the concept of 'combination' (*ibid.*, p. 177). Balibar's list of elements is composed of laborer, means of production – which includes both the object of labor and the means of

labor, and the non-laborer; for Balibar these same elements are linked into a 'single combination, i.e., to the structure of a single mode of production by two connections: the property connection and the real or material appropriation connection' (*ibid.*, pp. 214–15).

11. The four preceding quotations are from *Reading Capital*, pp. 171, 175, 176 and 215, respectively, Althusser's emphasis.

12. Althusser, *Reading Capital*, p. 212, Balibar's emphasis. The International Publishers' edition of *Capital*, trans. Samuel Moore and Edward Aveling (New York, 1967) has 'unify' where Balibar translated 'combine.' It uses the word 'unity' for Balibar's 'combination.' Other differences in translation that stand out include Balibar's 'eternalizes' for the International Publishers' 'reproduces' (*Reading Capital*, p. 269), Althusser's 'articulated combination' (*Reading Capital*, p. 64) for 'order' in *Grundrisse* (London: Penguin, 1976), p. 107, and 'connection established historically' (*Reading Capital*, p. 98) for 'historic position' on p. 108 in *Grundrisse*. For an even more pronounced difference compare Althusser's quotation from Marx on p. 191 of *Essays in Self Criticism* with the standard English translation.

13. Althusser, *Reading Capital*, p. 173, Althusser's emphasis.

14. *Ibid.*, pp. 185 and 179, Althusser's emphasis.

15. *Ibid.*, p. 237, Balibar's emphasis.

16. Marx, *Capital*, I, 173. This quotation is examined thoughtfully by Lucio Colletti, *From Rousseau to Lenin*, trans. John Merrington and Judith White (New York: Monthly Review Press, 1972), pt I.

17. Marx, *Capital*, I, 169.

18. Louis Althusser, *For Marx* (New York: Vintage Books, 1970).

19. *Ibid.*, p. 233.

20. *Ibid.*, p. 234, Althusser's emphasis.

21. *Ibid.*, p. 232, original is italicized.

22. *Capital*, I, 79 and 80.

23. There is a gap between Althusser's promise of a theory of ideology and his delivery of it. Althusser says that ideology constitutes subjects, and that they cannot comprehend the theory which explains this constitutive process. But he never actually shows how this process works. Instead, he argues that the repressive and ideological state apparatuses *function* to keep role-bearers bearing their roles. The question remains for Althusser: How does ideology constitute a subject, creating a framework of concepts and practices within which they are *necessarily* confined?

24. One can try to *reduce* the 'humanist' ingredients in this sketch to another set or to displace them with a more basic set. But, first, Althusser has not sought to do this; it would implicate him in a range of disputes he has sought to avoid. Secondly, the most impressive efforts to move in these directions represent, even in the eyes of their advocates, *possibilities* for future analysis; we presently lack the ability to explain complex conduct in such terms. Thirdly, such attempts must explain why role-bearers without the capacity, say, for autonomy require ideologies which recognize that capacity. Fourthly, attempts to displace such concepts and assumptions threaten the rational credential of the explaining agent. What is the status of the theory if such claims are true universally? What is the effect if the agents, having capacities not unlike the theorist, come to comprehend themselves as the theorist does and to take that account into consideration in forming future projects? These are issues structural theory must confront once its need for an anthropology is acknowledged and its resistance to humanist anthropologies reaffirmed. For a useful statement of some of these

issues see Richard Bernstein, *The Restructuring of Social and Political Theory* (New York: Harcourt Brace Jovanovich, 1976). The limits set by reflexive capacities to materialist philosophies of mind are discussed by Stuart Hampshire in 'A Kind of Materialism' in his *Freedom of the Mind* (Princeton: Princeton University Press, 1971), pp. 210–31.

25. For a complementary treatment of reciprocal connections between production relations, community life, and forms of consumption, see Marshall Sahlins, *Culture and Practical Reason* (Chicago: University of Chicago Press, 1976).

26. These arguments are developed more extensively in Michael Best and William E. Connolly, *The Politicized Economy* (Lexington: D. C. Heath, 1976), especially ch. 3.

27. Althusser, *Essays in Self Criticism*, p. 205, Althusser's emphasis. In this later text Althusser continues to theorize the participants as role-bearers. Thus he says 'Marx did not enter into this analysis (of superstructural relations), except in the form of a few brief remarks. But from everything that he said we can conclude that these relations too treat concrete human individuals as "bearers" of relations, as "supports" of functions, to which men are only parties because they are held within them. Thus legal relations abstract from the real man in order to treat him as a simple "bearer of the legal relation", as a simple subject of law, capable of owning property, even if the only property he possesses is that of his naked labour power. Thus too political relations abstract from the living man in order to treat him as a simple "support of the political relation", as a free citizen, even if his vote only reinforces his servitude. And thus too the ideological relations abstract from the living man in order to treat him as a simple subject either subjected to or rebelling against the ruling ideas. But all these relations, each of which uses the real man as its support, nevertheless determine and brand him in their flesh and blood, just as the production relation does.' *Ibid.*, pp. 203–4. The ambiguity in the new version of Althusser's theory emerges here. For now he says that it is capitalism which 'reduces' (*ibid.*, p. 203) the workers to role-bearers. And the question emerges, from what level of achievement are they reduced? If Althusser were to address this question, the firm refusal to introduce anthropological assumptions into theory would be challenged. But he does not address it.

28. Louis Althusser, *Lenin and Philosophy*, trans. Ben Brewster (New York: Monthly Review Press, 1971), p. 22.

29. *Ibid.*

30. *Ibid.*

31. *Ibid.*

32. Althusser, *Essays in Self Criticism*, p. 38, Althusser's emphasis.

33. *Lenin and Philosophy*, p. 18, Althusser's emphasis.

34. *Essays in Self Criticism*, p. 107, Althusser's emphasis.

35. Albert Camus, *The Rebel* (New York: Vintage Books, 1960), p. 294.

36. In the period between the first draft of this chapter and its final preparation for publication we came across the new text by by E. P. Thompson, *The Poverty of Theory* (London: Merlin Press, 1978), published in the United States by Monthly Review Press. His extended critique of Althusserian theory and its political implications complements and extends the argument here.

Notes to chapter 3, 'Appearance and reality in politics', pp. 63–89

1. The recent debates over Peter Winch's arguments in *The Idea of a Social*

Science (London: Routledge and Kegan Paul, 1958) explore these issues. Winch himself did not consistently support the relativist position attributed to him, but the critiques do point out weaknesses in such a relativism. See the collection by Bryan Wilson (ed.), Rationality (Oxford: Oxford University Press, 1970) as well as several chapters in Alasdair MacIntyre, *Against the Self Images of the Age* (New York: Schocken Books, 1971).

2. The interpretation at this first level is indebted directly to the study of Richard Sennett and Jonathan Cobb, *The Hidden Injuries of Class* (New York: Random House, 1973). Sennett and Cobb themselves reject theories of false consciousness, arguing that the ideology of the worker is a self-creation and not imposed on him from above. I will concur with the view that it is a self-creation and dissent from the conclusion that this makes false consciousness an impossibility. The Sennett–Cobb study has been widely criticized because the method they employ is closer to a *dialogue* with the respondent than a *survey* of their attitudes. Such methodological critiques, are unfounded. Taken seriously, they would make it impossible to inquire into the depth interpretations of any segment of the population. Of course these methods run the risk of introducing biases into the findings. But the proper approach here is not to perfect and thus sterilize the interview instrument but to devise a series of indirect tests. Does the ideology of sacrifice emerging out of these dialogues help to render intelligible modes of conduct which seemed mysterious before this background interpretation was present? If so, we have impressive evidence that the interpretation uncovered through dialogue actually enters into the self-interpretation of the respondents. To criticize these methodological critiques of the Sennett–Cobb study is to repudiate not the quest for evidence but rather its narrow confinement to the instrument of survey analysis.

3. It is not my intention now to show why these changes are implied by a successful program to reduce inequality and provide job security for everyone. Michael Best and I have offered such arguments in *The Politicized Economy* (Lexington: D. C. Heath, 1976). More immediately to the point, the new version of Liberalism to be examined later in this study now concedes that such objectives are not attainable within the prevailing institutional structure.

4. My argument at this point is indebted to the analyses by Jurgen Habermas in *Legitimation Crisis*, trans. Thomas McCarthy (Boston: Beacon Press, 1973) and Charles Taylor, 'Interpretation and the Sciences of Man,' *The Review of Metaphysics* (Spring, 1971), pp. 4–51.

5. Charles Taylor puts the point this way: 'The notion of a horizon to be attained by future greater production verges on the absurd in contemporary America. Suddenly the horizon which was essential to the sense of meaningful purpose has collapsed, which would mean that like so many other enlightenment dreams, the free productive, bargaining society can only sustain man as a goal, not as a reality.' 'Interpretation and the Sciences of Man,' p. 43.

6. This escalation of pressure for positions in law, medicine, and college teaching occurred even when high-paying jobs were more available in business, accounting, and public bureaucracies.

7. This analysis does not make reference to the earlier wrenching of people from the land to fill the cities and the factories. My argument does not presuppose that people once ran eagerly from the country to the city. But once in the city for a few generations the abstract goals of the civilization of productivity begin to take hold. The differences between the United

States and European countries in this respect would play a central role in any theory designed to compare and contrast their modes of development, and, particularly, the comparative rates of skepticism and resistance to that development.

8. The pressures for an expansion of Taylorism and the extensive inroads already made in this direction are examined effectively in Harry Braverman, *Labor and Monopoly Capital* (New York: Monthly Review Press, 1974).

9. This second point is argued extensively in the next chapter.

10. Theodore Adorno, *Minima Moralia*, trans. E. F. N. Jephcott (London: New Left Books, 1974), p. 233.

11. Daniel Bell, in *The Cultural Contradictions of Capitalism* (New York: Basic Books, 1977), interprets the revolt of the 1960s as a new hedonism generated by the success of capitalism itself. He misses, I contend, the deeper disaffection inside that revolt, misconstruing the difficulties in formulating it and giving it concrete political expression within the established order as a manifestation of irrationalism on the part of the disaffected. His text is critically examined in ch. 5.

12. This finding remains intact even when it is acknowledged that the low quality, availability, or pertinence of any particular account may make its general influence negligible. One is tempted to say that the general likelihood of political indoctrination increases proportionately with the tendency amongst political intellectuals to obscure this intrinsic feature of political reflection and discourse. Very general, epistemological orientations set a framework for practical political judgment which is not neutral. For an excellent, short defense of this thesis, see Brian Fay, *Social Theory and Political Practice* (London: George Allen and Unwin, 1975).

13. See Peter Strawson, 'Freedom and Resentment' in his *Studies in the Philosophy of Thought and Action* (New York: Oxford University Press, 1968), pp. 71–96. Habermas, *Legitimation Crisis*, pt III. The import of Strawson's effort for political theory is discussed in William E. Connolly, *The Terms of Political Discourse* (Lexington: D. C. Heath, 1974), chs. 2 and 6.

14. Numerous examples of such shifts in the controlling rules and analogies are to be found in Jonathan Glover (ed.), *The Philosophy of Mind* (Oxford University Press, 1976). The collected essays deal with pertinent issues such as the criteria of psychoanalytic interpretation (B. A. Farrell), self-deception (Patrick Gardiner), roles and self-consciousness (Gerald Cohen), the expression of feelings (Stuart Hampshire), and personal identity (Derek Parfit).

15. Stuart Hampshire, *Thought and Action* (New York: The Viking Press, 1959), p. 67. A philosophy of mind and a social theory are properly viewed as mutually enabling and restraining modes of thought. If a social theory projects a complex anthropology in which unconsciousness, pre-conscious, conscious, and self-conscious levels of thought and action are recognized, its claims are increasingly subject to revision and adjustment by the conceptual distinctions required to *distinguish* between these levels and the *connections* required to support the assumption that, to some degree, ideas can move from one level to another. I believe that an interpretive theorist can do no better than to start with Hampshire's study. My own thinking on these questions, in particular on the role of a modified version of the transcendental argument, has been clarified through discussions with Alan Montefiore and Charles Taylor.

16. Though the specification of anthropological limits was not the central focus of this essay, perhaps I should note that I do not hold that the self can

become fully transparent to the agent or that we can anticipate a society in which all dimensions of life are transparent to the participants. Such a recognition, if it is correct, must be built into any formulation of a socialist ideal of political life, modifying some of the hopes conveyed by Marxist readings of socialist politics. This conclusion is not an abridgement of the view advanced in this essay, but grows out of the philosophy of mind providing it with its conceptual foundations. Here again, Stuart Hampshire is illuminating: 'More of human conduct than we had thought, and aspects of it that we had not expected, may be outside the possible control of practical reason; less of human conduct than we had thought may flow from an unalterable natural endowment.' *Thought and Action*, p. 254.

17. The Roman historian Livy, quoted by Hegel in *The Philosophy of History*, trans. J. Sibree (New York: Dover Publications, 1956), p. 277.

Notes to chapter 4, 'The public interest and the common good', pp. 90–119

1. Ernest Klieck, quoted by Herbert Marcuse in *Negations* (Boston: Beacon Press, 1968), p. 3.
2. John Stuart Mill, *Considerations on Representative Government* (New York: The Liberal Arts Press, 1958), p. 25.
3. *Ibid.*, pp. 18–19.
4. Ronald Dworkin, 'Liberalism' in Stuart Hampshire (ed.), *Public and Private Morality* (Cambridge: Cambridge University Press, 1978), pp. 113–43.
5. *Ibid.*, p. 126.
6. *Ibid.*, p. 121.
7. *Ibid.*, p. 127.
8. *Ibid.*, p. 130.
9. *Ibid.*, p. 141.
10. *Ibid.*, p. 137.
11. Charles L. Schultze, *The Public Use of Private Interest* (Washington, D.C.: The Brookings Institution, 1977), pp. 17–18.
12. Michel Foucault, *Discipline and Punish: The Birth of the Prison*, trans. Alan Sheridan (New York: Pantheon Press, 1977), p. 193. Readers of Tocqueville will recall how he anticipated the process which we are examining here.
13. Schultze, *The Public Use of Private Interest*, p. 79.
14. *Ibid.*, pp. 67, 73.
15. *Ibid.* p. 90.
16. Jean Jacques Rousseau, *On The Social Contract: With the Geneva Manuscript and Political Economy*, ed. Roger D. Masters, trans. Judith Masters (New York: St Martin's Press, 1978), p. 160.
17. The most sophisticated version of this theory of the public interest is developed by Brian Barry, 'The Public Interest,' *Proceedings of the Aristotelian Society*, vol. 38 (1964), pp. 1–18, and *Political Argument* (New York: Humanities Press, 1965). It is not clear to me, though, just how narrow or broad the concept of citizenship is supposed to be in Barry's theory. I presuppose a narrow conception here to bring out the necessity for a broad one.
18. Ludwig Wittgenstein, *Zettel*, ed. G. E. M. Anscombe and G. H. von Wright, trans. G. E. M Anscombe (Berkeley: University of California Press, 1970), p. 78.
19. Rousseau himself says this in *The Government of Poland*, trans. Wilmoore Kendall (New York: Bobbs-Merrill, 1972).

20. The way in which a shared set of concepts help to constitute a way of life and in which contests over aspects of those concepts is an essential ingredient in politics is explored more closely in William E. Connolly, *The Terms of Political Discourse* (Lexington: D. C. Heath, 1974). The first set of issues is discussed brilliantly by Julius Kovesi, *Moral Notions* (London: Routledge and Kegan Paul, 1967).

21. There are many issues to be explored here. Stuart Hampshire discusses most of them in *Thought and Action* (New York: The Viking Press, 1959). I return to them in the last chapter.

22. Marx, 'On a Proposed Divorce Law' in L. D. Easton and K. H. Guddat (eds.), *The Young Marx on Philosophy and Society* (New York: Anchor Books, 1967), pp. 139–40, emphasis in text.

23. *Ibid.*, p. 140.

24. That is not to say it would be adopted. For if the dialectic of dissolution had proceeded very far the path of least resistance would be to adopt compromises which ignored the claims of those not actively included in the political process – children. My point here is not to ask what extent the politics of the common good is possible in our society, but to ask how it would appear if it were feasible.

25. Rousseau, *Political Economy*, in Masters (ed.), *On The Social Contract, With Geneva Manuscript and Political Economy*, p. 221.

Notes to chapter 5, 'Some theories of state crisis', pp. 120–50

1. C. Wright Mills, *The Power Elite*, (New York: Oxford University Press, 1956). For an early discussion of the 'pluralist–elitist' debate which is confined within these terms see William E. Connolly, *Political Science and Ideology* (New York: Atherton Press, 1967).

2. The most interesting study of all in my judgment is Jurgen Habermas, *Legitimation Crisis*, trans. Thomas McCarthy (New York: Beacon Press, 1973). I do not examine his work here, limiting my consideration to texts written with special reference to the American setting. The particularities which define each country support the case for theories which carefully take the specific features on a single society seriously. I am, however, certainly indebted to the Habermas study. I summarize that debt, and certain areas of disagreement, in a review essay in *History and Theory* (Fall, 1979).

3. Theodore Lowi, *The End of Liberalism* (New York: W. W. Norton, 1968).

4. *Ibid.*, p. 19.

5. *Ibid.*, p. 9.

6. *Ibid.*, p. 259.

7. *Ibid.*, p. 304.

8. *Ibid.*, p. 306.

9. *The End of Liberalism* (second edition) (New York: W. W. Norton, 1979), p. 291.

10. *Ibid.*, p. 292.

11. *Ibid.*, p. 293.

12. James O'Connor, *The Fiscal Crisis of the State* (New York: St Martin's Press, 1973).

13. James O'Connor, *The Corporations and the State* (New York: St Martin's Press, 1974), p. 6.

14. These themes are developed in greater detail in the following texts: Habermas, *Legitimation Crisis*; Fred Hirsch, *The Social Limits to Growth*

(London: Routledge and Kegan Paul, 1977); and Michael Best and William E. Connolly, *The Politicized Economy* (Lexington: D. C. Heath, 1976).

15. O'Connor, *Fiscal Crisis of the State*, p. 226.
16. *Ibid.*, title page.
17. Daniel Bell, *The Cultural Contradictions of Capitalism* (New York: Basic Books, 1976).
18. *Ibid.*, p. 71.
19. *Ibid.*, p. 84.
20. *Ibid.*, p. 282–3, emphasis in text.
21. In my discussion of hedonism I will not explore the connection to its clinical cousin, narcissism. Christopher Lasch discusses this phenomenon in *The Culture of Narcissism* (New York: W. W. Norton, 1978). The new, paradigmatic case in therapy, he says, diverges from the classic guilt-ridden and rigid individual. The new symptoms typically include 'a putative shallowness in emotional relations . . . fantasies of omnipotence and a strong belief to exploit others and be gratified' projected by a person who is 'ravenous for admiration but contemptuous of those he manipulates into providing it' (pp. 37–8). The symptoms are rooted in 'feelings of oral deprivation originating in the pre-oedipal stage of psychic development' (p. 37). No member of a university faculty can miss examples of this phenomenon; it may require only a glance in the bathroom mirror. A thorough account of hedonism, as well as narcissism, would show how the syndrome is rooted in a particular structure of family relationships and cultivated by its normative acceptance by the wider society as belief wanes in the credibility of the social future available. I will focus here primarily on the second dimension, even while acknowledging that it is integrally interwoven with the first. Lasch's study is quite illuminating, but he too exaggerates the scope of the phenomenon. To treat the culture exclusively through these clinical categories is to deny the possibility of a democratic political response to the social conditions behind the symptoms. It reduces the political to the therapeutic and suggests a 'politics' in which elites must manipulate psychic energies to adapt behavior to larger agendas.
22. G. W. F. Hegel, *The Phenomenology of Spirit*, trans. A. V. Miller (Oxford: Clarendon Press, 1977), p. 218. What follows is inspired by Hegel's account of hedonism, though it does not follow it strictly.
23. *Ibid.*, p. 65.

Notes to chapter 6, 'Personal identity, citizenship, and the state', pp. 151–72

1. Ludwig Wittgenstein, *The Blue and Brown Books* (Oxford: Basil Blackwell, 1968), pp. 104–5.
2. Godfrey Vesey, *Personal Identity* (New York: Cornell University Press, 1974), p. 11.
3. Mary Douglas, *Purity and Danger*, (London: Routledge and Kegan Paul, 1966).
4. *Ibid.*, pp. 168–9.
5. Midge Decter, 'Looting and Liberal Racism,' *Commentary* (September 1977), p. 48.
6. *Ibid.*, p. 54.
7. The media polls are summarized in Robert Curvin and Bruce Potter, *Blackout Looting* (New York: Gardner Press, 1979). See especially the Introduction and the last chapter.

8. *Ibid.*, p. 200.
9. *Ibid.*, p. 194.
10. *Ibid.*, ch. 9.
11. *Ibid.*, p. 190.
12. Lucio Colletti (ed.), *Early Writings: Marx* (London: Penguin Books, 1975), pp. 401–20.
13. *Ibid.*, p. 408.
14. *Ibid.*, pp. 411, 412.

Notes to chapter 7, 'Socialism and freedom', pp. 173–94

1. Bertell Ollman, *Social and Sexual Revolution: Essays on Marx and Reich* (Boston: South End Press, 1979), p. 75. When writing the first draft of this essay in 1975 for delivery at a meeting of the Southern Political Science Association I wanted to bring out some implicit dimensions in the ideal of socialism which socialists themselves should criticize. Almost all of the features which I thought remained implicit, because they could not withstand the light of day, are now explicitly articulated by Ollman. This image of socialism, because it is so incredible, contributes to the refusal of most people to take the image seriously. Or rather they take it seriously as a threat and not as an ideal.

2. *Ibid.*, p. 89. We are told that there is no need for social rules or even self-restraint because the society is transparent to all and because each citizen loves all others. We are not told whether they are capable of intimacy (an exclusive relation), and if so whether they must sometimes become jealous; whether they die or fear death; why their commitment to some people or principles will never interfere with their commitment to others, and so on.

3. A structural theorist may, of course, opt for a non-revolutionary strategy on the basis of purely strategic considerations; he may not, though, do so on moral grounds. It is the moralism of the humanist which the structuralist holds in contempt.

4. Erik Olin Wright, *Class, Crisis and the State* (London: New Left Books, 1978). I believe that Wright's actual explanation of crisis tendencies in advanced capitalism implicitly goes beyond the epistemological straitjacket he endorses. But the philosophical commitment to structural theory (see the introductory chapter) nonetheless takes its toll in his understanding of prevailing ideology and of the sources of resistance to socialism.

5. *Ibid.*, p. 248.

6. *Ibid.*

7. The conception of freedom I am working with is developed and defended in my *The Terms of Political Discourse* (Lexington: D. C. Heath, 1974), ch. 4. Those characteristics most pertinent to the question of the relation between socialism and freedom will be delineated later in this chapter.

8. John Locke, *The Second Treatise of Government* (New York: Bobbs-Merrill, 1952), p. 32.

9. Milton Friedman, *Capitalism and Freedom* (Chicago: University of Chicago Press, 1962); Frederick Hayek, *The Road to Serfdom* (Chicago: University of Chicago Press, 1944).

10. Friedman, *Capitalism and Freedom*, p. 19.

11. Frank Parkin, *Class Inequality and Political Order* (New York: Praeger, 1971), pp. 181–2.

12. *Ibid.*, p. 183.

13. Quoted from Robert Tucker (ed.), *The Marx–Engels Reader* (New York: W. W. Norton, 1972), p. 41.
14. *Ibid.*, p. 44.
15. Anselm Strauss (ed.), *The Social Psychology of George Herbert Mead* (Chicago: University of Chicago Press, 1958), p. 39.
16. Isaiah Berlin, *Two Concepts of Liberty* (Oxford: Clarendon Press, 1958), p. 39.
17. Jean Jacques Rousseau, *The Social Contract*, trans. Willmoore Kendall (Chicago: Henry Regnery, 1954), p. 18.
18. There are many issues which would have to be confronted in a thorough comparison of Marx and Rousseau on this question. Whether, for instance, Rousseau's commitment to force dissidents to be free takes back what was given with the property condition. Are the citizens forced to abide by the law on the familiar ground that the rule of law is a precondition of freedom or forced to believe that the law is true? I am interested here with what Rousseau gives to independence, not with those tendencies in his thought to take it back. One interesting text which provides the more liberal reading of that phrase 'forced to be free' is Stephen Ellenburg, *Rousseau's Political Philosophy: An Interpretation From Within* (Ithaca: Cornell University Press, 1976). There is a further complexity in the dialogue between Rousseau and Marx. Marx celebrated self-consciousness without worrying much whether a measure of independence was one of its essential preconditions, while Rousseau provided a measure of independence while trying to limit the scope for self-consciousness. I will support a theory of freedom in which a measure of independence and the pursuit of self-consciousness are celebrated, and in which the partial identification with larger purposes can thereby become reflective.
19. This theoretical defect contributes to the practical inability on the part of some western socialists to distinguish indoctrination from reflective identification in communist systems. It discourages critical examination, for instance, of this analogy enunciated by Khruschev: 'As an orchestra conductor sees to it that all the instruments sound harmonious and in proportion, so in social and political life does the Party direct the efforts of all people toward achievement of a single goal.' Quoted in Charles Lindblom, *Politics and Markets* (New York: Basic Books, 1977), p. 258.
20. These dimensions of freedom are developed more closely in my *The Terms of Political Discourse*, ch. 5–6, and Steven Lukes, *Individualism* (New York: Oxford University Press, 1973), chs 19–20. The most profound exploration of the relation between self-consciousness (or reflexivity) and freedom is to be found in Stuart Hampshire, *Thought and Action* (New York: The Viking Press, 1959). Those with socialist aspirations who also prize the ideal of self-consciousness can attain a deeper sense of the implications of their own aspirations, and especially of its social conditions of existence, from a close study of this text.
21. My thinking on the nature of the bond between the citizen and the state and on the institutional arrangements needed to nourish and protect freedom within that relationship is immediately indebted to Paul Ricoeur, 'The Political Paradox' in Hwa Yol Jung (ed.), *Existential Phenomenology and Political Theory* (Chicago: Henry Regnery, 1972), pp. 337–67. The larger influence is Rousseau, who understood that since the bonds of community cannot be stretched very far, large states require institutional arrangements that would be detrimental in small states: 'What, gentlemen,' he asked those who wished to write a new constitution for Poland, 'is the business you

are about? Reforming the government of Poland, which is to say: giving to the constitution of a large kingdom the stability and vigor of that of a tiny republic. You should first ask yourselves, before laboring to accomplish that purpose, whether your efforts can possibly be successful.' Jean Jacques Rousseau, *The Government of Poland*, trans. Willmoore Kendall (New York: Bobbs-Merrill, 1972), p. 25.

22. Rousseau, *The Social Contract*, ed. Roger D. Masters (New York: St Martin's Press, 1978), p. 61.

23. There are only three routes, as I see it, for the socialist who would reject some form of constitutionalism. One could try to show that the bonds of community life could be extended to encompass the space of the modern nation-state. One could try to show how an indefinitely large number of homogeneous and self-sufficient communities could coexist, unthreatened by the nation-states remaining in the world. One could expunge freedom from the socialist ideal, justifying the system in terms of the material discipline, material welfare, and security it promotes. To state my objection in a few words: the first view is a mindless daydream; the second a dangerous utopia; and the third a lapse into barbarism.

24. Theodore Adorno, *Minima Moralia*, trans. E. F. N. Jephcott (London: New Left Review, 1974), pp. 112–13.

Bibliography

Adorno, Theodore. *Minima Moralia*. Translated by E. F. N. Jephcott. London: New Left Books, 1974.

Althusser, Louis. *Essays in Self Criticism*. Translated by Ben Brewster. London: New Left Books, 1976.

For Marx. New York: Vintage Books, 1970.

Lenin and Philosophy. Translated by Ben Brewster. New York: Monthly Review Press, 1971.

Althusser, Louis and Etienne Balibar. *Reading Capital*. Translated by Ben Brewster. London: New Left Books, 1970.

Barry, Brian. *Political Argument*. New York: Humanities Press, 1965.

'The Public Interest,' *Proceedings of the Aristotelian Society*. Vol. 38, 1964.

Bell, Daniel. *The Cultural Contradictions of Capitalism*. New York: Basic Books, 1977.

Berlin, Isaiah. *Two Concepts of Liberty*. Oxford: Clarendon Press, 1958.

Bernstein, Richard. *The Restructuring of Social and Political Theory*. New York: Harcourt, Brace Jovanovich, 1976.

Best, Michael, and William E. Connolly. *The Politicized Economy*. Lexington: D. C. Heath, 1976.

Braverman, Harry. *Labor and Monopoly Capital*. New York: Monthly Review Press, 1974.

Brodbeck, May. 'Explanation, Prediction, and Imperfect Knowledge.' In *Readings in the Philosophy of The Social Sciences*. Edited by May Brodbeck. New York: Harcourt Brace, 1968.

Camus, Albert. *The Rebel*. New York: Vintage Books, 1960.

Colletti, Lucio, ed. *Early Writings: Marx*. London: Penguin Books, 1975.

From Rousseau To Lenin. Translated by John Merrington and Judith White. New York: Monthly Review Press, 1972.

Connerton, Paul, ed. *Critical Sociology*. New York: Penguin Books, 1976.

Connolly, William E. 'The Critical Theory of Jurgen Habermass.' *History and Theory*. Fall 1979, pp. 397–416.

Political Science and Ideology. New York: Atherton Press, 1967.

The Terms of Political Discourse. Lexington: D. C. Heath, 1974.

Curvin, Robert and Bruce Potter. *Blackout Looting*. New York: Gardner Press, 1979.

Davidson, Donald. 'Philosophy and Psychology.' In *The Philosophy of Mind*. Edited by Jonathan Glover. London: Oxford University Press, 1976.

Decter, Midge. 'Looting and Liberal Racism.' *Commentary*. September 1977, pp. 48–54.

Douglas, Mary. *Purity and Danger*. London: Routledge and Keegan Paul, 1966.

Duverger, Maurice. *Political Parties: Their Organization and Activity in the Modern State.* New York: John Wiley and Sons, 1954.

Dworkin, Ronald. 'Liberalism.' In *Public and Private Morality.* Edited by Stuart Hampshire. Cambridge: Cambridge University Press, 1978.

Ellenburg, Steven. *Rousseau's Political Philosophy: An Interpretation From Within.* Ithaca: Cornell University Press, 1976.

Fay, Brian. *Social Theory and Political Practice.* London: George Allen and Unwin, 1975.

Foucault, Michel. *Discipline and Punish: The Birth of the Prison.* Translated by Alan Sheridan. New York: Pantheon Books, 1977.

Madness and Civilization. New York: Vintage Books, 1975.

Friedman, Milton. *Capitalism and Freedom.* Chicago: University of Chicago Press, 1962.

Glover, Jonathan, ed. *The Philosophy of Mind.* Oxford: Oxford University Press, 1976.

Gorz, Andre. *Socialism and Revolution.* Garden City: Anchor Books, 1973.

Habermas, Jurgen. *Knowledge and Human Interests.* Translated by Jeremy J. Shapiro. Boston: Beacon Press, 1971.

Legitimation Crisis. Translated by Thomas McCarthy. Boston: Beacon Press, 1973.

Hampshire, Stuart. *Freedom of the Individual.* Princeton: Princeton University Press, 1965.

Freedom of the Mind. Princeton: Princeton University Press, 1971.

Thought and Action. New York: The Viking Press, 1959.

Hayek, Frederick. *The Road to Serfdom.* Chicago: University of Chicago Press. 1944.

Hegel, Georg Wilhelm Friedrich. *The Phenomenology of Spirit.* Translated by A. V. Miller. Oxford: Clarendon Press, 1977.

The Philosophy of History. Translated by J. Sibree. New York: Dover Publications, 1965.

Hempel, Karl. 'Rational Action.' In *Readings in the Theory of Action.* Edited by Norman S. Care and Charles Landesman. Bloomington: Indiana University Press, 1968.

Hirsch, Fred. *The Social Limits to Growth.* London: Routledge and Kegan Paul, 1977.

Hollis, Martin. *Models of Man.* Cambridge: Cambridge University Press, 1977.

'Reason and Ritual.' In *Rationality.* Edited by Bryan Wilson. Oxford University Press, 1970.

Jarvie, I. C. 'Understanding and Explanation in Sociology and Social Anthropology.' In *Explanation in the Behavioral Sciences.* Edited by Robert Borger and Frank Cioffi. Cambridge: Cambridge University Press, 1970.

Key, Bryan Wilson. *Media Sexploitation.* New York: The New American Library, 1976.

Kirkpatrick, Jean K. 'Changing Patterns of Electoral Competition.' In *The New American Political System.* Edited by Anthony King. Washington, D.C.: American Enterprise Institute, 1978.

Kovesi, Julius. *Moral Notions.* London: Routledge and Kegan Paul, 1967.

Lasch, Christopher. *The Culture of Narcissism.* New York: W. W. Norton, 1978.

Lindblom, Charles. *Politics and Markets.* New York: Basic Books, 1977.

Locke, John. *The Second Treatise of Government.* New York: Bobbs-Merrill, 1952.

Lowi, Theodore. *The End of Liberalism.* New York: W. W. Norton, 1968. Second edition, 1979.

Bibliography

Lukes, Steven. *Essays in Social Theory*. Cambridge: Cambridge University Press, 1977.

　Individualism. New York: Oxford University Press, 1973.

　'Some Problems About Rationality.' In *Rationality*. Edited by Bryan Wilson. Oxford: Oxford University Press, 1970.

MacIntyre, Alasdair. *Against the Self Images of the Age*. New York: Schocken Books, 1971.

Marcuse, Herbert. *Negations*. Boston: Beacon Press, 1968.

Marx, Karl. *Capital: A Critique of Political Economy*. Vol I. Translated by Samuel Moore and Edward Aveling. New York: International Publishers, 1967.

　'Critical Notes on the Article "The King of Prussia and Social Reform. By a Prussian." ' In *Early Writings: Marx*. Edited by Lucio Colletti. London: Penguin Books, 1975.

　'On a Proposed Divorce Law.' In *The Writings of The Young Marx on Philosophy and Society*. Edited by L. D. Easton and K. H. Guddat. New York: Anchor Books, 1967.

Mill, John Stuart. *Considerations on Representative Government*. New York: The Liberal Arts Press, 1958.

Mills, C. Wright. *The Power Elite*. New York: Oxford University Press, 1956.

Montefiore, Alan, ed. *Philosophy and Personal Relations*. London: Routledge and Kegan Paul, 1973.

Nielson, Kai, 'Rationality and Relativism.' *Philosophy of the Social Sciences*. Spring 1974, pp. 313–31.

Norman, Richard. *Hegel's Phenomenology: A Philosophical Introduction*. Brighton: Sussex University Press, 1975.

O'Connor, James. *The Corporations and The State*. New York: St Martin's Press, 1974.

　The Fiscal Crisis of the State. New York: St Martin's Press, 1973.

Ollman, Bertell. *Social and Sexual Revolution*. Boston: South End Press, 1979.

Oppenheim, Felix. 'Power Revisited' and 'Power: One More Visit.' *Journal of Politics*. Fall 1978, pp. 589–608 and 620–1.

Parkin, Frank. *Class Inequality and Political Order*. New York: Praeger, 1971.

Rae, Douglas. *The Political Consequences of Electoral Laws*. New Haven: Yale University Press, 1967.

Ricouer, Paul. 'The Political Paradox.' In *Existential Phenomenology and Political Theory*. Edited by Hwa Yol Jung. Chicago: Henry Regnery, 1972.

Rousseau, Jean Jacques. *The Government of Poland*. Translated by Willmoore Kendall. New York: Bobbs-Merrill, 1972.

　On the Social Contract: With the Geneva Manuscript and Political Economy. Translated by Judith Masters. Edited by Roger Masters. New York: St Martin's Press, 1978.

Sahlins, Marshall. *Culture and Practical Reason*. Chicago: University of Chicago Press, 1976.

Sartre, Jean-Paul. *Search For a Method*. Translated by Hazel Barnes. New York: Vintage Books, 1963.

Schultze, Charles. *The Public Use of Private Interest*. Washington, D.C.: The Brookings Institution, 1977.

Sellars, Wilfred. *Science, Perception and Reality*. New York: Humanities Press, 1963.

Sennett, Richard and Jonathan Cobb. *The Hidden Injuries of Class*. New York: Random House, 1973.

Shapiro, Michael. *Language and Politics*. New Haven: Yale University Press forthcoming.

Strauss, Anselam, ed. *The Social Psychology of George Herbert Mead.* Chicago: University of Chicago Press, 1958.

Strawson, Peter. 'Freedom and Resentment.' In *Studies in the Philosophy of Thought and Action.* Edited by Peter Strawson. New York: Oxford University Press, 1968.

Taylor, Charles. 'The Explanation of Purposive Behavior.' In *Explanation in the Behavioral Sciences.* Edited by Robert Borger and Frank Cioffi. Cambridge: Cambridge University Press, 1970.

   Hegel. Cambridge: Cambridge University Press, 1975.

   'Interpretation and The Sciences of Man.' *Review of Metaphysics.* Spring 1971, pp. 4–51.

   'Neutrality in Political Science.' In *Philosophy, Politics and Society.* Edited by Peter Laslett and W. G. Runciman. Oxford: Basil Blackwell and Mott, 1967.

   'The Opening Arguments of the Phenomenology.' In *Hegel.* Edited by Alasdair MacIntyre. New York: Anchor Books, 1972.

Thompson, E. P. *The Poverty of Theory.* London: Merlin Press, 1978.

Tucker, Robert, ed. *The Marx-Engels Reader.* New York: W. W. Norton, 1972.

Vesey, Godfrey. *Personal Identity.* New York: Cornell University Press, 1974.

Williams, Bernard. *Problems of the Self.* Cambridge: Cambridge University Press, 1973.

Wilson, Bryan, ed. *Rationality.* Oxford University Press, 1970.

Winch, Peter. *Ethics and Action.* London: Routledge and Kegan Paul, 1972.

   The Idea of A Social Science. London: Routledge and Kegan Paul, 1958.

   'Understanding a Primitive Society.' In *Rationality.* Edited by Bryan Wilson. Oxford: Oxford University Press, 1970.

Wittgenstein, Ludwig. *The Blue and Brown Books.* Oxford: Basil Blackwell, 1968.

   Zettel. Translated by G. E. M. Anscombe and edited by G. E. M. Anscombe and G. H. von Wright. Berkeley: University of California Press, 1970.

Wolin, Sheldon. 'Political Theory as a Vocation.' In *Machiavelli and the Nature of Political Thought.* Edited by Martin Fleisher. New York: Atheneum, 1972.

   Politics and Vision. Boston: Little, Brown, 1960.

Wright, Erik Olin. *Class, Crisis and the State.* London: New Left Books, 1978.

Index

accountability
  dual nature of, 165–8, 190
Adorno, Theodore, 82, 193
advertising
  and manipulation, 20–1, 39
affirmative action, 106–8
affluence, the pursuit of, 130–2
  see also civilization of productivity
allegiance: *see* legitimacy
Althusser, Louis
  and humanism, 44–7, 176–7
  and ideology, 49–52
  and the mode of production, 46–7
  and the subject, 45–6, 55–6, 202
  self-critique of, 58–62
anti-abortionism
  interpretation of, 32–3
anti-humanism
  and Althusserian theory, 44–7, 58–60
appearance
  alterations in, 138–9
  as constituting reality, 63–6, 82–3
  and personal identity, 54–6, 66,
    67–70, 163–5
articulation
  of disaffection, 54–5, 82–4, 162–4,
    168–70

bachelorhood
  the contestability of, 106
Balibar, Etienne, 46
belief
  and conduct, 26–7, 54–7
  and personal identity, 66, 67–70, 153–6
  and rationale, 37–9
  and reflexivity, 14–16, 38–40
  and self-interpretation, 68–70
  and social relations, 70–2
  the two dimensions, 14–15
Bell, Daniel, 121, 142–5, 147–50
Berlin, Isaiah, 183

Camus, Albert, 61, 92
cause and effect
  in social relations, 24–6
citizenship
  the abstract character of, 182, 187–8
  and the common good, 91–2, 113–19
  and personal identity, 165–6
  and the state, 3, 155–6, 165–8
civic virtue
  and the dialectic of dissolution, 103–8
  the dilemma of, 188–9
  and liberalism, 95–6, 97–8
  and self-consciousness, 92–3
  see also common good
civilization of productivity
  and hedonism, 142–7
  and legitimacy, 136–9, 188–9
  and personal identity, 154–6
  as the common good, 70–1, 163–6
  declining allegiance to, 71–2, 136–9,
    162–3
  repressive tendencies in, 79–80,
    103–8, 141–2, 149–50, 171–2
  the structural dimension of,
    77–9
class
  the injuries of, 67–9
common good
  and civilization of productivity,
    71–3, 163–6
  the conception of, 90, 91, 111–12
  and equality, 118
  and Fascism, 92
  and institutional life, 96
  and liberalism, 97–8
  and self-interest, 116–17
  see also public interest
community, limits to, 186–8
consumption
  the social infrastructure of, 56–8,
    97–8, 130–2, 148–50

contradiction
  and social life, 57–8, 128–31
counterfactuals
  in political inquiry, 9, 14, 66–7
Curvin, Robert, 158–9

death
  hedonist view of, 146
Decter, Midge, 157–60
delegitimation
  indirect expressions of, 134–5,
    139–40, 162–4, 168–70
  see also legitimacy
disability, 7
disaffection
  and civilization of productivity,
    70–5, 137–9, 144–7
  and hedonism, 142–5
  and the welfare state, 168–9
  its political articulation, 54–5, 82–4,
    162–4, 168–70
dispositionals, 14
Dostoevski, Fyodor
  and the underground man, 164
Douglas, Mary, 153–4
Duverger, Maurice, 9–10
Dworkin, Ronald, 95–7

economy
  sectors of, 127–9, 135–6
egalitarianism
  and the common good, 118
  and freedom, 181
elections, 10–17, 134–5
environment
  and the public interest, 103–4
epistemology
  the dilemma of, 34–5
explanation
  as interpretation, 13–18, 30–3,
    35–9, 56–8
  of irrationality, 37–9, 199
  the law-like model of, 10–14, 19–22,
    23–5
  the politics of, 1, 8, 18–21, 28,
    38–40, 58–60, 84–9
  two dimensions of, 26

false consciousness, 114, 203
family
  and the common good, 115
Fascism, 92
Foucault, Michel
  and individualization, 100

freedom
  and personal identity, 73–5, 154–6,
    163–5, 182–3
  and political interpretation, 165–8
  and way of life, 96–7
  the dimensions of, 184–6
  the individualistic theory of, 181–2
  Rousseau's view of, 209
free rider, the, 91, 101–2, 103–7
Friedman, Milton, 180

gender
  contestability of, 106–7
general will, 109
Gorz, André, 42, 43

Habermas, Jurgen, 49, 206
Hampshire, Stuart, 26, 88–9, 196, 204
Hayek, Frederick, 180
hedonism
  and the civilization of productivity,
    139, 142–7
Hegel, G. W. F., 34–6, 52, 145–7
Hempel, Karl, 196
Hollis, Martin, 199
humanism
  and moral limits, 176–7
  and structural theory, 44–6

identification
  and freedom, 182–5
  and personal identity, 172
  and social structure, 154–6
ideology
  and theory, 49–52
  end of, 121
  function of, 53
  of sacrifice, 66, 76, 83–4
individualization
  and regimentation, 100, 108–9
inflation
  sources of, 128–32
interpretation, 4
  and personal identity, 68–70, 111,
    137–9, 153–6
  and politics, 38–40, 83–5
  and rationality, 28–32, 36–8, 199
  and the structural dimension, 56–8,
    65, 77–9
  and the subject, 19, 176
  and test procedures, 85–9, 203
  criticisms of, 24–6, 34–8, 39–40, 84–5
intersubjective relations, 54–6, 71–2,
    79–80, 84–5, 137–9

irrationality
  and social ends, 71–2
  in social practices, 28–33, 35–8,
    73–6, 79–80

Jarvie, I. C., 28–31
juridical democracy, 124–5

Kirkpatrick, Jean, 10

legitimacy, 135
  and intersubjective relations, 70–1,
    73–6, 136–9
  and self-consciousness, 92–4
  and the welfare state, 126–7, 128–9,
    136–9, 189–91
  thin theory of, 133–4, 136, 138
Lele, the, 153–4
liberalism
  the circle of, 97–100
  and civic virtue, 94–5
  and the civilization of
    productivity, 80–3
  and regimentation, 94–7
  and socialism, 191–3
  and welfare state, 95–7, 122–3
  interest group, 123–4
  the two priorities of, 192–3
life-styles
  and institutional forms, 97–8
Locke, John, 180
looting, 157–9
Lowi, Theodore, 121
  and interest-group liberalism, 123–4
  and juridical democracy, 124–5
  and legitimacy, 141–2
  on capitalism, 122
  on citizenship, 127–8

McCarthyism, 36–7
manipulation
  and persuasion, 64–5
market
  and the state, 99–100, 167
  politicization of, 99–101, 127–9
Marx, Karl
  and abstract citizen, 182–3
  on divorce, 115–16
  on elections, 100–2
  on labor power, 49
Marxism
  and structural theory, 45–7, 175–6
  and theory of state, 121, 127–30
Mead, G. H., 182

Mill, John Stuart, 94–5
Mills, C. Wright, 120
mind
  and mechanism, 25–6
  and social theory, 204
mode of production
  as structure, 45–8

narcissism, 207
nature
  orientations to, 30, 76–7, 153–6
New Left, 5, 42, 75–7

O'Connor, James, 121
  and theory of state, 128–31
  and thin theory of legitimacy, 137–
    40
Ollman, Bertell, 173–4

Parkin, Frank, 180–1
party competition, 9–13, 160–1, 164–6
patriotism, 166–7
pauperism, 160–1
personal identity, 151–6
  and beliefs, 38–40
  and citizenship, 165–7
  and disaffection from welfare state,
    168–72
  and freedom, 73–5, 153–6, 165–6
  and political interpretation, 54–6,
    68–70, 73–6, 80, 83–4, 158–60,
    164–5
  and responsibility, 68–9, 153–6
  and social identification, 163–5, 172
  social confirmation of, 154–6
persuasion
  and manipulation, 64–5
plagiarism, 32
political theory
  and ideology, 49–52
  and political engagement, 4–5,
    87–9, 177–9
politicization
  of the market, 93–4, 99–100
  of social relations, 7–8, 93, 123–4,
    134–6
  of tradition, 93–4
politics
  and barriers to change, 77–9
  and the common good, 111–
    14
  see also: explanation, politics of;
    politicization
Porter, Bruce, 158–9

public interest, 90, 124
  and the common good, 90–4
  and the free rider, 101–7
  and private escapes, 102–3
  and the problem of knowledge,
    105–8
  the thin theory of, 101–9, 119

Rae, Douglas, 10
rationalism, 28–34
rationality
  and belief, 14–15, 38–9, 196
  and explanation, 14–16
  and interpretation, 29–31
  criteria of, 29–30, 199
reactive attitudes, 52
reflexivity
  and belief, 14–15
  and interpretation, 25–8
  and the subject, 87–8
  barriers to, 38–9, 54–7
Reich, Charles, 76
Rousseau, Jean Jacques, 101–2, 105,
    108–9
  and the dilemma of change, 190
  and freedom, 183–9, 209
  and limits of community, 209
  and limits of law, 118–19

sacrifice
  and hedonism, 146–7
  ideology of, 66–9
Sartre, Jean-Paul, 42, 43, 61
Schultze, Charles
  and the public interest, 99–100
self-consciousness, 111
  and freedom, 185–6
  in modern life, 92–3
  limits of, 25–7, 49–52, 204–5
Sellars, Wilfred, 25–6
social change
  the dilemma of, 190–1
social coordination
  modes of, 94–5, 98–9
social dissolution
  dialectic of, 101–8
socialism
  American image of, 177–8, 189–90
  and capitalist idealism, 173–4
  and constitutionalism, 191
  and liberalism, 191–3
  and problematic of the state, 186–9

  barriers to, 41–2, 176–8
  revisions of, 189–93
  two images of, 174–5
Stalinism, 43
state
  contradictory imperatives of, 128–30
  priority of, 120–1
  role of, 132–4
strategy
  problems of, 135–6, 177–8
structural theory
  and class struggle, 59–60
  and humanism, 44–6
  and ideology, 43, 49–50
  and interpretation, 44–5, 55–7
  and Marxism, 175–6
  and self-consciousness, 49–52
  and the subject, 48–52, 60–2
subject
  and pre-understandings, 204–5
  and reflexivity, 14–15, 87–8
  the defenses of, 86–8
  the ideology of, 44–6, 202
  reinserted into structural theory,
    48–52, 55–7

Taylor, Charles, 44, 195, 203, 204
technocratic theory, 76–88
test procedures, 85–8, 203
transcendental argument
  reconstitution of, 87–8

unconscious, the, 84, 197–8
underground man
  and personal identity, 164–5

voting
  and beliefs, 13, 16–17
  see also elections

welfare state
  and the civilization of productivity,
    78–9, 167–9
  and fiscal crisis, 128–38
  as target of disaffection, 140–1,
    168–9
  dual accountability of, 140–1, 165–8
Winch, Peter, 28–30, 34–6, 198
witchcraft, 28–31
Wittgenstein, Ludwig, 105–6, 152
Wright, Erik Olin, 177–8